GOD

EXISTS

BUT GAWD

DOES NOT

GOD
EXISTS
BUT GAWD
DOES NOT

FROM EVIL TO NEW
ATHEISM TO FINE-TUNING

DAVID RAY GRIFFIN

PROCESS
CENTURY
PRESS
ANOKA, MINNESOTA 2016

God Exists but Gawd Does Not: From Evil to New Atheism to Fine-Tuning

Process Century Press
RiverHouse LLC
802 River Lane
Anoka, MN 55303

Process Century Press books are published in association with the International Process Network.

Cover design: Susanna Mennicke

VOLUME 2: THEOLOGICAL EXPLORATIONS SERIES

JEANYNE B. SLETTOM, GENERAL EDITOR

ISBN 978-1-940447-15-5
Printed in the United States of America

This series aims to explore the implications of Whiteheadian philosophy and theology for religious belief and practice. It also proposes that process religious thinkers, working from within many different traditions—Buddhist, Confucian, Christian, Hindu, Indigenous, Jewish, Muslim, and others—have unique insights pertinent to the critical issues of our day.

In 1976, we published a book, *Process Theology: An Introductory Exposition,* in which we aimed to "show the creative potentiality of a process perspective in theology." In addition to its explanation of process concepts and their application to Christian doctrine, the book noted the contribution of Whiteheadian thought toward "intercultural and interreligious understanding" and took an early stance on the ecological threat, claiming that process theology was prepared to "make a distinctive contribution" to this challenge.

Since the publication of that book, we have seen many others explore these and other themes in articles, books, and conferences. At the same time, the threat to planetary health and the need for "intercultural and interreligious understanding" has only accelerated. This series is an effort to support theologians and religious philosophers in their ongoing exposition of possible Whiteheadian solutions.

John B. Cobb, Jr.
David Ray Griffin

This book is dedicated to
John B. Cobb, Jr.,
who as my professor inspired my love
for philosophical theology,
and who at 91
is still inspiring people
to contribute to the common good.

Table of Contents

Preface

In my view, it is important for individuals and societies to believe that our world has been brought forth by a divine creator, which has been called "God" in the West. But I also believe that the dominant view of God has been based on a fundamental, and disastrous, mistake.

I wrote this book with the hope that it would be the best book on the existence of God ever written. Readers will, I trust, let me know how far short I fell.

David Ray Griffin
Isla Vista, California
January 2016

Introduction

Some years ago, while I was on sabbatical leave in Cambridge, England, I was told an amusing story by a colleague about a British philosopher with extremely conservative theological views. During a meeting of a theological discussion group, another member of the group made a statement with which this philosopher disagreed. "Are you talking about God," this philosopher asked, "or Gawd?"

By "Gawd," he meant the omnipotent creator of the universe as portrayed by traditional theism, Thomism in particular, in which he believed. By "God," he meant an alleged divine reality without some of the attributes of the Thomistic deity, including omnipotence—a divine reality he considered entirely fictitious.[1]

In this book, I employ the same distinction, but in the opposite way, arguing that Gawd does not exist, although God does. By speaking of Gawd with reference to Thomism—that is, the philosophical theology of St. Thomas Aquinas—the philosopher was defining Gawd as not only omnipotent but also impassible and immutable, meaning that the divine existent is unaffected by the world and, in fact, unchanging in all respects. This idea resulted in a strong tension between this theology and the scriptures on which it was supposedly based.

1

In the century before St. Thomas, twelfth-century theologian St. Anselm faced this problem directly, writing in a prayer:

> Although it is better for thee to be . . . compassionate, passionless, than not to be these things; how art thou . . . compassionate, and, at the same time, passionless? For, if thou art passionless, thou dost not feel sympathy; and if thou dost not feel sympathy, thy heart is not wretched from sympathy for the wretched; but this it is to be compassionate.

The best that Anselm could do to resolve this paradox was to say: "Thou art compassionate in terms of our experience, and not compassionate in terms of thy being."[2] In other words, God is not really compassionate, but only seems so to us.

When it was time for Thomas to deal with this issue, he did not do any better. In his *Summa Theologica,* Thomas addressed the following argument: "[I]n God there are no passions. Now love is a passion. Therefore love is not in God." Rather than denying the first premise, Thomas solved the problem by simply saying that God "loves without passion."[3]

But in more recent times, many conservative theologians, while affirming divine omnipotence, no longer think of Gawd as impassible and immutable. (In other words, they still affirm traditional theism, but not the classical version of traditional theism.) So in this book, the distinction between God and Gawd is stated only in terms of whether the divine power is held to be omnipotent in the traditional sense.

This distinction is crucial for the rise of atheism and the resulting debates between theists and atheists, including the so-called New Atheists, because almost all arguments for the "non-existence of God" are really objections to Gawd. This book argues, in fact, that there are many good reasons to deny the existence of Gawd, but no good reasons to reject the existence of God.

To say that Gawd is omnipotent means that the creator of the universe is able to bring about any state of affairs in the world unilaterally, as long as that state of affairs is not self-contradictory. So, for example, Gawd cannot create a round square or change the past; nor could Gawd bring about something that Gawd could not unilaterally change. But

Gawd *could* unilaterally prevent plague, cancer, and the destruction of civilization by either nuclear holocaust or global warming.

Part I of this book discusses six good reasons people have had for rejecting theism conceived in terms of Gawd. Part II then discusses eight good reasons to affirm theism conceived in terms of God.

The stipulation that the reasons must be *good* reasons raises the question of criteria. The question of the existence or non-existence of a deity should be judged in terms of the normal criteria employed in philosophical and scientific reasoning, namely, self-consistency and adequacy to all the relevant evidence. Each of these criteria requires discussion.

SELF-CONSISTENCY

To say that a position cannot be considered true unless it is self-consistent means that it cannot contain any ideas that contradict each other. This is the logical principle of non-contradiction, which says that an assertion and its contradictory cannot both be true. If a position contains contradictory ideas, the only rational conclusion is that at least one of those ideas is false. For example, one cannot say that the Divine Reality is perfectly good while also saying that it has arbitrarily caused horrendous evils.

With regard to philosophical, theological, or scientific thought, the charge of self-contradiction is generally discussed in terms of verbal affirmations, as when people endorse the existence of a divine being who is both omnipotent and perfectly good. But there is also another kind of self-contradiction.

Philosophers Jürgen Habermas and Karl-Otto Apel have both criticized what they call "performative contradiction," in which the performance of making a statement contradicts the statement's meaning. For example, if a lecturer tells his audience that he is a solipsist, meaning that he doubts the existence of anything beyond himself, the fact that he is addressing the people in the audience contradicts his professed doubt.[4]

Philosopher John Passmore said that such a contradiction is "absolutely self-refuting," because "to assert p is equivalent to asserting both p and not-p." Alfred North Whitehead made the same point by saying that to avoid self-contradictions requires avoiding "negations of what in practice is presupposed."[5] In a longer statement Whitehead said:

> [W]e must bow to those presumptions, which, in despite of criticism, we still employ for the regulation of our lives. Such presumptions are imperative in experience. . . . Rationalism is the search for the coherence of such presumptions.[6]

A philosophical position is irrational, accordingly, insofar as it denies some ideas that we inevitably presuppose in our daily lives. In another statement, Whitehead said:

> Whatever is found in 'practice' must lie within the scope of the metaphysical description. When the description fails to include the 'practice,' the metaphysics is inadequate and requires revision. There can be no appeal to practice to supplement metaphysics.[7]

The final sentence in this statement was made in criticism of Hume, who said that he had various "natural beliefs," which he and others all presupposed in practice. But he was not able to affirm some of these beliefs in his philosophical position, he said, because they conflict with other beliefs that he considered well-founded.

For example, when he drank and played cards with his friends, he presupposed the reality of his friends, the cards, the table, and the wine. But through philosophical analysis, he concluded that all of our knowledge, except for our knowledge about our own conscious experiences, comes through sensory perception, and sensory perception gives us only sense-data, not the real existence of objects. So as a philosopher he had to be a solipsist, although in practice, he had to presuppose the real existence of his friends, the cards, the table, and the wine.

Whitehead argued, by contrast, that these "natural" beliefs, which we inevitably presuppose in practice, should be taken as the ultimate evidence for us as philosophers.

Harvard's Hilary Putnam has also made this point, saying that the classical pragmatists—Peirce, James, and Dewey—rejected the idea that there is a "first philosophy" higher than the practice that we take most seriously when the chips are down. There is no Archimedean point from which we can argue that what is indispensable in life *gilt nicht in der Philosophie.*

Charles Hartshorne also endorsed this idea as the "pragmatic principle," which says that "what we have to be guided by in our decision-making, we should not pretend to reject theoretically."[8]

ADEQUACY TO ALL THE EVIDENCE

Whereas self-consistency is a necessary condition for having a reasonable position, it is not sufficient. "It is easy enough to find a [logically harmonious] theory," observed Whitehead, "provided that you are content to disregard half your evidence." Discussing "the moral temper required for the pursuit of truth," Whitehead described it as an "unflinching determination to take the whole evidence into account."[9] What would this criterion imply in relation to the question of the truth of theism?

It would mean, first, not disregarding any of the ideas that we inevitably presuppose in practice. If rationalism is the search for such presuppositions, then a position cannot be rational if it rejects or ignores any of "the moral intuitions which are presupposed in the concrete affairs of life."[10]

This criterion would also mean taking into account *all* of the relevant evidence. This is typically done by philosophers who argue for the existence of God, building a *cumulative case* for theism. For example, Richard Swinburne's book *The Existence of God* has chapters on the cosmological argument, teleological arguments, arguments from consciousness and morality, an argument from providence, arguments from history and miracles, and an argument from religious experience—along with an explanation of why the problem of evil does not disprove traditional theism.[11]

But also, as Caroline Franks Davis points out, problems in traditional theism provide the basis for a cumulative case *against* it.[12] Accordingly, to consider all the relevant evidence requires that we consider the cumulative case *against* theism, which is commonly done in books by atheists. For example, Michael Martin's *Atheism: A Philosophical Justification* has chapters on the meaningfulness of religious language, the ontological argument (in various forms), the cosmological argument, the teleological argument (in various forms), the argument from religious experience, the argument from miracles, the moral argument, arguments from scripture, and the argument from consciousness, concluding with the argument from cumulative evidence.[13]

RESULTS OF A CUMULATIVE CASE FOR THEISM

Following Whitehead's dictum—to "take the whole evidence into account"—would mean giving equal attention to the cumulative arguments for both theism and atheism. What would be the result?

Swinburne argued that the cumulative argument against theism weakens, but does not destroy, the positive case for it. Leaving aside the argument from religious experience, he said, the evidence shows theism to be *somewhat* "more probable than not," which is enough to allow us to take the argument from religious experience seriously. Adding that argument, he argued, makes theism "significantly more probable than not."[14]

By contrast, Martin, after reviewing the arguments for and against theism, concluded that the evidence justifies "disbelief in God."[15]

John Hick argued for a third position. The arguments for and against theism, he said, render the world religiously "ambiguous," meaning that atheism and theism are equally rational positions. Contrary to Swinburne, therefore, theism cannot be "shown to be in any objective sense more probable than not," and, contrary to Martin, the same is true of atheism.[16]

Taking an even-handed approach with regard to these three options might seem to require us to reach Hick's conclusion. However, I argue for a fourth position: Insofar as there are good arguments against theism, they are arguments against a deity understood as omnipotent. For example, although Michael Martin said that he wrote his book "to provide good reasons for being an atheist," he in fact argued only against "an all-good, all-powerful, and all-knowing being," so that his book provided a philosophical justification only for "atheism in the sense of disbelief in a being who is omniscient, omnipotent, morally perfect, and completely free."[17]

In other words, Martin's book provides a philosophical justification for the rejection of the existence of Gawd. But many theists had already reached that conclusion. For example, referring to "that masterpiece, Hume's *Dialogues Concerning Natural Religion*," Whitehead said that it criticized the best-known theistic ways of understanding the world "unanswerably." In the *Dialogues,* of course, Hume used his skeptical position (voiced by Philo) to attack both traditional theism (represented by Demea) and deism (represented by Cleanthes). Having referred to these three positions, Whitehead introduced his own idea of God by calling it "an attempt to add another speaker to that masterpiece."

In addition to Hume, Kant is the other philosopher whose arguments against the theistic arguments have been cited by countless philosophers as having refuted all such arguments. It is relevant, therefore, to see what Charles Hartshorne said about Kant's refutation. Pointing out that Kant claimed "to have defined the one and only philosophically legitimate 'ideal of reason' or idea of God," Hartshorne said that Kant's *ens realissimum* ("most real being") is not simply indemonstrable, as Kant argued, but "demonstrably impossible." Moreover, Hartshorne added, Kant's concept of God is "not what 'God' as a religious term ought to mean."[18]

Writing about the classical version of traditional theism, according to which God is immutable and impassible in all respects as well as omnipotent, Hartshorne said that the arguments against it are "as conclusive as philosophical arguments could well be."[19]

Accordingly, Part I of this book, which provides a cumulative case against the thesis that Gawd exists, argues for a position that is already widely supported by philosophers and theologians.

Part II then presents a cumulative case for the existence of God, using the types of arguments employed by Swinburne and rejected by Martin, with the difference that they are here used for the existence of God, not Gawd. Given this distinction, one need not accept Hick's conclusion that, if we look at the cumulative cases both for and against theism, we must conclude that the world is religiously ambiguous. Whereas Hick suggested that the arguments for theism are canceled out by the arguments against it, the cumulative cases show that while the arguments *against* theism provide strong evidence for the non-existence of Gawd, the cumulative case *for* theism provides strong evidence for the existence of God.

ENDNOTES

1. It has been suggested that this philosopher was Peter Geach (1916–2013), who taught logic at the University of Leeds; wrote many books, including *God and the Soul;* wrote many articles, including "Omnipotence"; and was evidently the founder of the movement known as Analytical Thomism. If this is correct, the incident likely occurred at a meeting of the Philosophical Enquiry Group, which was formed by Dominican priest and philosopher Columba Ryan, and to which Geach and his wife, the analytic philosopher Elizabeth Anscombe, were among the first to be invited. Geach's *God and the Soul* (1969; Thoemmes Press, 1997) included an essay entitled "On Worshipping the Right God," which said: "[W]e dare not be complacent about confused and erroneous thinking about God. . . . If anybody's thoughts about God are sufficiently confused and erroneous, then he will fail to be thinking about the true and living God at all; and just because God alone can draw the line, none of us is in a position to say that a given error is not serious enough to be harmful" (112). See Edward Feser, "Geach on Worshipping the Right God," 26 June 2013, and "Columba Ryan," Wikipedia, accessed 29 August 2014.

2. Saint Anselm, *Proslogium; Monologium; An Appendix in Behalf of the Fool by Gaunilon;* and *Cur Deus Homo,* trans. S. N. Deane (Open Court, 1903), 11, 13.

3. St. Thomas Aquinas, *Summa Theologica,* trans. Fathers of the English Dominican Province, rev. Daniel J. Sullivan. A volume in *Great Books of the Western World,* ed. Robert M Hutchins (W. Benton, 1952), I, Q.20, art. 1.

4. Martin Jay, "The Debate over Performative Contradiction: Habermas versus the Poststructuralists," in Martin Jay, *Force Fields: Between Intellectual History and Cultural Critique* (Routledge, 1993), 25–37.

5. John Passmore, *Philosophical Reasoning* (Basic Books, 1961), 60; Alfred North Whitehead, *Process and Reality*, corrected edition, ed. David Ray Griffin and Donald W. Sherburne (Free Press, 1978), 13.

6. Whitehead, *Process and Reality*, 151.

7. Ibid., 13.

8. Hilary Putnam, *Words and Life,* ed. James Conant (Harvard University Press, 1994), 154; Charles Hartshorne, "A Reply to My Critics," in *The Philosophy of Charles Hartshorne,* Library of Living Philosophers Vol. 20, ed. Lewis Edwin Hahn (Open Court, 1991), 569–731, at 624.

9. Alfred North Whitehead, *Science and the Modern World* (1925; Free Press, 1967), 187.

10. Ibid., 80.

11. Richard Swinburne, *The Existence of God* (Oxford University Press, 2004).

12. Caroline Franks Davis, *The Evidential Force of Religious Experience* (Clarendon Press, 1989), 113, 140–42.

13. Michael Martin, *Atheism: A Philosophical Justification* (Temple University Press, 1992).

14. Richard Swinburne, *Is There a God?* (University Press, 1996), 138–39.

15. Martin, *Atheism*, 456.

16. John Hick, *An Interpretation of Religion: Human Responses to the Transcendent* (Macmillan, 1989), 211, 227.

17. Martin, *Atheism*, 24, 30, 315.

18. Charles Hartshorne, *Creative Synthesis and Philosophic Method* (Open Court; London: SCM Press, 1970), 277.

19. Hartshorne, *Man's Vision of God and the Logic of Theism* (Harper & Row, 1941), 58.

PART I

WHY GAWD

DOES NOT

EXIST

I

Evil

Of all the reasons for the decline of theism in the West, the most important, it is widely agreed, has been the fact that the world's evils seem to refute the existence of a divine creator.[1] This issue is called "the problem of evil." Catholic theologian Hans Küng has called this problem "the rock of atheism."[2]

An attempt to answer this problem is called a "theodicy." Derived from the Greek words *theos* (God) and *dike* (justice), the word, which was coined in the 18th century by Leibniz, means to justify God. The question is whether God can be justified as truly good in light of the world's evils. In other words, can there be a satisfactory answer to the problem of evil?

In what has come to be called the "evidential argument from evil," David Hume, in his *Dialogues Concerning Natural Religion*, had Philo ask:

> Is the world considered in general, and as it appears to us in this life, different from what a man or such a limited being would, beforehand, expect from a very powerful, wise, and benevolent Deity? It must be strange prejudice to assert the contrary.

13

This evidential argument is inductive, arguing that the world's evils make it unlikely that a deity, thus conceived, exists.

A recent example of this kind of argument has been provided in a book entitled *God's Problem,* written by New Testament scholar Bart Ehrman. Having been raised in a conservative family, Ehrman was "born again" in high school, after which he attended fundamentalist schools. But some years after he had become a university professor, Ehrman announced: "I no longer go to church, no longer believe, no longer consider myself a Christian." Having written his book to explain why, he said:

> I could no longer explain how there can be a good and all-powerful God actively involved with this world, given the state of things. . . . The problem of suffering became for me the problem of faith.[3]

Not merely rejecting traditional theodicy, Ehrman provided an *anti-theodicy,* which—in the words of a review of Ehrman's book—"is permanent rebellion. It is not quite atheism but wounded theism, condemned to argue ceaselessly against a God it is supposed not to believe in."[4]

This anti-theodicy is exemplified in numerous passages. For example, having discussed terrible evils, such as the Jewish Holocaust, the killing fields of Cambodia, and the five people who die of malaria every minute, Ehrman asked: "How could [Gawd] allow it to happen? . . . How could [Gawd] allow this to happen to anyone, let alone his 'chosen people'?"[5] In another passage, Ehrman said:

> It is hard to believe that [Gawd] inflicts people with cancer, flu, or AIDS in order to make sure they praise him to the end. Praise him for what? Mutilation and torture? For his great power to inflict pain and misery on innocent people? . . . What kind of God is this?[6]

[Note: In direct quotations, the word "Gawd" is put in square brackets to indicate that the word "God" has been replaced by "Gawd."]

The answer to Ehrman's rhetorical question is, of course, the "kind of God" that in this book is called "Gawd." The kinds of arguments provided by Ehrman are the kinds that have led countless people to reject belief in Gawd. But such inductive arguments against the existence of Gawd cannot be conclusive, because there may be various facts about deity and the world that, if we understood them, would explain how theism and horrible evil can co-exist.

To avoid this weakness in inductive arguments, philosophers usually formulate the problem of evil as a *logical* problem, according to which the existence of evil is logically incompatible with theism.

I. THE LOGICAL PROBLEM OF EVIL

The logical problem of evil results from the idea that, if there is a deity that is both all-good and all-powerful—that is, if Gawd exists—then evil should not exist. But if it does exist, as seems to be the case, then Gawd must not exist. The argument for this conclusion can be formulated as a six-step argument, in which five premises lead to the conclusion:

1. The word "Gawd" refers, by definition, to the all-powerful and all-good creator of the world.

2. Because Gawd is all-powerful, Gawd would be able to prevent all evil.

3. Because Gawd is all-good, Gawd would want to prevent all evil.

4. Because logic applies to Gawd, premises 2 and 3 together imply that Gawd would prevent the occurrence of evil.

5. But evil does occur.

6. Therefore Gawd does not exist.

This argument is *valid*, meaning that the conclusion follows from the five premises. The only question is whether the argument is *sound*, which would mean that, besides being valid, the argument's premises are true. Accordingly, this argument's conclusion can be avoided only by rejecting one of the premises.

PREMISE 3

One way to avoid the conclusion is to reject Premise 3, that "Gawd would want to prevent all evil." People could argue instead that Gawd would not necessarily want to prevent all evil, because Gawd could have good reasons for allowing evil. For example, some evils, such as a painful root canal treatment, may help one to prevent worse pain in the future; having some terrible experiences can lead people to be more grateful for their good experiences; and being mistreated by others gives one the opportunity to develop patience and practice forgiveness.

But this type of argument does not refute the claim that an all-good and all-powerful creator would imply the non-existence of evil. It only points out that some *prima facie* evils—things that may at first glance seem evil—may not be *genuinely* evil, because the apparent evils are necessary conditions for good things that more than compensate for them, so the *prima facie* evils are not really evil.

Accordingly, to remove ambiguity, the word "genuine" needs to be inserted into Premise 3, so that it reads: "If Gawd is all-good, then Gawd would want to prevent all *genuine* evil." To call evils genuine is to say that they make the world worse than it would have been without them, all things considered. With this clarification, Premise 3 is a truism, because it is analytic that a perfectly good deity would want to prevent the world from being worse than it might have been.

If the word "genuine" had been inserted, a lot of spilt ink could have been avoided. For example, a famous 1964 article by John Mackie entitled "Evil and Omnipotence" argued that the existence of an omnipotent and morally perfect deity is inconsistent with the existence of evil. Alvin Plantinga then pointed out that this was not necessarily true, as there may be good reasons for evil. In particular, perhaps the highest good is the existence of intelligent beings who freely worship Gawd and love their neighbors as themselves, and they could not do this freely if Gawd had coerced their obedience to the divine will. Therefore, Plantinga argued, the "free-will defense" defeats the problem.[7]

Mackie was also to blame for a lot of extra words by arguing that Gawd could have created beings who are free but sinless, because as omnipotent, Gawd could have done so. Mackie said, "If their being of this sort is logically possible, then Gawd's making them of this sort is logically possible." But this, Plantinga could easily point out, is a fallacy, because it is not possible for Gawd to create beings who are genuinely free and yet *guaranteed* to be sinless.[8]

Mackie then further confused the issue. After conceding the correctness of Plantinga's argument, Mackie agreed that the problem of evil does not, after all, show that the central doctrines of theism are logically inconsistent with one another.

But Mackie could have saved his inconsistency argument by simply inserting the word "genuine" before "evil." This was done by, for example, H. J. McCloskey. Saying that the problem of evil involves a logical contradiction, McCloskey made clear that he was not talking simply about *prima facie* evil, which might be necessary to produce higher goods, but "unnecessary" or "superfluous" evil.[9]

In fact, even Plantinga has agreed. Although he has devoted much of his energy to arguing that all sorts of evil, even natural evils, could be justified as perhaps needed for goods that outweigh the evils, he granted that if any "unjustified" evil occurs, "it follows that there is no omnipotent, omniscient, wholly good being."[10] In other words, Plantinga conceded that the existence of genuine evil would disprove the existence of Gawd.

PREMISE 2

It would seem, therefore, that the only way to avoid the atheistic conclusion would be to deny the truth of Premise 2, according to which the deity, being all-powerful, "would be able to prevent all evil." That is, perhaps our creator could be defined as "all-powerful" in the sense of having the unique power to create a universe, while not being "omnipotent," meaning the power to override the creatures' power. But the possibility of rejecting the omnipotence of God, thus understood, was ruled out for most of Christian history by the idea of *creatio ex nihilo*, which solidified the Christian view of the world's creator as "Gawd." Given this understanding of the creator's being "all-powerful," the argument is sound, disproving the existence of Gawd.

2. THE ADOPTION OF *CREATIO EX NIHILO*

According to the doctrine of *creatio ex nihilo*, Gawd created the world out of absolutely nothing. This view was not contained in the Hebrew

Bible and hence in what Christians have called the Old Testament. *Creatio ex nihilo* was suggested, to be sure, by the customary Christian translation of the first verses of Genesis, "In the beginning God created the heaven and the earth. The earth was without form and void." More accurately translated, however, the passage says, "When God began to create the heaven and the earth, the world was without form and void." Rather than suggesting that the earth's being "without form and void" came *after* the deity's initial creative activity, the more accurate translation suggests a version of the view articulated in most cosmogonies of the Ancient Near East, as well as Plato's *Timaeus*, namely, that our universe was created out of a primeval chaos.

This view suggests that our world was created out of material with some power of its own, so that it would not be wholly subject to the divine will. Plato implied this in saying that the creator willed that everything should be good "as far as possible."[11]

According to the traditional Christian rendition of Genesis 1:1–2, however, the deity first created the raw material out of nothing, then used this material to create our world. This view suggests that the creator is absolutely omnipotent, because the basic elements of the world, owing their existence wholly to the creator's will, would have no *inherent* power with which to offer any resistance. This understanding was expressed by Millard Erickson, a contemporary Calvinist theologian, who said:

> [Gawd] did not work with something which was in existence. He brought into existence the very raw material which he employed. If this were not the case, [Gawd] would . . . have been limited by having to work with the intrinsic characteristics of the raw material which he employed.[12]

The idea that the world was created *ex nihilo* meant that the liturgical statement that God is "all-powerful" had to be interpreted in terms of the technical doctrine of divine *omnipotence*, according to which the creatures have no inherent power that cannot be overridden by divine power. But perhaps the adoption of *creatio ex nihilo* was a huge mistake.

CREATIO EX NIHILO NOT BIBLICAL

For one thing, the idea of *creatio ex nihilo* is not grounded in the Bible. Jewish biblical scholar Jon Levenson of Harvard University has emphasized this fact in a book entitled *Creation and the Persistence of Evil.* If properly understood, said Levenson, the first verses of Genesis "cannot be invoked in support of the developed Jewish, Christian, and Muslim doctrine of *creatio ex nihilo*."[13]

Likewise, besides not being in the Hebrew Scriptures, the doctrine of creation out of nothing was also not in the New Testament, as shown by Christian theologian Gerhard May in a book entitled *Creatio Ex Nihilo: The Doctrine of "Creation out of Nothing" in Early Christian Thought.*

To be sure, many Christian scholars have claimed otherwise, saying that *creatio ex nihilo* was expressed in John 1:3, Romans 4:17, Colossians 1:16, and Hebrews 11:3. Although these passages taken alone are ambiguous, argue these scholars, they can safely be assumed to reflect *creatio ex nihilo*, because "primitive Christianity found the doctrine ready-made in the Jewish tradition," specifically in the intertestamental literature.

The primary passage that has been cited in this regard is 2 Maccabees 7:28, which says that God created the world and humanity "out of non-being." However, said May, this formula does not necessarily imply *creatio ex nihilo* in the strict sense, according to which the very stuff of which this world is composed was itself created out of nothing. This is shown by the fact that the Hellenistic Jewish philosopher Philo spoke of God as creating "out of non-being," even though Philo accepted the existence of a pre-existent matter alongside God.[14]

The absence of *creatio ex nihilo* from the Hebrew and Christian writings fits, May said, with the fact that in the first two centuries A.D., Jewish thinkers, such as Philo, and early Christian thinkers later considered orthodox—such as Justin Martyr, Athenagoras, and Clement of Alexandria—held that the "acceptance of an unformed matter was entirely reconcilable with biblical monotheism." Justin even argued that Plato "took over the doctrine that God made the cosmos out of unoriginate matter from the opening verses of Genesis."[15] As some scholars have paraphrased this point, Justin said that Plato plagiarized Genesis!

How, then, did the doctrine of *creatio ex nihilo* become the orthodox Christian position (which was later adopted by most Jewish and Muslim theologians)? It developed in reaction to the ideas of the second-century gnostic Marcion, according to whom the world was created out of evil matter by the Hebrew Bible's creator-deity, in distinction from the supreme divine reality revealed by Jesus. To fence the Church off from this heretical view, Christian thinkers rejected entirely the idea of creation out of unformed matter, replacing it with the idea of creation out of nothing.[16]

One Christian theologian who warned against this solution was Hermogenes, who was, May said, the Platonic Christian theologian who was the primary victim of this development. Being "emphatically anxious to ensure the absolute goodness of the creator God," Hermogenes pointed out that the idea of unoriginate matter allowed for an explanation of the origin of evil in a way that protected God's goodness. According to this explanation, "the trace of the original disorder of matter remain[ed] in every created thing." But this trace of disorder did not mean that matter was evil, Hermogenes added, because "matter before its ordering is without qualities," therefore "neither good nor evil."[17]

By contrast, Hermogenes said, the idea of *creatio ex nihilo*, by saying that the creator is the source of literally everything, including evil, would threaten the creator's perfect goodness. But in their zeal to fence the church off from Marcion's ideas, other theologians were in no mood to listen, and Hermogenes was attacked as a heretic. The attack was begun by Theophilus of Antioch, the first church theologian known "to use unambiguously the substance and the terminology of the doctrine of *creatio ex nihilo*."[18]

Theophilus's polemic then influenced Hippolytus and Tertullian and probably also Irenaeus, the other founder, along with Theophilus himself, "of the church doctrine of *creatio ex nihilo*."[19] This rejection of creation out of chaos, which had been the understanding of the biblical tradition for over a millennium, occurred very suddenly: "For Tertullian and Hippolytus it is already the fixed Christian position that

God created the world out of absolutely nothing."[20] In other words, God had suddenly become Gawd.

This sudden transition from creation out of chaos to creation out of nothing, with its fateful implications, seems to have been made with little reflection. For example, May said that the doctrine of *creatio ex nihilo*, "which removes all restrictions on [the deity's] creative activity by declaring the free decision of [the creator's] will [to be] the sole ground of creation," was bound to make the biblical concept of the divine creator "a philosophical problem." However, May added, "this is a question far beyond Theophilus."[21]

Irenaeus also rejected the Platonic view, according to which the creator can only will "the best possible," in favor of the "the absolute freedom and omnipotence of the biblical [Gawd]," which "must rule and dominate in everything," so that "everything else must give way to it." However, May said, this position was "only attainable because Irenaeus is quite unaware of philosophical problems." Indeed, "cosmological questions scarcely worried Irenaeus."[22]

The change was spearheaded by theologians who, besides being uninterested in taking a circumspect view because of their single-minded focus on the threat from Marcionite gnosticism, were perhaps intellectually unequipped to do so. The adoption of *creatio ex nihilo* was evidently made without due regard to the warning by Hermogenes about the threat to Christian faith implicit in *this* doctrine—the threat to the perfect goodness of the creator. Hermogenes' worry was borne out by the subsequent history, after God had become Gawd.

3. TRADITIONAL THEODICY

The doctrine of *creatio ex nihilo* implies, in Erickson's words, "God's will is never frustrated. What he chooses to do, he accomplishes."[23] Erickson was, of course, talking about Gawd. Has it been possible, within the framework of this doctrine, to formulate a believable theodicy?

A theodicy within this framework, in which the creator is assumed to be omnipotent, is a *traditional* theodicy, which comes in two types. One type says that Gawd uses his power to determine all things. The other type holds that Gawd allows some of the creatures to have a degree of freedom to make their own decisions. The present chapter looks at the all-determining type of traditional theodicy as exemplified by Augustine, Calvin, and Leibniz and then at three examples of traditional free-will theism.

AUGUSTINE'S THEODICY

Aurelius Augustinus of Hippo (354–430), who would be elevated to sainthood, began his justification of Gawd's doings by stipulating that all evil results from freely-chosen sin. Aside from the problem of how all natural evil could be due to sin, Augustine had to defend the reality of free choice by humans.

Saying that the majority of the human race will be sent to ever-lasting suffering, Augustine defended Gawd's goodness on the grounds that all people sin, so all deserve damnation. Gawd's merciful goodness is shown by the fact that he freely saves a few. The damnation is just, Augustine insisted, because human volition does not come from Gawd. The evil will is not created by Gawd; otherwise, Gawd would be the author of sin.[24]

However, with reference to the creedal affirmation of faith in Gawd the Father Almighty, Augustine said: "For he is called Almighty for no other reason than he can do whatsoever he willeth and his omnipotent will is not impeded by the will of any creature." Anyone who denies that "all things are in the hands of the one Almighty," he added, "is a madman," because "the will of the Omnipotent is always undefeated."[25]

In spite of Augustine's claim to the contrary, therefore, it seems that Gawd must be the author of sin. This conclusion is made even more explicit in Augustine's conclusion: "Nothing, therefore, happens unless the Omnipotent wills it to happen."[26]

How could Gawd cause people to sin without being the author of their sin? Augustine said: "[Gawd] works in the hearts of men to incline their wills whithersoever He wills, whether to good deeds according to His mercy, or to evil after their own deserts." But if Gawd causes every-thing, how could anyone deserve punishment?

Augustine implored people to have a "fixed and immovable convic-tion" that "there is no unrighteousness with [Gawd]," because "[Gawd's] causation does not take away our free agency." With regard to our free acts, we must understand "both that we do them, and that [Gawd] makes us to do them." But although a few philosophers have professed to believe the idea that human action can be free even though it is completely determined—whether by Gawd above or molecules below—this notion is self-contradictory. The goodness of Augustine's Gawd cannot be saved by a self-contradictory claim about human freedom.[27]

In any case, Augustine's ultimate defense of Gawd is based on his claim that there is finally no evil: Just as the beauty of the world is achieved by means of contraries, Gawd uses human wickedness for good, "thus embellishing the course of the ages, as if an exquisite poem were set off with antitheses." Put otherwise:

> [Gawd] judged it better to bring good out of evil than not to permit any evil to exist. . . . If it were not good that evil things exist, they would certainly not be allowed to exist by the Omnipotent Good.[28]

Augustine's theodicy, hence, involves the rejection of Premise 5, according to which "(genuine) evil does occur."

In response to this type of theodicy, Ivan in Dostoevsky's *The Brothers Karamazov* protested. He realized that the world may end with a "higher harmony," and if he were present he might cry out with the rest, "Thou art just, O Lord, for Thy ways are revealed." But Ivan wanted to state on the record in advance that he hopes that he would not join that chorus, because he could not accept the idea that any "higher harmony" could justify all the evils that were allegedly necessary for it, such as the suffering of innocent children.

Many people would want to stand with Ivan, saying that if the omnipotent deity portrayed by Augustine existed, they would not want to spend eternity in its presence, because the denial of the existence of genuine evil cannot save the goodness of Gawd.[29]

CALVIN'S THEODICY

Writing in the sixteenth century, John Calvin had substantially the same view of Gawd as Augustine, so his theodicy was similar. But he had some emphases that made his theodicy seem even worse.

Gawd is called omnipotent, Calvin said, because "he regulates all things according to his secret plan, which depends solely upon itself." Although Augustine and Thomas Aquinas had distinguished between Gawd's "causing" things and merely "permitting" them, Calvin rejected this distinction. Recognizing that the motive for this distinction was that it seemed absurd to some people "for man, who will soon be punished for his blindness, to be blinded by [Gawd's] will and command," Calvin retorted with Scripture's statement that "men can accomplish nothing except by [Gawd's] secret command."[30]

Calvin thereby brought out explicitly the doctrine of "double pre-destination," calling it childish to say that Gawd elects some to salvation without condemning others to damnation. "Those whom [Gawd] passes over, he condemns; and this he does for no other reason than that he wills to exclude them from the inheritance which he predestines for his own children." Many sinners fail to repent because Gawd does not will the repentance of all.[31]

Calvin also rejected the attempt by Thomas to protect Gawd's justice by saying that predestination is based on Gawd's foreknowledge of sin and merit. Criticizing this "quibbling," Calvin said that Gawd "foresees future events only by reason of the fact that he decreed they take place."[32]

Although Calvin often said that Gawd is not blameworthy for damning people for things they could not have avoided, he did in one passage show an ounce of humanity. In response to the question, "Whence does it happen that Adam's fall irremediably involved so many peoples, together with their infant offspring, in eternal death unless because it so pleased [Gawd]?" Calvin replied: "The decree is dreadful indeed, I confess."

But Calvin said that this dreadful decree does not mean that Gawd is unjust, because Gawd's will is by definition right: "[Gawd's] will is so much the highest rule of righteousness that whatever he wills, by the very fact that he wills it, must be considered righteous." In other words, there is no genuine evil, because Gawd is omnipotent, and might makes right![33]

LEIBNIZ'S THEODICY

In contrast with the pugnacity of Calvin, Gottfried Wilhelm Leibniz (1646–1716) was an eminently reasonable philosopher. But in spite of the enormous differences in tone and emphasis, he fully endorsed the traditional doctrine of omnipotence, so his theodicy ended up with similar conclusions.

Leibniz is most famous for defining ours as the "best of all possible worlds." Although he thereby emphasized the divine reason rather than the divine will, this emphasis meant no qualification of divine omnipotence: The world was not created out of preexistent matter, said Leibniz, so Gawd's power is absolute and infinite. To say that Gawd is limited in power would deny that Gawd is the greatest conceivable being, hence not truly divine. Being the master of all things, Gawd's will is infallibly successful.[34]

Although some interpreters have said that Leibniz, with his focus on ours as the best possible world, thereby implied that there is sin and suffering in any possible world, that is inaccurate. He said that, if the happiness of rational creatures had been the sole aim of Gawd, "perhaps neither sin nor unhappiness would ever occur." Gawd could also have made all rational creatures so that they would always have a good will, and if Gawd had loved virtue and hated vice unreservedly, "there would be no vice in the world."[35]

Although divine omnipotence could have prevented all sin and suffering, the creation of the world was also based on the Gawd's infinite wisdom and goodness. Having perfect wisdom, Gawd knows which of the possible worlds is best and, being perfectly good, Gawd necessarily chooses to create that best world. That our world, with all its sin and suffering, is the best possible world is, therefore, true by definition, being implied by the definition of Gawd as omnipotent and perfectly good. So there can be no reasonable basis, held Leibniz, for criticizing Gawd.

But if Leibniz considered his theodicy beyond criticism, it did not work out that way. Most famously, Voltaire's *Candide* lampooned Leibniz's view in a story about a young man who had accepted his professor's idea that ours is the best of all possible worlds. The young man experienced a series of catastrophes, which finally made him lose faith. Like most satirists, Voltaire was somewhat unfair to his subject, because Leibniz had based his affirmation of ours as the best of all possible worlds not upon an empirical survey, but as a logical implication of Gawd's wisdom, goodness, and power. Also, Leibniz had never denied that our world is full of sin and suffering. Rather, he said that our world, with all of its sin and suffering, was the best world possible.[36]

Nevertheless, Voltaire's satire illustrated a serious point—that no one could consistently affirm that ours is the best of all possible worlds, containing no genuine evil. As argued above in the Introduction, to have a self-consistent position requires, in Whitehead's words, that we must avoid "negations of what in practice is presupposed."[37] And in practice, no one can consistently maintain that everything that happens is for the best.

4. TRADITIONAL FREE-WILL THEODICY

More recently, the most popular type of traditional theodicy has been what is known as the "free-will defense." The basic idea is that, although Gawd is all-powerful as well as all-good, Gawd gave humans free will, because it is better for them to have free will than to be in an evil-free world devoid of freedom.

This approach, having been popularized in the mid-twentieth century by C. S. Lewis, has been developed more recently not only by Alvin Plantinga, whose position was already mentioned above,[38] but also John Hick and Richard Swinburne.

JOHN HICK

John Hick's version will be examined at length, after which Swinburne's will be examined more briefly.

Hick's Theodicy: When he began formulating his theology, Hick set out to explain how Christian belief, according to which the universe was created by "a limitless good and limitlessly powerful Being," is not "rendered irrational by the fact of evil."[39]

To be successful, a theodicy must be not only coherent and adequate to the facts of the world, but also plausible. This is a requirement upon which Hick himself insisted. For example, he was critical of Plantinga's defense of the Augustinian explanation of evil, according to which humanity was created perfect but fell into sin. Although Plantinga's theodicy may be self-consistent, said Hick, it is not plausible, given the fact that our world has been created through a long evolutionary development.[40]

A much better starting point, Hick said, is what can be called an "Irenaean theodicy," not because it was developed by St. Irenaeus himself, but because it employs his two-stage conception of the creation of human beings. According to this conception, humans were created with the potentiality for friendship with Gawd, but they were immature, so they would need to grow into this friendship. Hick adapted this view by putting the two stages in an evolutionary context, according to which humankind, arising from its animal past, necessarily had to be immature at the beginning. So, human perfection did not exist at the beginning, but it is to be expected at the end.[41]

However, if Gawd is limitlessly good and powerful, why did Gawd create humans as "an imperfect and developing creature rather than as the perfect being whom [Gawd] is intending to create"? This cannot be because human beings had to be formed through an evolutionary process:

> [A]n omnipotent deity, creating *ex nihilo*, and determining solely by His own sovereign will both the nature of the beings whom He creates and the character of the environment in which He places them, could if He wished produce perfect persons who, while free to sin and even perhaps tempted to sin, remain for ever sinless.[42]

Rather, the reason is that Gawd wants human beings to come "freely to know and love their Maker." If humans had been created with the knowledge of "the limitless reality and power, goodness and love" of Gawd, then the "disproportion between Creator and creatures would be so great that the latter would have no freedom in relation to [Gawd]." They would, accordingly, "not exist as independent autonomous persons." So humans must be born at a distance from Gawd. However, the needed distance is not spatial but *epistemic*: Humans must be in an autonomous system in which the existence of Gawd is not obvious. They must be in a world that is "religiously ambiguous, capable of being seen either as a purely natural phenomenon or as [Gawd's] creation." Only in such a context could people come to love and worship their creator freely.[43]

Of course, the fact that we are immature, retaining many of our animalistic characteristics, opened the way for horrendous evils in human history. Some people may agree with the wisdom of Gawd in allowing creatures to have freedom to make mistakes and even to inflict pain and suffering on others, but still ask why Gawd does not intervene now and then to prevent the most horrible evils. Hick agreed that Gawd, being omnipotent, could do this. However, Hick said, Gawd's primary concern is not to prevent terrible suffering. Far from creating this world to be a "hedonistic paradise," Gawd created it to be a "vale of soul-making," and the worst evils may serve that goal the best.[44]

If this provides a plausible answer to the question of moral evil, which often results in pain, there is still the problem of natural evil, in which horrendous death and suffering is caused by storms, earthquakes, and diseases. "We have to ask," Hick said, "why an unlimitedly good and unlimitedly powerful [deity] should have created so dangerous a world." He answered:

> In a world devoid both of dangers to be avoided and rewards to be won, we may assume that virtually no development of the human intellect and imagination would have taken place, and hence no development of the sciences, the arts, human civilization, or culture.[45]

In response, people may say that there are many evils that, rather than producing virtues, such as faith, hope, and patience, produce atheism and despair. It seems far from evident that Gawd has created a world in which the pain and suffering would be just the right amount. However, said Hick, "at this point we meet the paradox that if we *could* see that, then the world would no longer serve a person-making purpose!"[46]

Even if one were to accept this answer, there is still the problem of animal suffering. Animals are presumably not undergoing moral and spiritual development, so their suffering serves no purpose. A partial answer, Hick said, was that "the teeming multitude of life-forms, each nourishing and nourished by others in a continuous recycling of life, constitutes the vast evolutionary process within which humanity has emerged," so this is "an aspect of our epistemic distance from [Gawd]." However, he added, "if we ask why so many animals are carnivorous rather than vegetarian, killing and eating other species, no evident answer is available." But one thing can be said:

> [P]ain is an aspect of the process of biological evolution as it has actually occurred, and is to us part of the same mysterious totality as earthquakes, volcanic eruptions, storms, hurricanes, and tidal waves. The very fact that it is mysterious may, however, itself have value.[47]

Finally, having promised to provide a theodicy that is plausible, Hick said that the principal threat to its plausibility comes from the "sheer amount and intensity of both moral and natural evil." The only answer, he said, is the "eschatological answer," namely, "in the end we shall participate in the divine kingdom. . . . Without such an eschatological fulfillment, this theodicy would collapse."[48]

Critique of Hick's Theodicy: Hick rightfully said that a theodicy, to be helpful, must be plausible. But it seems to me that he failed. Indeed, the problems with his position are many. I will mention six:

- Hick's theodicy is based entirely on the idea that the free development of moral and spiritual virtues is so valuable that it justifies the world's evils. But for whom is the free development of these virtues so valuable? Only to Gawd: Being omnipotent, Gawd could have programmed us so that we would think that we had developed our virtues freely, even though we would not be free in relation to Gawd: "He alone would know," Hick said. So, this whole divine-human drama, with its tens of thousands of years of horrendous human evil, is all for the benefit of Gawd. That hardly seems like a deity that is "limitlessly good."[49]

- In response to the fact that people experience so much pain and suffering, Hick advocates the "eschatological answer," that we should "trust in [Gawd] even in the midst of deep suffering, for in the end we shall participate in the divine kingdom." However, it is one thing when a theologian recommends trust in a deity for which there is abundant evidence. It is quite different to get this recommendation from Hick, who says that the evidence is "ambiguous," so that Gawd "is not evident."[50]

- If animals were not created to develop virtues, their sufferings serve no purpose for them. They, with their millions of years of suffering, are justified by their role in giving us epistemic distance from Gawd. However, being omnipotent, Gawd could have created them simultaneously with *homo sapiens*, so that all of the prior animal suffering would have been avoided. This solution need not have ruined the epistemic distance gained by humankind's assumption that it was part of a long evolutionary development, because Gawd, being omnipotent, could have made the creation appear to be many billions of years old, even if it were not (as some creationists have, in fact, suggested; see Chapter 3).

- Holding the standard evolutionary view, Hick said that the universe has existed for over 13 billion years. If the history of the universe were to be written in a 12-volume work, with hundreds of pages in each volume, Homo sapiens would show up somewhere on the final page of the final volume. Is it plausible to hold that the universe was created solely for the sake of the divine-human drama?[51]

- In justifying the fact that no good answers can be given to the question of why Gawd would have set up the world as it is, Hick suggested that such mysteries serve the divine plan, by increasing the ambiguity of the world, thereby increasing epistemic distance. But Hick was thereby simply attempting to turn a vice into a virtue.

- Finally, Hick's intention was to reconcile the "ultimate omni-responsibility of [Gawd]" with "a serious facing of evil *as evil*." But Hick ended up, like the previous theologians, denying that there is any genuine evil—that is, anything that would have made the world worse than it might have been. Gawd permitted moral evil, Hick said, to "bring out of it an even greater good than would have been possible if evil had never existed."[52]

Therefore, Hick did, as he intended, to show that the existence of an omnipotent and perfectly good deity is not "rendered irrational by the fact of evil." And, as Voltaire implied in *Candide*, no one can really believe that everything happens for the best.

RICHARD SWINBURNE

Swinburne's free-will theodicy is essentially the same as Hick's, but with a different twist. Swinburne said:

> A [Gawd] who gives humans such free will necessarily brings about the possibility, and puts outside his own control whether or not that evil occurs. It is not logically possible . . . that [Gawd] could give us such free will and yet ensure that we always use it in the right way.[53]

In response to those who say that Gawd should not have given us the ability to inflict great suffering on others, Swinburne replied that this would have prevented us from developing really worthwhile free will, which requires the need to make "significant choices between good and evil"—choices that "make a big difference to the agent, to others, and to the world."[54] In explaining this point, Swinburne wrote:

> A world in which agents can benefit each other but not do each other harm is one where they have only very limited responsibility for each other. . . . A [Gawd] who gave agents only such limited responsibilities for their fellows would not have given much. [Gawd] would have reserved for himself the all-important choice of the kind of world it was to be, while simply allowing humans the minor choice of filling in the details. . . . A good [Gawd] . . . will delegate responsibility. In order to allow creatures to share in creation, he will allow them the choice of hurting and maiming, or frustrating the divine plan.[55]

Moreover, Swinburne argued, it is good to be made to suffer. One's suffering would be pure loss "if the only good thing in life was sensory pleasure." But life is about the development of fully human lives, so "[b]eing allowed to suffer to make possible a great good [for oneself or others] is a privilege."[56]

As for natural evil, its main role "is to make it possible for humans to have the kind of choice which the free-will defense extols." For one thing, for humans to make significant choices, the evils produced by nature give humans the knowledge of "how to bring about such evils themselves." This knowledge gives us the ability to make the meaningful choice between producing more of the evil or preventing it.[57]

But could Gawd "not just whisper in our ears from time to time what are the different consequences of different actions of ours?" Yes, said Swinburne, but by thereby leaving no doubt that all of our actions are "done under the all-watchful eye of [Gawd]," our freedom would be greatly inhibited by making it very difficult "to choose to do evil." Also, we "would be deprived of the [chance] to discover what the consequences were through experiment and hard cooperative work."[58]

In addition, natural evil "makes possible certain kinds of action towards it between which agents can choose." For example physical pain "gives to the sufferer a choice—whether to endure it with patience, or bemoan his lot."[59]

Given these elements in Swinburne's position, we are in position to see his central argument as to why Gawd, being omnipotent and perfectly good, allowed the world to be so filled with evil. If for Hick Gawd allowed so much evil for the sake of producing moral and spiritual values, Swinburne said that Gawd wants to produce heroes. In explaining why there needs to be natural as well as moral evil, Swinburne reflected on what human beings would be like if the world were devoid of "all the suffering of mind and body caused by disease, earthquake, and accident unpreventable by humans."

> Many of us would then have such an easy life that we simply would not have much opportunity to show courage or, indeed, manifest much in the way of great goodness at all. We need these insidious processes of decay and dissolution which money and strength cannot ward off for long to give us the opportunities, so easy otherwise to avoid, to become heroes.[6]

In light of the fact that he portrays Gawd as deliberately producing these "insidious processes of decay and dissolution," it is good that Swinburne began his discussion by saying: "I can only ask the reader to believe that I am not totally insensitive to human suffering."[61]

In any case, Swinburne did better than Hick at explaining how an omnipotent creator could be compatible with the existence of genuine evil. But he did no better in portraying Gawd as good and worthy of devotion.

5. CAN ANY TRADITIONAL THEODICY SUCCEED?

As the five theologians discussed above illustrate, the insistence on Premise 2, according to which "Gawd is all-powerful" in the sense of omnipotent, seems to make a successful theodicy impossible. Of course, an examination of only five examples would be insufficient for an inductive argument in support of such a sweeping conclusion. However, my book *God, Power, and Evil* also has chapters dealing with Thomas Aquinas, Baruch Spinoza, Martin Luther, Karl Barth, James Ross, and the Personal Idealism of Bishop Berkeley and E. S. Brightman. Moreover, I have also examined the theodical writings of still more thinkers, including David Basinger, Stephen Davis, William Hasker, John Knasas, Alvin Plantinga, John Roth, and Frederick Sontag—the latter two of whom admitted that Gawd must be partly evil.[62] This list would seem sufficient for an inductive argument that traditional theodicy could never succeed, because the only ways to affirm the existence of Gawd is to deny either genuine evil or divine goodness.

But does the acceptance of Premise 2 necessarily make impossible a theodicy reconciling Gawd's goodness with the world's evil? Perhaps not, because two more approaches have been suggested.

THEODICY AND LOGIC: EMIL FACKENHEIM'S APPROACH

Having accepted Premise 2's stipulation that Gawd is all-powerful, theologians have provided various ways to defend Gawd's goodness—with Augustine emphasizing human free will, Calvin emphasizing the divine will as the very standard of justice, Leibniz focusing on our world as the best of all possible ones, Hick focusing on the world as a vale of soul-making, and Swinburne offering a heroic theodicy. Although it might seem that these approaches exhaust the possible ways of defending Gawd's goodness, there is a another possibility: rejecting Premise 4, according to which "logic applies to Gawd."

This approach was taken by Jewish theologian Emil Fackenheim, whose writing on the problem of evil was preceded by that of Richard Rubenstein. According to Rubenstein, no Jew should believe in a deity understood as the omnipotent author of history. To believe in such a deity, he said, would mean accepting Hitler's action as expressing the divine will and the SS as divine instruments. These ideas, Rubenstein said, are simply too obscene to accept: The idea that the divine being is omnipotently active in history implies that historical events express the divine will, and combining this idea with that of divine goodness leads to the justification of the Nazi-Jewish holocaust. Rubenstein said that he would never do this.[63]

Rubenstein's solution was to give up divine providence in history, affirming only a God of nature, thereby replacing theism with a version of deism.[64] Fackenheim could not accept this solution, on the grounds that excluding divine guidance in history would mean the end of Judaism, thereby giving Hitler a posthumous victory. Fackenheim, however, agreed with Rubenstein's view that humans have freedom in relation to deity, so sinful human acts are not divinely caused.[65] Accordingly, Fackenheim rejected every idea of deity as a "sole power" that ruled out the reality of human freedom and evil, which, he said, vital religion requires.[66]

Nevertheless, Fackenheim insisted, belief in deity as the sole power is also required by vital religion. In addition, he maintained, any view that limits divine power, thereby making the deity finite, would be paganism. Accordingly, Fackenheim said, human freedom and divine omnipotence must both be affirmed.[67]

But how is this possible, given the fact that holding both beliefs is logically contradictory? Fackenheim's answer was that religion is not to be judged by the standard of "objective rationality," because it has its own logic. Within Judaism, religious discourse is called Midrash, which, according to Fackenheim, has contradictory affirmations in stories, parables, and metaphors.[68]

Fackenheim solved the problem of evil, in other words, by rejecting Premise 4, according to which logic, and hence the law of non-contradiction, applies to the deity. Accordingly, he said, one can reconcile human evil with divine goodness and omnipotence by simply stipulating that logic does not apply to religious discourse.

This approach, however, does not provide a satisfactory solution. In the first place, although Fackenheim did not mean to deny logic in every topic, only in religious discourse, it is not easy to draw a clear line between religious and non-religious discourse. For example, many people have considered Nazism and Communism religions. Would Fackenheim also excuse them from responsibility to be logical?

There would also be problems within unquestionably religious traditions. Would Fackenheim give traditional Christianity a pass on its contradictory statements within trinitarian discourse, with its claim that the deity is both one and three? Would he say that there is nothing problematic about Christian talk about Jesus as being "fully divine" while also being "fully human," and with Jesus' being omniscient while being ignorant about some things? Would he say that contradictions within Advaita Vedanta do not count against its claim to be truth? He surely would not.

Therefore, the logical problem of evil—according to which the affirmation of Gawd as good and omnipotent contradicts the affirmation of genuine evil—cannot be resolved by dismissing the need for logic.

THE DIVINE PLAYWRIGHT: THE APPROACH OF JAMES ROSS

Thus far, this chapter have provided two reasons to reject the doctrine of *creatio ex nihilo*, which provides the basis for Premise 2. Namely, (a) this doctrine is not biblical and (b) this doctrine makes a successful theodicy impossible. But there is also a third reason: Christian theology, like both Jewish and Islamic theology, has insisted that the world's creator created a *real* world, not merely an idea in the divine mind. What makes our world's creatures *real*, moreover, is the fact that they have power of their own. If they did not, they would be indistinguishable from mere ideas in the divine mind.

This was illustrated by philosophical theologian James Ross, who argued that, although the actions of human beings are totally determined by Gawd, we act freely. To explain how this is possible, he spoke about characters in plays. For example, Othello's murdering Desdemona was totally determined by Shakespeare, but Othello nevertheless acted freely, insisted Ross, so he was responsible for the murder. Likewise, in bringing about events that cause pain, Gawd is not guilty for causing evil, because "a person who deliberately imagines a suffering lion is committing no moral crime."[69]

As Ross's examples slow, if the actions and feelings of creatures are wholly determined by their creators, the creatures are not really real, but merely ideas in the minds of their creators. The doctrine of *creatio ex nihilo*, by giving the divine creator the power to determine all actions and feelings, in effect denies the reality of the world.

6. RECONSIDERATION: WHY NOT REJECT PREMISE 2?

The existence of a good creator could be affirmed by rejecting Premise 2's stipulation that the deity is "all-powerful" in the sense that the deity, having created the world *ex nihilo*, could override the power of the creatures. But the existence of an all-powerful and good creator could be affirmed by specifying that being "all-powerful" means having the unique power to create a universe, but it does not mean being omnipotent, having the power to override the power of the creatures. With this definition, the deity is God rather than Gawd, so the deity's goodness and power are not inconsistent with the genuine evil in the world.

Alfred North Whitehead developed a version of this approach, rejecting the idea of "one supreme reality, omnipotently disposing a wholly derivative world." Plato's conviction "that the divine element in the world is to be conceived as a persuasive agency and not as a coercive agency," added Whitehead, was "one of the greatest intellectual discoveries in the history of religion."[70]

However, the Western idea of deity has been so shaped by divine omnipotence based on *creatio ex nihilo* that philosopher after philosopher has said that no other kind of deity is worthy of worship. For example:

- C. A. Campbell said that worship is not possible "once the infinitude of the creator has been compromised, and forces independent of the deity and either actually or potentially hostile to Him have been admitted."

- M. B. Ahern said that if the creator lacks the power to prevent evil, unrestricted obedience would not be justified.

- Terrence Penelhum wrote: "From time to time thinkers suggest that there is a [divine being] who is all-good but not all-powerful." But although suggestions of this type avoid the problem of evil, "we are merely bored by them. The alternatives are always tacitly restricted to two—either there is a [divine being] who is all-powerful and all-good, or there is no [deity] at all. Christianity may not have convinced everybody, but it has certainly made us all very finicky."[71]

Of course, this "finicky" view assures that theodicy is impossible. In fact, some philosophers seem to have affirmed divine omnipotence for the very purpose of showing theism to be false because incoherent. For example:

- J. M. Findlay, referring to a "consensus" that it is "wholly anomalous to worship anything limited in any thinkable manner," said that this consensus leads us "to demand that our religious object . . . shouldn't stand surrounded by a world of *alien* objects, which . . . set limits to its influence." Findlay then used this demand to give an affirmative answer to the question asked by his article's title, "Can [Gawd's] Existence Be Disproved?"[72]

- Having equated Christian theism with traditional, all-determining theism, Antony Flew argued that Christian theism is incoherent, because it holds that nothing happens without Gawd's consent while maintaining that human beings sin by violating the will of Gawd. Then, with reference to views denying that the deity could control all events, Flew said that they would not be "true theism," so the advocates of such positions could be dismissed with the rebuke, "Your God is too small."[73]

- Roland Puccetti, after describing a divine being who cannot save a person from a raging flood or pull off a threat to end the world, said that such a deity "could hardly provoke the unstinted adoration and fearsome awe appropriate to total religious commitment," because the very concept of Gawd involves omnipotence. Then, stipulating that the idea of omnipotence is required by "reflective theism," he concluded that "all reflective theists hold an absurd or impossible concept of [Gawd]," because "the concept of [Gawd] is self-contradictory."[74]

- Having rejected traditional theism as incoherent, Kai Nielsen then dismissed all other concepts of divinity as anthropomorphic, "Zeus-like conceptions," which speak of the deity "as if he were some kind of great green bird" or "a sort of cosmic Mickey Mouse."[75]

- The same type of theological "Catch-22" is contained in the argument of Dewey Hoitenga, who rejected the type of free-will argument defended by Plantinga. In response to the claim that moral evil is incompatible with divine omnipotence, because it is inconsistent to speak of Gawd's *causing* us to do good *freely*, Hoitenga retorted by saying that Augustine and Calvin did not think so. Moreover, giving any iota of independence to the human will would set a limit to the deity's control over the world and hence "conflict with the theist's belief in providence." Then, after having blocked every possible way of making theism intelligible, Hoitenga concluded that theism is "a faith lacking understanding," in which theists employ propositions using terms that are unintelligible.[76]

The positions thus dismissed as *not really theistic* by Ahern, Campbell, Findlay, Flew, Nielsen, Penelhum, and Puccetti would include, by implication, those of such respected philosophers and theologians as John B. Cobb Jr., William James, Catherine Keller, C. Lloyd-Morgan, Reinhold Niebuhr, Schubert Ogden, Otto Pfleiderer, Andrew Seth Pringle-Pattison, Hastings Rashdall, Charles Raven, Marjorie Suchocki, William Temple, Frederick Tennant, James Ward, and Daniel Day Williams, as well as Hartshorne and Whitehead.

Although the type of argumentation used by Findlay, Flew, Puccetti, Nielsen, and Hoitenga is outrageous, it is not surprising, given their zeal to defeat the idea of a divine creator. What is surprising is that people who wish to promote theism would continue to define it in a way that makes it, in Puccetti's words, either "absurd or impossible."

CONCLUSION

The long history of theodicy has borne out the warning of Hermogenes: If the world is said to have been created *ex nihilo*, then the defense of the creator's goodness will be impossible. As long as Premise 2, with its acceptance of this view of creation is accepted, the best answer to the problem of evil is that which Stendhal reportedly gave: "[Gawd's] only excuse is that he does not exist." But to have a successful theodicy, one needs only to revise Premise 2, making it say instead that although God is all-powerful, God's power is "merely" the unique power to create a universe, not also omnipotence, understood as the power, once creatures are created, to override their power.

ENDNOTES

1. Richard Swinburne, *Providence and the Problem of Evil* (Oxford, 1998), 29.

2. Hans Küng, *On Being a Christian*, trans. Edward Quinn (Doubleday, 1976), 432.

3. Bart D. Ehrman, *God's Problem: How the Bible Fails to Answer Our Most Important Question—Why We Suffer* (HarperOne, 2008), 3.

4. James Wood, "Holiday in Hellmouth," *New Yorker*, 9 June 2008.

5. Ehrman, *God's Problem*, 26.

6. Ibid., 171.

7. Alvin Plantinga, *The Nature of Necessity* (Oxford University Press, 1974), and *God, Freedom, and Evil* (Eerdmans, 1977).

8. Ibid. I have referred to this false idea as the "omnipotence fallacy" in David Ray Griffin, "Worshipfulness and the Omnipotence Fallacy," Chapter 17 of *God, Power, and Evil: A Process Theodicy* (1976; Westminster John Knox, 2004).

9. J. L. Mackie, *The Miracle of Theism* (Oxford University Press, 1982), 154; H. J. McCloskey, "God and Evil," in Nelson Pike, ed., *God and Evil* (Prentice-Hall, 1964), 84.

10. Alvin Plantinga, *God and Other Minds* (Cornell University Press, 1967), 129.

11. Plato, *The Timaeus*, 30A.

12. Millard J. Erickson, *Christian Theology* (Baker Book House, 1985), 374.

13. Jon D. Levenson, *Creation and the Persistence of Evil: The Jewish Drama of Divine Omnipotence* (Harper & Row, 1988), 121.

14. Gerhard May, *Creatio Ex Nihilo: The Doctrine of "Creation out of Nothing" in Early Christian Thought*, trans. A. S. Worrall (T. & T. Clark, 1994), xi–xii, 7–8, 11, 16, 21, 27.

15. Ibid., xiii, 61, 74, 122.

16. Ibid., 40, 43, 56.

17. Ibid., 140, 141, 142, 145, 146.

18. Ibid, 140, 141, 146, 147.

19. Ibid., 147, 159, 178.

20. Ibid., 147, 159, 178.

21. Ibid., 161.

22. Ibid., 167–68, 174.

23. Erickson, *Christian Theology*, 277.

24. St. Augustine, *On the Spirit and the Letter,* trans. John H. S. Burleigh, LIV.

25. St. Augustine, *Enchiridion*, trans. J. F. Shaw, XIV.96; XVI.102; *The City of God*, trans. Marcus Dods, X.14, Encyclopedia Britannica.

26. *Enchiridion*, XXIV.95.

27. St. Augustine, *On the Predestination of the Saints*, XXII.

28. *The City of God*, XI.18; *Enchiridion*, XXIV.96.

29. For a more extensive summary of Augustine's theodicy, see Chapter 6 of Griffin, *God, Power, and Evil.*

30. John Calvin, *Institutes of the Christian Religion*, ed. John T. McNeill, trans. Ford Lewis Battles, Vol. III, xxiii. 7; Vol. I. xviii. 1, Encyclopedia Britannica.

31. Ibid., Vol. III, xxiii.1; xiv.15.

32. Ibid., Vol. III, xxiii.6.

33. Ibid., Vol. XX, xxiii.7; xxiii.2. For a more complete summary of Calvin's theodicy, see Chapter 10 of Griffin, *God, Power, and Evil.*

34. Gottfried Wilhelm Leibniz, *Theodicy: Essays on the Good of God, the Freedom of Man, and the Origin of Evil*, trans. E. M. Huggard, from C. J.

Gerhardt's edition of the *Collected Philosophical Works* 1875–1890 (Yale University Press, 1952), 117.ii; 122.vi; 22, 80.

35. Ibid., 120.v; 117.ii.

36. Ibid., 123.viii. For a more extensive summary of Leibniz's theodicy, see Chapter 11 of Griffin, *God, Power, and Evil.*

37. John Passmore, *Philosophical Reasoning* (Basic Books, 1961), 60; Alfred North Whitehead, *Process and Reality,* corrected edition, ed. David Ray Griffin and Donald W. Sherburne (Free Press, 1978), 13.

38. Plantinga, however, said that he needed to present only a "defense," not a theodicy. He meant thereby that he did not feel obligated to explain why the decisions made by Gawd were justified.

39. John Hick, "An Irenaean Theodicy," Stephen T. Davis, ed., *Encountering Evil: Live Options in Theodicy* (Westminster John Knox Press, 2001).

40. Ibid., 38–39.

41. Ibid., 40–41.

42. John Hick, *Evil and the God of Love* (Harper & Row, 1966), 33.

43. Hick, "An Irenaean Theodicy," 42.

44. Ibid., 46–47.

45. Ibid., 46.

46. Ibid., 50.

47. Ibid., 47–48.

48. Ibid., 49, 51.

49. Hick, *Evil and the God of Love*, 183.

50. Hick, "An Irenaean Theodicy," 50.

51. Hick, *Evil and the God of Love*, 173, 263.

52. Ibid., 182.

53. Richard Swinburne, *Is There a God?* (Oxford University Press, 2010), 86.

54. Ibid., 87.

55. Ibid., 87–88.

56. Ibid., 89.

57. Ibid., 94.

58. Ibid., 94–95.

59. Ibid., 95.

60. Ibid., 96.

61. Ibid., 85.

62. David Ray Griffin, *Evil Revisited: Responses and Reconsiderations* (State University of New York Press, 1991); Stephen T. Davis, ed., *Encountering Evil: Live Options in Theodicy* (John Knox, 1981); Griffin, "In Response to William Hasker," in John B. Cobb, Jr., and Clark H. Pinnock, eds., *Searching for an Adequate God: A Dialogue between Process and Free Will Theists* (Eerdmans, 2000), 246–62; and Griffin, "Traditional Free Will Theodicy and Process Theodicy: Hasker's Claim for Parity," *Process Studies* 29/2 (Fall–Winter 2000), 209–26.

63. Richard L. Rubenstein, *After Auschwitz: Radical Theology and Contemporary Judaism* (Bobbs-Merrill, 1966), 46, 48, 64–65, 153.

64. Ibid., 67, 68, 70, 152.

65. Emil Fackenheim, *Quest for Past and Future: Essays in Jewish Theology* (Indiana University Press, 1968), 18, 20; *God's Presence in History: Jewish Affirmations and Philosophical Reflections* (Harper & Row, 1972), 18, 26, 73.

66. Fackenheim, *God's Presence,* 19; *Quest,* 197.

67. Fackenheim, *God's Presence*, 13–14; *Quest,* 16–17, 199, 201.

68. Fackenheim, *Quest,* 16–17, 200–02.

69. James F. Ross, *Philosophical Theology* (Bobbs-Merrill Company, 1969), 258, 264.

70. Alfred North Whitehead, *Adventures of Ideas* (1933; Free Press, 1967), 166.

71. Charles A. Campbell *On Selfhood and Godhood* (MacMillan 1957), 291; M. B. Ahern, *The Problem of Evil* (Routledge & Kegan Paul, 1971), ix; Terence Penelhum, "Divine Goodness and the Problem of Evil," *Religious Studies*, II (1966), 99.

72. J. N. Findlay, "Can God's Existence Be Disproved?" in *New Essays in Philosophical Theology*, ed. Antony Flew and Alasdair MacIntyre (SCM Press, 1955), 51–52. In "Has God's Existence Been Disproved? A Reply

to Professor J. N. Findlay" (in same volume), George E. Hughes said that Findlay had given such a good account of "what is involved in theism" that one could not rebut Findlay's argument by saying, "that is not at all the kind of being in whose existence I believe"—thereby illustrating how theists often aid atheists by defining theism in terms of Gawd.

73. Antony Flew, *God and Philosophy* (Dell, 1966), 51–52. (Many decades later, Flew came to affirm a deistic deity, as mentioned below in Chapter 14.)

74. Roland Puccetti, "The Concept of God," *Philosophical* Quarterly, XIV (1964), 245.

75. Kai Nielsen, *God, Scepticism and Modernity* (University of Ottawa Press, 1989), 2, 244; Nielsen, *An Introduction to the Philosophy of Religion* (St. Martin's Press), 1982), ix.

76. Dewey J. Hoitenga, Jr., "Logic and the Problem of Evil," *American Philosophical Quarterly* IV (1967), 121–22.

2

Scientific Naturalism

In addition to being contradicted by the problem of evil, the existence of Gawd is also ruled out by scientific naturalism, which most fundamentally is the doctrine that there are no supernatural interruptions of the world's normal cause-effect relations. Stated more fully, scientific naturalism holds that the universe involves an unbroken web of cause-and-effect relations; that every event occurs within this web, having causal antecedents and causal consequences; and that every event exemplifies a common set of causal principles.

This has been the scientific worldview since at least the end of the 19th century. For example, in his 1925 book, *Science and the Modern World*, Alfred North Whitehead said that the scientific mentality "instinctively holds that all things great and small are conceivable as exemplifications of general principles which reign throughout the natural order," so that "every detailed occurrence can be correlated with its antecedents in a perfectly definite manner, exemplifying general principles."[1]

Unfortunately, the name "scientific naturalism" has been hijacked to refer to a sensationistic version of this doctrine, according to which the only acceptable data and theories are ones that are based on our physical senses. According to this worldview, to affirm naturalism is to affirm atheism, materialism, and sensate empiricism, according to which we cannot perceive anything except by means of our physical senses.

In this book, the term "scientific naturalism" refers to the definition of naturalism given two paragraphs above, which can be called *generic* naturalism, because it is common to all species of naturalism. In a book entitled *Religion, Science and Naturalism,* theologian Willem Drees employed this definition, saying that naturalism rejects the belief "that God intervenes occasionally in the natural world."[2]

The term "scientific naturalism" should be used only in this sense. Naturalism does not necessarily imply atheism, materialism, and sensate empiricism. When one refers to naturalism in this more restrictive sense, it should be labeled *sensationist naturalism.*

I. THE EMERGENCE OF SCIENTIFIC NATURALISM

Scientific naturalism (in the generic sense) had emerged in Greece in the sixth-century BCE, as pioneered by philosophers such as Thales, Heraclitus, Anaximander, and Anaximenes. Prior to them, Greek culture, as represented in the works of Homer and Hesiod, had fully accepted, as did other cultures at the time, the idea of supernatural incursions into the world. As David Lindberg said in his book *The Beginnings of Western Science*, the world of Homer and Hesiod was "a capricious world, in which nothing could be safely predicted because of the boundless possibilities of divine intervention."[3]

By contrast, the sixth-century philosophers started portraying the world as a "cosmos," an *ordered* world in which intervening gods were excluded, so "explanations are entirely naturalistic." Among these philosophers, "there was a wide agreement that causes . . . are to be sought only in the nature of things," not in the "personal whim or the arbitrary fancies of the gods."[4]

Plato's cosmology, it is true, did include a divine creator. However, Lindberg pointed out, "Plato's deities never interrupt the course of nature." Accordingly, "Plato's reintroduction of divinity does not represent a return to the unpredictability of the Homeric world." Likewise, although Aristotle also had a deity, it was not even a creator, but only an "unmoved mover."[5]

2. THE CONTEST BETWEEN NATURALISM AND SUPERNATURALISM

But this period of scientific naturalism in the West was broken by the adoption of Christian thought, especially after the acceptance of *creatio ex nihilo*. In his book *Science and Religion*, John Hedley Brooke, looking back over Western civilization prior to the Enlightenment, wrote:

> [I]t is almost impossible to exaggerate the extent to which belief in [divine] intervention once permeated European societies, creating popular images of the disruption of nature that could hardly have been congenial to a critical science of nature.[6]

However, some Christian thinkers, once they were exposed to the naturalism of Aristotle, tried to accommodate it. Already in the 12th century, some Christian thinkers said that we need to refer to divine causation only for the original creation of the world. From then on, virtually all things could be explained in terms of natural causes, except for the Christian miracles, in which Gawd suspended, or over-rode, the ordinary laws of nature in order to give testimony to Christianity as the true religion.

Even this allowance for supernatural interruptions of the ordinary causal processes was mitigated by the scheme of primary and secondary causation. According to this scheme, Gawd is the *primary* cause of all events, but most events are brought about by Gawd *indirectly*, by means of natural causes, called *secondary* causes; miracles are simply events that Gawd chose to bring about directly, without using secondary causes. Given this view, miracles are not complete exceptions to the normal order, because Gawd is the primary cause of *all* events.

Nevertheless, some thinkers in the 12th and 13th centuries decided that their task, as natural philosophers, was to explain as much as they could in purely naturalistic terms, with a few thinkers even suggesting naturalistic explanations for some of the biblical miracles. The more radical of these philosophers said, under Aristotle's influence, that natural philosophy, employing only experience and reason, comes to conclusions that contradict Christian doctrines.

Natural philosophy, in particular, was said to support the idea that the world is eternal, not created, and that there are certain things that the divine being could not do. On this last point, Christian theologians had always held that Gawd could not do that which is *logically* contradictory, such as create round squares. But some of these philosophers said that there were certain things that, even though they involved no logical contradiction, the divine being could not create.[7]

This movement produced a reaction from the church in the form of the Condemnation of 1277, in which 219 propositions drawn from Aristotelian writings were forbidden. The forbidden propositions included the idea that the world is eternal; that nature is a system of natural causes closed to divine providence and hence miracles; and that there are some things beyond logical contradictions that the divine being cannot do.[8]

As this list shows, the issue involved divine omnipotence and freedom over against the Aristotelian claim that our world embodies various necessary principles, so that it could not, in some fundamental respects, be otherwise. In condemning this claim, says Lindberg, the church's spokesmen "declared, in opposition to Aristotle, that the world is whatever its omnipotent Creator chose to make it."[9] In other words, the church declared the creator to be Gawd.

THE CENTRALITY OF *CREATIO EX NIHILO*

Central to this conflict was the question of whether the world was eternal or created *ex nihilo*. Aristotle's position was based on the insight that the eternal and the necessary are identical: whatever is eternal is necessary, and whatever is necessary is eternal. Combining this insight with his view that our world had always existed, Aristotle considered all the principles of our world, including what would later be called the "laws of nature," to be necessary.

By contrast, Christian theologians, because of the doctrine of *creatio ex nihilo*, had to say that not only our particular world but finitude itself was freely created by Gawd. Thomas Aquinas thought so highly of Aristotle that he referred to him as simply "the philosopher," who had shown what reason would come to on its own, without the aid of super-natural revelation. However, although Thomas agreed with Aristotle that reason could not prove the world had a beginning, he stated that this fact had been revealed. "According to our faith," said Thomas, "nothing has always existed except [Gawd] alone."[10]

The Condemnation of 1277 led in the 14th century to a preoccu-pation with the theme of divine omnipotence. The goal of emphasizing the absolute omnipotence of Gawd, without undercutting the regularity presupposed by natural philosophy, led to the distinction between the *absolute* and the *ordained* power of Gawd. "When we consider [Gawd's] power absolutely," explained Lindberg in summarizing this position,

> we acknowledge that [Gawd] is omnipotent and can do as he wishes; at the moment of creation there were no factors other than the law of noncontradiction limiting the kind of world he might create. But in fact we recognize that [Gawd] chose from among the infinity of possibilities open to him and created *this* world; and, because he is a consistent [Gawd], we can be confident that he will (but for a rare exception) abide by the order thus established, and we need not worry about perpetual divine tinkering.[11]

For the most part, therefore, we can, according to this position, ignore the absolute power of Gawd, focusing on only the ordained power of Gawd—the divine decision to work, at least most of the time, through the laws of this world.

Once this point had been established, the use of Aristotle to under-stand the contingent laws of this world was allowed. In fact, shortly after Thomas was elevated to sainthood, teachers at the University of Paris were required to swear that they would teach "the system of Aristotle. . . . except in those cases that are contrary to the faith."[12]

THE RISE OF VOLUNTARISM

However, whereas Thomas had emphasized divine *reason*, saying that Gawd acts on the basis of what divine omniscience sees to be good, a 14th-century movement called "voluntarism" emphasized the divine *will*, saying that there is nothing prior to the divine will that compromises the divine freedom, not even the idea of the good. Insofar as anything is good, it is so only because the divine will made it such. This voluntarist position was embodied in both the Protestant Reformation and the Roman Catholic movement sometimes called the Counter-Reformation.

On the Protestant side, voluntarism was exemplified by the position of Calvin, mentioned above in Chapter 1. A representative statement of the implications of Calvinism for science was provided by 19th-century theologian Charles Hodge, who said in response to the question of how Gawd is related to the laws of nature:

> The answer to that question . . . is, First, that He is their author. . . . Secondly, He is independent of them. He can change, annihilate, or suspend them at pleasure. He can operate with or without them. The "Reign of Law" must not be made to extend over Him who made the laws.[13]

3. THE HERMETIC TRADITION

Histories of science had long portrayed the "modern scientific worldview" as having developed in opposition to Aristotelian science. According to this history, the Aristotelian worldview, with its organic and teleological concepts, was replaced by the "new mechanical philosophy," with its exclusion of all such ideas in favor of mathematical and mechanistic notions. In the 1970s, however, it became recognized that the mechanical philosophy had battled at least as vigorously against a third worldview, which is sometimes called "neoplatonic," sometimes "spiritualist," and sometimes "magical." Brian Easlea wrote:

> "Modern science" emerged, at least in part, out of a three-cornered contest between proponents of the established view and adherents of newly prospering magical cosmologies, both to be opposed in the seventeenth century by advocates of revived mechanical world views. Scholastic Aristotelianism versus magic versus mechanical philosophies.[14]

This neoplatonic or magical cosmology arose as part of the Greek Renaissance, which began in Italy in the latter part of the fifteenth century. This Greek Renaissance, which superseded the Latin Renaissance that had begun in Italy in the 14th century, dealt with philosophy, theology, mathematics, and science.

The so-called Hermetic or magical tradition was rooted in the writings attributed to Hermes Trismegistus—supposedly an ancient Egyptian author—which were made prominent by Marsilio Ficino, one of the founders of the Greek Renaissance.[15]

Although there was a distinction between "black" and "white" magic, the intellectuals focused primarily on white magic, which included medicine, natural philosophy (physics), astrology, alchemy, and mathematics. Given the association today of the term "magic" with tricks, as well as so-called black magic, it is best to follow the practice of referring to this third movement as the "Hermetic tradition."[16]

One of the features of the Hermetic movement was the notion of "action at a distance" as a natural phenomenon. From this perspective, the "miracles" of Jesus—such as mind-reading, physical healings, the multiplication of food, and walking on water—were extraordinary occurrences, but they were fully natural. They were, therefore, not different in kind from similar events that have occurred in other traditions, such as Hinduism and Buddhism.[17]

This Hermetic tradition was deeply threatening to the church, because the church held that the Christian miracles showed Christianity, alone among the religions on the face of the earth, to have been ordained by Gawd as the vehicle of truth and salvation. These miracles, understood as events produced by Gawd's supernatural intervention in the world, were Gawd's signal of the singular truth and saving power of the Christian religion. Without this signal, the church's claim to possess the "keys to the kingdom" would have seemed groundless. If the miracles could be given a naturalistic interpretation, the church's authority would be in peril.

4. THE "SCIENTIFIC REVOLUTION"

The so-called scientific revolution of the 16th and 17th centuries was in the first place the creation of a new worldview, in which theological voluntarism was joined with Democritean atomism (Democritus was a fifth-century BCE Greek philosopher), which had been revived by Galileo.[18] The joining of these two traditions resulted in supernaturalistic mechanism.

Although this supernatural-mechanical philosophy was the basis for what is normally called the "scientific revolution," it arose in large part to protect the authority of the church, which was seen as important to the social order. Besides threatening the supernatural character of the Christian miracles, the Hermetic worldview was also threatening to those who favored the status quo, given the almost universal assumption that the authority of the government depended upon the support of the church, with its power over people's extramundane status: What would prevent rebellion if the church were no longer seen to possess such power?

MARIN MERSENNE

Foundational for the use of the mechanical philosophy to protect the supernatural nature of Jesus' miracles was Fr. Marin Mersenne. Along with Pierre Gassendi, Mersenne preceded Descartes in introducing the mechanical philosophy into France (just as Robert Boyle preceded Isaac Newton's development of the mechanistic worldview in England).

In 1623, Mersenne published a criticism of the Hermetic philosophy, dealing especially with Giordano Bruno ("one of the wickedest men whom the earth has ever supported . . . who seems to have invented a new manner of philosophizing only in order to make underhand attacks on the Christian religion") and Thomas Fludd ("Bruno's vile successor and principal enemy of Christian religion").[19]

When Fludd replied, Mersenne, realizing that he needed an alternative system to defeat Fludd's Hermetic philosophy, appealed for help to Pierre Gassendi. Mersenne learned from Gassendi about the Democritean, mechanistic philosophy, which had recently been revived in Italy by Galileo.[20] Mersenne thereby became a major figure in the ascendancy of the mechanistic philosophy of nature, as indicated by the title of Robert Lenoble's book, *Mersenne ou la naissance du méchanisme* ("Mersenne or the Birth of Mechanism").

According to Lenoble, Mersenne came to see the Hermetic tradition as "public enemy number one" by virtue of the fact that, by affirming universal magic, it denied the supernatural character of the miracles upon which the Catholic Church was built. By regarding all wonders as natural, the magical philosophy in effect denied laws of nature, and without laws of nature to be broken, there could be no miracles in the true sense.[21]

The mechanistic philosophy was superior, Mersenne held, because it, by denying the possibility of influence at a distance, made clear that certain miraculous effects are naturally impossible. Mersenne acknowledged that similar events were reported in other religious traditions, but he said that they were produced by the devil. (Although truly supernatural power is possessed by Gawd alone, the devil had *preternatural* power, through which miracles could be simulated.)[22]

Accordingly, far from being used to undermine the belief in miracles, as older studies suggested, the mechanistic philosophy was used to support it.

DESCARTES

Carrying out the new approach pioneered by Mersenne (drawing on Galileo and Gassendi), Descartes said that "there exists nothing in the whole of nature which cannot be explained in terms of purely corporeal causes." This position meant that action at a distance was impossible. According to Richard Westfall, "the fundamental tenet of Descartes' mechanical philosophy of nature [was] that one body can act on another only by direct contact."[23]

ROBERT BOYLE

Having adopted this perspective, Robert Boyle denounced the views of a man named Henry Stubbe, who had attacked Christianity from a Hermetic perspective. In a 1666 letter to Boyle, Stubbe argued that the miracles of Jesus, being similar to miracles in other traditions, were fully natural. Boyle replied that Stubbe's view depended upon a false worldview, involving an "animated and intelligent universe." Unlike the mechanical philosophy, said Boyle, this worldview fails to recognize the distinction between the divine creator and the created nature.[24]

Against such "enemies of Christianity," who grant the truth of the New Testament's reports of miracles but, employing a "vulgar" philosophy, give a naturalistic account of them, Boyle recommended the virtues of the mechanical philosophy. The most important virtue is that, contrary to the vulgar philosophy, the mechanical philosophy insists that matter interacts only by contact.[25] Because no natural explanation of miracles is possible consistent with the principles of the mechanical philosophy, Boyle said, people who accept it will "frankly acknowledge, and heartily believe, divers effects to be truly miraculous, that may be plausibly ascribed to other causes in the vulgar philosophy."[26]

Besides using the mechanical philosophy to protect the supernatural character of the New Testament miracles, Boyle also used it to defend the existence of the transcendent deity described by the theologians of the Reformation and Counter-Reformation, in opposition to the view, common to Renaissance and Aristotelian naturalists, that creatures have "internal principles of motion." Criticizing these "vulgar" views for making nature "almost divine," Boyle argued that motion is not inherent in matter. The creatures do not need the power to move themselves, Boyle said, because an external, omnipotent agent can do everything directly.[27]

The idea that motion is externally imposed was important, because some people had used the idea of matter as self-moving to portray the world as a self-organizing whole, thereby denying the need for a transcendent creator of the world. Boyle argued for inert matter in order to support a wholly transcendent deity who had created the world out of nothing and therefore exercised absolute dominion over it.[28] Boyle wrote:

> [S]ince motion does not essentially belong to matter, . . . the motions of all bodies, at least at the beginning of things, . . . were impressed upon them . . . by an external immaterial agent, [Gawd].[29]

ISAAC NEWTON

The idea of inert material particles was also used by Isaac Newton to prove the existence of an omnipotent deity. Having pointed out that inertia is merely a passive principle, Newton said:

> By this Principle alone there never could have been any Motion in the World. Some other Principle was necessary for putting Bodies into Motion [and hence] a powerful ever-living Agent

[who] in the Beginning form'd Matter in solid, massy, hard, impenetrable, moveable Particles.[30]

5. THE TRANSITION TO COMPLETE NATURALISM

However, although these thinkers used the mechanistic philosophy of nature to support a supernatural deity who could intervene in the world, the mechanistic way of thinking quickly led to, in Brooke's words, "a growing aversion among natural philosophers to talk of divine intervention."[31] This aversion soon led to a virtual deism, which allowed for only a few divine interventions, perhaps only one. The allowance for one supernatural intervention is illustrated by the famous geologist Charles Lyell, whose view will be discussed in the following chapter.

Soon, moreover, some members of the scientific community moved to a *complete* deism, according to which there could not be even a single interruption of the normal pattern of cause-effect relations. "[T]he more we know of the fixed laws of nature," wrote Charles Darwin in his *Autobiography*, "the more incredible do miracles become."[32]

Darwin's consistently deistic version of scientific naturalism quickly became *the* scientific worldview—except for one more modification, which was required by the fact that deism was not completely naturalistic: By saying that the world was originally created *ex nihilo*, it implied that the basic causal principles of our world were not really *natural*, in the sense of lying in the very nature of things. Darwin's affirmation of a divine creator, in other words, allowed in principle for the possibility that the imposed causal principles could be interrupted by their divine creator. This possibility was removed by the movement known as neo-Darwinism.

Although the move to a complete naturalism was made only in the latter half of the 19th century, this is to speak only of the English-speaking world. It occurred more quickly in Germany, as shown by the fact that philosopher and biblical critic David Friedrich Strauss, reflecting German currents of thought, declared in his 1835 book, *Life of Jesus*, that the biblical miracles must be interpreted as myths. The reason why they had to be considered myths was that modern thought presupposes that "all things are linked together by a chain of causes and effects, which suffer no interruption."[33]

The transition occurred even earlier in France, when Denis Diderot, arguably the most important figure of the French Enlightenment, rejected deism in favor of an atheistic version of naturalism in the middle of the 18th century.[34]

In any case, after the long retreat from Greek naturalism because of Christian supernaturalism, especially the doctrine of *creatio ex nihilo*, the world of science, including science-based philosophy, made its way back to full-fledged naturalism. By the beginning of the 20th century, scientific naturalism had become the framework of the worldwide scientific community. If, like Plato, science-based philosophers affirm a divine reality, this reality cannot be Gawd.

6. PHILOSOPHICAL AND THEOLOGICAL HOLD-OUTS

However, among philosophers and theologians, there are many hold-outs. Some of them affirm the view of the 14th-century Voluntarists. "Nature," wrote Calvinist theologian Millard Erickson,

> is under [Gawd's] control; and while it ordinarily functions in uniform and predictable ways in obedience to the laws he has structured into it, he can and does also act within it in ways which contravene these normal patterns (miracles).[35]

According to Richard Swinburne, who is in the tradition of Greek Orthodoxy:

> [Gawd] can bring about . . . any event he chooses. . . . [Gawd] is not limited by the laws of nature; he makes them and can change or suspend them. . . . [Gawd] is *omnipotent*: he can do anything.[36]

Likewise, aforementioned Calvinist philosopher Alvin Plantinga, who is in some respects a sophisticated philosopher, holds a similar view. Explicit about his acceptance of supernatural exceptions to the normal causal processes, Plantinga wrote: "[Gawd] has often treated what he has made in a way different from the way in which he ordinarily treats it," illustrating this point by reference to miracles.

Plantinga even argues that there is no reason why scientists *qua* scientists could not refer to supernatural causation: "If after considerable study, we can't see how some event could have happened by way of the ordinary workings of matter," wrote Plantinga, it is natural for theists to think that Gawd did something different and special. "And why couldn't one," continued Plantinga rhetorically, "conclude this precisely as a scientist? Where is it written that such a conclusion can't be part of science?"[37]

Plantinga refers to his position as "theistic science." But fellow conservative religious philosopher William Hasker, reflecting the completeness with which the scientific community now presupposes naturalism, has quipped that Plantinga's view "might better be termed 'quixotic science.'"[38]

However, even Hasker himself, while rejecting Plantinga's Calvinism, affirms a version of supernaturalism. As a member of a school of thought known as "methodological naturalism," Hasker holds that science should be recognized to be "methodologically naturalistic" (or "methodologically atheistic"), because "scientific explanation cannot appeal to supernatural intervention."[39]

Another member of this school, Ernan McMullin, explained that the atheism of scientific naturalism is only "a way of characterizing a particular *methodology,* no more." Then, arguing that the natural sciences by definition deal only with a limited domain (the "natural" or "creaturely" domain), these thinkers say that scientific naturalism should be placed within a supernaturalistic framework.[40]

According to McMullin, although Gawd has chosen to work through natural or secondary causes, "[Gawd] *could* also, if He so chose, relate to His creation in a different way, in the dramatic mode of a grace that overcomes nature." Hasker, moreover, adds that Gawd actually does this. Having said that "scientific explanation cannot appeal to supernatural intervention," he announced that Christians should "refuse to make the assumption that every actual event has a scientific explanation."[41]

Noting that the distinction between the domains of *nature* and *grace* was meant to avoid conflicts between science and religion, McMullin admitted that conflicts could not be completely avoided. However, he assured readers, "the domain of such potential conflict is quite limited."[42] Likewise, William Alston, writing from this same point of view, claimed that "the odd miracle would not seem to violate anything of importance to science," because it would probably not conflict with any actual observations.

CONCLUSION

Willem Drees, who was quoted earlier, rightly replied to Alston, saying:

> By undermining scientific reasoning, this argument for the possibility of occasional miracles does undermine something "of importance to science," even though it does not conflict with any observations. The argument undermines the integrity of science . . . , the underlying spirit, the larger web of belief, intentions and procedures of which it is a part.[43]

For many scientists, indeed, the fact that traditional theism allows for the possibility of miracles is central to their atheism, at least as important as the problem of evil. For example, in a response to the question of why he is so hostile to religion, Richard Dawkins said: "As a scientist, I am hostile to fundamentalist religion because it actively debauches the scientific enterprise."[44]

Harvard biologist Richard Lewontin, while admitting the "patent absurdity" of some explanations of evolution based on materialistic atheism, said that scientists must hold fast to it anyway. They "cannot allow a Divine Foot in the door," said Lewontin: "To appeal to an omnipotent deity is to allow that at any moment the regularities of nature may be ruptured, that miracles may happen."[45]

Although Lewontin was wrong to assume that scientific naturalism requires materialistic atheism, he correctly indicated that the scientific worldview now rules out Gawd.

In Part II of this book, however, we will see that God is compatible with scientific naturalism—as long as it is not the sensationist and materialistic version of naturalism.

ENDNOTES

1. Alfred North Whitehead, *Science and the Modern World* (1925; Free Press, 1967), 5, 12.

2. Willem Drees, *Religion, Science and Naturalism* (Cambridge University Press, 1996), 14.

3. David C. Lindberg, *The Beginnings of Western Science: The European Scientific Tradition in Philosophical, Religious, and Institutional Context, 600 B.C. to A.D. 1450* (Chicago: University of Chicago Press, 1992), 24.

4. Ibid., 26, 27.

5. Ibid., 42–43.

6. John Hedley Brooke, *Science and Religion: Some Historical Perspectives* (Cambridge: Cambridge University Press, 1991), 44.

7. Lindberg, *The Beginnings of Western Science*, 197–201, 234–35.

8. Ibid., 236–38.

9. Ibid., 239.

10. Brooke, *Science and Religion*, 60.

11. Lindberg, *The Beginnings of Western Science*, 243.

12. Ibid., 241.

13. Charles Hodge, *Systematic Theology* (1872; Eerdmans, 1982), Vol. I: 607.

14. Brian Easlea, *Witch Hunting, Magic, and the New Philosophy: An Introduction to the Debates of the Scientific Revolution 1450–1750* (Humanities Press, 1980), 89.

15. Frances Yates, *The Rosicrucian Enlightenment* (Shambhala, 1978), 79–84.

16. See Frances Yates, *Giordano Bruno and the Hermetic Tradition* (University of Chicago Press, 1964).

17. Easlea, *Witch Hunting, Magic and the New Philosophy*, 94–95.

18. Ibid., 108.

19. A. C. Crombie, "Marin Mersenne," C. G. Gillispie, ed., *Dictionary of Scientific Biography*, Vol. 9 (Scribner's, 1974), 316–22.

20. Easlea, *Witch Hunting, Magic and the New Philosophy,* 108.

21. Robert Lenoble, *Mersenne ou la naissance du méchanisme* (Librairie Philosophique J. Vrin, 1943), 9, 120, 133, 157.

22. Ibid., 133, 157–58, 210, 375, 381; Margaret Galitzin, "The Supernatural and the Preternatural," Tradition in Action, 14 November 2008.

23. Easlea, *Witch Hunting, Magic and the New Philosophy,* 111; Richard J. Westfall, *Never at Rest: A Biography of Isaac Newton* (Cambridge University Press, 1980), 381.

24. Easlea, *Witch Hunting, Magic and the New Philosophy,* 94–95; James R. Jacob, "Boyle's Atomism and the Restoration Assault on Pagan Naturalism," *Social Studies of Science* 8 (1978): 211–33, at 218–19.

25. Robert Boyle, *The Works of the Honourable Robert Boyle* (London: A. Millar, 1744), Works III: 453, 457; Works IV: 416.

26. Jacob, "Boyle's Atomism," 219.

27. Eugene M. Klaaren, *Religious Origins of Modern Science: Belief in Creation in Seventeenth-Century Thought* (Eerdmans, 1977), 149, 162, 166.

28. Ibid., 163.

29. *The Works of the Honourable Robert Boyle,* Vol. IV, 394.

30. Alexandre Koyré, *From the Closed World to the Infinite Universe* (The Johns Hopkins Press, 1957), 216, 217, 219.

31. Brooke, *Science and Religion,* 155.

32. Ibid., 271.

33. David Friedrich Strauss, *The Life of Jesus Critically Examined,* trans. George Eliot (1855; Fortress Press, 1972).

34. "Denis Diderot: 1713–1784" (Brandeis University); Brooke, *Science and Religion,* 270.

35. Millard J. Erickson, *Christian Theology* (Baker Book House, 1985), 54.

36. Richard Swinburne, *Is There a God?* (Oxford University Press, 1996), 7.

37. Alvin Plantinga, "Reply to the Basingers on Divine Omnipotence," *Process Studies* 11/1 (Spring 1991): 25–29.

38. William Hasker, "*Darwin on Trial* Revisited: A Review Essay," *Christian Scholar's Review* 24/4 (May 1995): 479–88, at 483.

39. Ibid.

40. Ernan McMullin, "Plantinga's Defense of Special Creation," *Christian Scholar's Review* 21/1 (1991): 55–79, at 57.

41. Ibid., 76–77; Hasker, *"Darwin on Trial Revisited,"* 483.

42. McMullin, "Plantinga's Defense of Special Creation," 62.

43. Drees, *Religion, Science and Naturalism,* 94–95.

44. Richard Dawkins, *The God Delusion* (Houghton Mifflin, 2006), 321.

45. Richard Lewontin, "Billions and Billions of Demons," *New York Review of Books*, 9 January 1997: 28–32, at 31.

3

Evolution

Whereas the problem of evil and the rise of scientific naturalism have both been described as the main reason for atheism, some writers give this distinction to the rise of Darwinian evolution. Michael Denton said:

> [T]he decline in religious belief can probably be attributed more to the propagation and advocacy by the intellectual and scientific community of the Darwinian version of evolution than to any other single factor.[1]

Pointing out that most evolutionary scientists are atheists, historian of science William Provine said: "[M]any have been driven there by their understanding of the evolutionary process and other science."[2]

The evolutionary perspective was radically new in at least two respects. First, when this perspective developed in the 19th century, society for the most part, especially in the English-speaking world, still largely accepted the biblically based idea that life was only a few thousand years old. The evidence for evolution showed that life was much, much older.

Closely related, the evidence for evolution showed that today's plants and animals emerged from very simple organisms through a long, slow evolutionary process. Accordingly, the evolutionary process, including the process that brought forth human beings, required a very long time (known today to have taken about 3 billion years since life first emerged on this planet).

1. EVOLUTION VS. GAWD

There are three major ways in which this new perspective on life militated against the traditional belief that the universe was created by Gawd.

BIBLE AS INERRANTLY INSPIRED

When the evolutionary perspective emerged, Christian doctrine was still widely assumed to be based on infallible revelation, which was protected from error by means of the inerrant inspiration of the Bible. But the historical study of the Bible showed that it was not inerrant.

The idea that the Bible, alone among the world's writings, was inerrant implied that it was produced in a unique way. Usually, authors are influenced by all sorts of factors—including ignorance, bias, and historically and culturally conditioned ideas—that prevent their writings from being error-free. Whatever truth is expressed in such writings is always mixed with error. But authors of inerrant writings would need to be protected from all such sources of error.

There is, however, no natural process through which this protection could be provided. The writing of an inerrant book would, therefore, require protection from error by supernatural agency. The idea that the Bible was inerrantly inspired implied, accordingly, that the deity had supernaturally protected this book from error.

The inerrancy of the Bible was hence considered one of the exceptions to the natural cause-effect processes. Indeed, the production of the Bible was considered a divine miracle. Although the various books of the Bible had the names of human authors attached to them (such as Isaiah, Matthew, and John), the Holy Spirit, the third Person of the Trinity, was said to be the true author.

This view of the Bible had been rejected by some intellectuals since at least the 17th century, when the Jewish philosopher Baruch Spinoza provided the beginning of the critical study of the Bible. In line with the new emphasis on empirical-mathematical science, Spinoza called false any biblical passages implying that nature's system of causal laws was violated. A crucial example was the story in Joshua 10:12–13, in which God, in response to a request from Joshua, made the sun stand still (so that there would be time to defeat the Amorites). This same passage was also crucial, incidentally, in Galileo's argument for heliocentrism, which led him to be charged with heresy. More radical than Galileo, Spinoza used this passage to argue that the Bible was not divinely inspired.[3]

After Spinoza, many other scholars provided abundant evidence that the Bible is not inerrant, and that it was written in the same ways as other books. For a long time, however, the scientific study of the Bible did not have much influence on society in general.

The widespread confrontation with evidence that the Bible could not have been inerrantly inspired was brought about by the evidence for the evolution of our world. This evidence made the inerrant inspiration of the Bible implausible, given the fact that the Bible indicated that the world had been created only a few thousand years ago. The evidence for evolution indicated that the authorship of the Bible did not constitute a supernatural exception to the processes by which writings are normally produced. By virtue of showing that the Bible was not written by Gawd, scholars removed one of the supports for Gawd's existence.

HUMAN BEINGS CREATED IN THE IMAGE OF THE DIVINE CREATOR

A particular implication of the loss of biblical inerrancy is important enough to be treated as a separate point. According to the biblically based idea of human origins, humans were unique in having been created in the image of the divine creator, but the evolutionary perspective implied that this was a myth.

The idea that human beings alone were created in the divine image implied that they were special creations. But the evolutionary perspective implied that humans, like other animals, evolved from lower-grade beings. The conclusion that humans were not special creations easily led to the idea that the world was not created by Gawd. If the human soul was not supernaturally created, resulting instead from the same evolutionary processes that created all the other animals, then perhaps the world came about without any supernatural agency.

THE SLOWNESS OF THE EVOLUTIONARY PROCESS

In addition, the evolutionary process raised a very difficult question with regard to divine omnipotence: Why did the process go on so long before human beings were created?

This question was given special urgency by the traditional Christian assumption that the world was created as a stage for the divine-human drama. That is, the only ultimately important question was whether, after humans die, they spend eternity in heaven or hell. Indeed, the whole world was created to provide souls suitable for eternal life with the divine creator. But if the world's value consisted only in being a stage for the drama of the human soul in relation to its creator, why did the creator take so long to get to the main act?

The traditional view, according to which the world was created in a week, entailed that there was no long wait. But the new view entailed that human beings, especially civilized human beings, have existed for only a tiny portion of the history of the world. In Darwin's time, the world was considered to be about a hundred million years old. Human civilization arose only about 10,000 years ago. So roughly 99.9 percent of the Earth's history occurred before human civilization arose.

The problem is that the deity of traditional theism, which in this book is called Gawd, could have created the world, complete with human beings, as quickly as suggested by the book of Genesis. In fact, Gawd is by definition omnipotent, so everything could have been created in a split second. The question is why Gawd, after creating the Earth, would have waited hundreds of millions of years before bringing forth the creature for whom the whole world was created.

Even if we reject the anthropocentric view, according to which humans alone have intrinsic value, it is still reasonable to hold that humans and the other higher animals have more intrinsic value than more elementary creatures. The question can hence be reformulated: Why would Gawd have allowed most of the Earth's history to go by before bringing forth the most valuable creatures? The most likely answer, many people concluded, is that Gawd simply does not exist.

More recent timelines have made the problem even worse. Rather than merely hundreds of millions of years, the Earth was formed over four billion years ago. And if Big Bang cosmology is correct, the universe as a whole was created over 13 billion years ago. Assuming that humans and the other higher animals are the most valuable creatures to have been produced in the evolutionary process, is it plausible that an omnipotent creator would have used such an extremely slow evolutionary process, taking over 13 billion years, to have produced these results? One can say, of course, that "evolution is the deity's way of creating." But the question remains: Unless this were the only way to create a world such as ours, why would the deity have used this method?

Moreover, whereas the discussion thus far has been about evolution as such, the distinctively Darwinian view of evolution creates even more problems for Gawd.

2. DARWINIAN AND NEO-DARWINIAN EVOLUTION

The basic idea of evolution had been discussed long before Charles Darwin. Indeed, his grandfather, Erasmus Darwin, was one of the earliest evolutionists. But Charles Darwin's conception of evolution had some distinctive elements.

One of these elements reflected the fact that Darwin was a member of a movement insisting on a completely consistent scientific naturalism, according to which an exception to the normal causal principles is not conceivable. Darwin's adoption of this view was illustrated by his insistence on a strict adherence to the position known as "uniformitarianism," according to which explanations of things in the past should not employ causes that are not operating today.

This doctrine, which was advocated by a few scientists in the 18th century, was held most influentially by geologist Charles Lyell in the early 19th century. Lyell's epoch-making book on geology was subtitled, "An Attempt to Explain the Former Changes of the Earth's Surface by Reference to Causes Now in Operation."

Although Lyell was called the "father of uniformitarianism," he affirmed an exception: Believing that the origin of the human mind could not be explained in terms of natural causes alone, Lyell argued that divine intervention added "the moral and intellectual faculties of the human race, to a system of nature which had gone on for millions of years without the intervention of any analogous cause." This suggestion meant, Lyell added, that we must "assume a primeval creative power which does not act with uniformity."[4]

However, Lyell's younger friend Charles Darwin developed a theory of how humans could have evolved through the natural selection of random variations. In a letter to Lyell, Darwin rejected the idea of divine additions to explain the distinctive capacities of the human mind, saying: "I would give nothing for the theory of natural selection, if it requires miraculous additions at any one stage of descent."[5]

Darwin still believed in a divine creator, thinking evolution intelligible only on the assumption that the deity, in creating the universe, had built in laws of evolutionary development. But Darwin insisted on a consistently deistic view, with not a single interruption of these laws. As a member of the movement promoting scientific naturalism, Darwin considered the fulfillment of this movement's ideal to require the complete rejection of divine interventions.

Given the traditional way of understanding special divine causation in the world, according to which divine causation brings about effects by replacing natural causes, Darwinian evolution ruled out divine causation, except in the creation of the universe and the laws that govern it.

Next, in the view that would come to be called neo-Darwinism, Darwin's deistic creator was rejected in favor of the idea that there is nothing that requires reference to deity to explain it, not even the existence of the world. This view was expressed emphatically by an outspoken advocate of scientific naturalism, John Tyndall, who famously declared, "We claim, and we shall wrest from theology, the entire domain of cosmological theory."[6]

Darwin believed that the evolutionary process was directed, in the sense that the divine creator had built in various laws and tendencies, so that the evolutionary process would be progressive, with the aim being the creation of beings with moral and intellectual qualities. According to the neo-Darwinian view, by contrast, there is no guidance to evolution whatsoever, and no progress. In the words of Steven Weinberg, evolution "demystified" life by showing "how the wonderful capabilities of living things could evolve through natural selection with no outside plan or guidance."[7]

To summarize: Although Darwin accepted the traditional view that the universe was created by an omnipotent deity, he excluded Gawd from having any ongoing activity in the evolutionary process. In neo-Darwinism, this half-way position was left behind in favor the rejection of the very existence of Gawd.

However, in spite of the fact that Gawd seems to be ruled out by the evolutionary worldview, and even more by Darwinian and neo-Darwinian evolution, many thinkers have tried to reconcile Gawd and evolution.

3. ARE GAWD AND EVOLUTION COMPATIBLE?

Many Christians in the West, especially Americans, do not feel a need to reconcile Gawd with evolution, for they simply reject evolution. According to a 2013 Pew Research poll:

- 33 percent of Americans reject evolution, holding instead that "humans and other living things have existed in their present form since the beginning of time";

- 32 percent of Americans say that evolution is "due to natural processes such as natural selection";

- and 24 percent believe that "a supreme being guided the evolution of living things for the purpose of creating humans and other life in the form it exists today."[8]

Because most people in the West who believe in a supreme being think of it as omnipotent, probably close to 20 percent of Americans consider Gawd to be compatible with evolution, or at least the appearance of it. How could this compatibility be explained?

OMNIPOTENT DECEIT

One possibility would be that Gawd, while creating all the species separately, did this so as to give the appearance of evolution. For example, in an 1857 book entitled *Omphalos* (the Greek word for "navel"), Philip Henry Gosse argued that, given *creatio ex nihilo*, there would be traces of previous existence that had never occurred. For example, Adam had a navel, even though he was not born, trees were created with rings, and hippopotamuses with worn-down teeth.[9]

Duane Gish, a 20th-century creationist, dealt with the question of how we can see light from stars that are millions of light-years away. Gish argued that the astronomers are wrong to say that we are seeing stars as they existed millions of years ago. Rather, the universe was "supernaturally created," so the light did not start from the stars, but was created in-transit. Because Gawd created the stars, as the Bible tells us, to be signs, "obviously he'd have to make them visible immediately."[10]

A contemporary version of this view has been argued by Rabbi David Gottlieb, who wrote:

> [T]he real age of the universe is 5755 years, but it has misleading evidence of greater age. The bones, artifacts, partially decayed radium, potassium-argon, uranium, the red-shifted light from space, etc.—all of it points to a greater age which nevertheless is not true.[11]

As Eugenie Scott explained (in writing about this position, which is not hers), "An omnipotent being could create the universe to appear as if it had evolved but actually have created everything five minutes ago"—a view that Bertrand Russell stated long ago to be a logical possibility, saying: "We may all have come into existence five minutes ago, provided with ready-made memories, with holes in our socks and hair that needed cutting."[12]

Of course, most people emplying the idea of divine deceit believe that Gawd did not create the world five minutes ago, but a few thousand years ago. In any case, although some creationists have espoused this view, most traditional theists would consider it contrary to Gawd's character to use deception.

PROGRESSIVE CREATIONISM

Another approach is called "progressive creationism." According to this view, the timeline of evolutionary theorists is followed, so it took billions of years before humans emerged. But each species was created *ex nihilo*. This view is defended by some intellectuals, such as philosopher

Alvin Plantinga, who was quoted in the previous chapter as saying that "[Gawd] has often treated what he has made in a way different from the way in which he ordinarily treats it." From a theistic perspective, Plantinga said, "the claim that [Gawd] created mankind as well as many kinds of plants and animals separately and specially" is more probable than the claim that all living things have a common ancestry.[13]

THEISTIC EVOLUTION

The normal way to reconcile Gawd and evolution is called "theistic evolution." But there is no standard definition of the term. Rather, "Theistic evolution encompasses a wide array of different approaches and views."[14] For one thing, the label can be applied to approaches that portray evolution as guided by God, not Gawd. In the present chapter, however, the label is applied only to attempts to reconcile evolution with divine omnipotence.

For example, Darwin's own view was a version of theistic evolution, because Gawd created initial conditions, laws, and principles that guaranteed that evolution would be progressive, culminating in human beings.

Theistic evolution nowadays usually refers to the view that combines neo-Darwinian evolution with the position known as "methodological naturalism" (or "methodological atheism"), which was mentioned in the previous chapter. This approach is intended to allow scientists who are Christians to hold true to their Christian faith while accepting the currently accepted standards for membership in the scientific community. According to this view, the scientist qua scientist does not speak of Gawd, so as not to violate the convention that divine action is not discussed within science. But the scientist qua Christian places scientific evolution within a traditional Christian worldview.

For example, William Hasker, who made the famous quip that Plantinga's position is best called "quixotic science," says that "scientific explanation cannot appeal to supernatural intervention." Accordingly, he rejects Plantinga's progressive evolutionism, according to which Gawd has directly created the various species. Rather, Hasker says, "divine purpose enters into the process at another level—not in the origins of specific creatures, but in establishing the process as a whole."[15] In other words, Hasker recommends essentially the same view of creation as did Darwin.

Similarly, speaking about the creator suggested in Genesis, Job, Isaiah, and the Psalms, Ernan McMullin, also quoted in the previous chapter, asked rhetorically: "Would such a Being be likely to 'intervene' in His creation in the way that Plantinga describes?" Instead, Gawd "must be thought of as creating in that very first moment the potencies for all the kinds of living things that would come later, including the human body itself."[16]

However, although these thinkers describe Gawd's relation to the evolutionary process in the same way as did Darwin, they are not deists. For example, after saying that scientific explanation cannot appeal to Gawd, Hasker said that there may be *events that have no scientific explanation*. In particular, he said, it may be that "there just *is no* scientific (i.e. naturalistic) explanation of the origin of life." Likewise, McMullin justified speaking of miracles by appealing to the "old and valuable distinctions between nature and supernature, between the order of nature and the order of grace."[17]

These thinkers claim that this perspective shows neo-Darwinism, which excludes any appeal to supernatural interventions, to be fully compatible with Christian theism.[18] But it is not, as shown by their own statements. For example, Hasker said that he does not believe "that the kinds of processes described by neo-Darwinism are capable of producing some of the unique attributes of human beings." And McMullin, after having distinguished the order of nature from that of grace or salvation, says that "the story of salvation *does* bear on the origin of the first humans," meaning that "[Gawd] somehow 'leant' into cosmic history at the advent of the human."[19]

INTELLIGENT DESIGN

Still another attempt to reconcile Gawd and evolution is called "intelligent design" (ID), which has been expounded most authoritatively by William A. Dembski in his books *Intelligent Design* (1999) and *The Design Revolution* (2004).[20] The subtitle of the former book, *The Bridge between Science and Theology*, points to Dembski's claim that ID is a "third way" between supernaturalistic creationism, traditionally called "scientific creationism," and neo-Darwinian naturalism. This third way, Dembski claims, could in principle be acceptable to both the scientific and the religious communities.[21]

With regard to Dembski's statement that there is no good reason for the scientific community to consider ID unacceptable, he claims that it is very different from scientific creationism. The most obvious difference, according to Dembski, is that ID "has no prior religious commitments."[22]

In particular, besides not regarding the Genesis account as scientifically accurate, ID does *not*, Dembski asserts, identify the intelligent cause responsible for nature's design as "a supernatural agent" who "create[d] the world out of nothing."[23] Accordingly, he says, the charge that ID is committed to supernaturalism is a "red herring."[24] But then Dembski indicates otherwise:

- Speaking of a kind of theism that rejects supernaturalism, he says that it is "incompatible with Christian theism," primarily because "Christian theology . . . regards the doctrine of *creatio ex nihilo* . . . as nonnegotiable."[25] Dembski goes on for several pages in this vein without explaining why this discussion is relevant if ID has no prior religious commitments.

- Dembski even says that only a God who creates *ex nihilo* can be a designer in the true sense of the term.[26]

- Dembski also claims that ID "does not require miracles." But he then indicates otherwise:

- "[I]n a naturalized world that positively excludes miracles," Dembski says, "design becomes increasingly implausible."[27]

- Dembski then defends the reality of miracles, which occur when "[Gawd] over-rules the inherent capacities of an entity, endowing the entity with new capacities,"[28] as in "the bodily resurrection of Jesus Christ" and "the virgin birth."[29]

Dembski's claim to have a "third way," which would be acceptable to the scientific community, is also contradicted by his rejection of macroevolution, according to which present species have evolved out of previous species:

- While pointing out that some ID advocates accept macroevolution, as least provisionally, Dembski insists that the discussion should remain open.[30]

- He seems to accept the special creation of each species, as suggested by his comment that the Christian God, being omnipotent, is capable of "creating species from scratch," along with Dembski's statement that he regards CSI (complex specified information) as emerging "through discrete insertions over time."[31]

- It seems, therefore, that Dembski accepts progressive creationism.

Accordingly, Dembski has not presented a position that could in principle be accepted, even in principle, by the scientific community.

CONCLUSION

The rise of the evolutionary perspective provided challenges to the existence of an omnipotent deity that defenders of traditional theism have not been able to answer. The Darwinian and neo-Darwinian versions of evolution have increased the incompatibility. But the basic challenges have been provided by evolution as such:

- The evolutionary timeline is radically different from the biblical timeline, which was supposedly based on inerrant scripture.

- The evolutionary perspective undermines the idea that human beings were created all at once in the divine image—a notion that was also derived from supposedly inerrant scripture.

- The idea that the very long, slow process of evolution was the product of an omnipotent deity is simply implausible.

Accordingly, the science of evolution has provided an additional argument—along with the problem of evil and the conflict of divine omnipotence with scientific naturalism—against the existence of Gawd.

Although Dembski has not provided it, a third way is clearly needed. For example, Thomas Nagel wrote: "I reject both supernaturalism and neo-Darwinism's explanation of the sources of evolutionary change." That twofold rejection is expressed in his statement that a naturalistic teleology is needed.[32] An example of such a third way is sketched below in Chapters 13 and 14.

ENDNOTES

1. Michael Denton, *Evolution: A Theory in Crisis* (Burnett Books, 1991), 66.

2. William Provine, "Progress in Evolution and Meaning in Life," in Matthew H. Nitecki, ed., *Evolutionary Progress* (University of Chicago Press, 1988), 49–74, at 68.

3. T. M. Rudavsky, "Galileo and Spinoza: Heroes, Heretics, and Hermeneutics," *Journal of the History of Ideas*, 62/4 (October 2001): 611–31.

4. Lyell's statements are quoted in R. Hooykaas, *Natural Law and Divine Miracle: A Historical-Critical Study of the Principle of Uniformity in Geology, Biology, and Theology* (E. J. Brill, 1959), 114.

5. *The Life and Letters of Charles Darwin*, ed. Francis Darwin, Vol. 2: 6–7.

6. John Tyndall, "Belfast Address," in Tyndall, *Fragments of Science*, 5th ed. (Longmans, Green, & Co., 1876), 530.

7. Steven Weinberg, *Dreams of a Final Theory: The Scientist's Search for the Ultimate Laws of Nature*, 2nd edition (Vintage Books, 1994), 246.

8. "Public's Views on Human Evolution," Pew Research, 30 December 2013.

9. Ann Thwaite, *Glimpses of the Wonderful: The Life of Philip Henry Gosse, 1810–1888* (Faber & Faber, 2002), 209, 216.

10. "The Apparent Age Argument," The Age of the Earth, Creation/Evolution, Don Lindsay Archive.

11. Rabbi David Gottlieb, "The Age of the Universe" (blog), David-Gottlieb.com.

12. Eugenie C. Scott, *Evolution vs Creationism: An Introduction*, second ed. (Greenwood Press, 2009), 20; Bertrand Russell, *Religion and Science* (1935; Oxford University Press, 1961), 70.

13. Alvin Plantinga, "When Faith and Reason Clash: Evolution and the Bible," *Christian Scholar's Review* 21/1 (1991): 8–32, at 22.

14. John C. West, "What is Theistic Evolution?" Discovery Institute,

1 May 2009.

15. William Hasker, "*Darwin on Trial* Revisited: A Review Essay," *Christian Scholar's Review* 24/4 (May 1995): 479–88, at 483, 485.

16. Ernan McMullin, "Plantinga's Defense of Special Creation," *Christian Scholar's Review* 21/1 (1991): 55–79, at 75.

17. Hasker, "*Darwin on Trial* Revisited," 483; McMullin, "Plantinga's Defense," 74.

18. Hasker, "*Darwin on Trial* Revisited," 484.

19. Ibid., 486; McMullin, "Plantinga's Defense," 74–75.

20. William A. Dembski, *Intelligent Design: The Bridge between Science and Theology* (InterVarsity Press, 1999); *The Design Revolution: Answering the Toughest Questions about Intelligent Design* (InterVarsity Press, 2004).

21. Dembski, *The Design Revolution*, 26–27.

22. Dembski, *Intelligent Design*, 247; *The Design Revolution*, 41.

23. *Intelligent Design*, 247; *The Design Revolution*, 41.

24. *The Design Revolution*, 190.

25. Ibid., 173, 174.

26. Ibid., 176.

27. *Intelligent Design*, 51.

28. Ibid., 67.

29. Ibid., 42–43.

30. Ibid., 250.

31. *The Design Revolution*, 173; *Intelligent Design*, 171.

32. Thomas Nagel, *Mind and Cosmos: Why the Materialist Neo-Darwinian Conception of Nature Is Almost Certainly False* (Oxford University Press, 2012), 7.

4

Consciousness

Unlike the first three chapters, which discuss phenomena that have been widely used in anti-theistic arguments, the present chapter and the next deal with phenomena that have been held to provide evidence for Gawd, although they do not. The present chapter treats human consciousness.

As we saw in Chapter 3, Charles Lyell considered the human mind so miraculous that he violated his otherwise consistent uniformitarianism to account for it. To explain the existence of humanity's intellectual and moral capacities, he said, we must "assume a primeval creative power which does not act with uniformity."[1] Some philosophers have used human consciousness, perhaps along with consciousness in general, in an argument for the existence of an omnipotent deity. This chapter explains why this argument is not sound.

1. DUALISM AND DIVINE OMNIPOTENCE

The doctrine that the human mind is absolutely different from the brain was used by traditional theists in the 17th century as a proof for the existence of an omnipotent creator. Essentially the same argument has been repeated in present times.

RENÉ DESCARTES

The most famous philosopher to use this argument was René Descartes. Besides saying that the mind is *numerically distinct* from the brain—the brain is one thing, the mind is another—he argued that the mind is also *ontologically different in kind* from the brain's components, made of different stuff: The mind is composed of consciousness, whereas the brain is composed of matter, the essence of which is spatial extension. Being composed entirely of insentient matter, the brain is completely devoid of experience.

Being different in kind, according to this way of thinking, the mind and the brain cannot interact naturally: The mind has consciousness, which involves temporal duration, whereas matter, consisting solely of spatial extension, has no duration. Moreover, material things are moved by physical contact—being impacted by other material things—whereas the mind is moved by non-material things, such as ideals and purposes. Given this absolute dualism, it seemed impossible to explain how mind and matter could interact. There is no way, therefore, to understand how the movement of a person's finger could have been moved by the person's wish to move it.

For a long time, philosophers and historians of philosophy had said that the seeming impossibility of mind-body interaction was a serious problem, perhaps fatal, for Descartes' dualistic worldview. However, in a book entitled *Descartes' Dualism*, Gordon Baker and Katherine Morris showed that he was not embarrassed by the fact that his position made mind-body interaction impossible. Rather, this impossibility was part and parcel of his position. Baker and Morris wrote:

> It is ironic that one common criticism of Descartes' dualism points to the *a priori* impossibility of his *explaining* mind-body interaction. This is precisely his doctrine, not a *problem* for it.

Descartes' doctrine was that mind and body can appear to influence each other only because this relationship has been ordained by divine omnipotence. In other words, Descartes used his dualism for a proof of the existence of an omnipotent deity.[2]

The appeal to divine omnipotence to render the mind-body relation intelligible was more explicitly made by subsequent Cartesians. Most famously, Nicolas Malebranche taught "occasionalism," according to which mind and matter could not really interact: They appear to interact only because Gawd causes them to do so. For example, upon the occasion of my hand being on a hot stove, Gawd causes me to feel pain; and upon the occasion of my decision to move my hand, Gawd causes my hand to move. Baker and Morris showed that this was already Descartes' position.[3]

William James, referring to the 17th century, wrote: "For thinkers of that age, '[Gawd]' was the great solvent of all absurdities."[4] However, the use of mind-body dualism to prove the existence of an omnipotent deity did not disappear after the 17th century.

RICHARD SWINBURNE

As we saw in Chapter 2, Oxford University's Richard Swinburne defends the existence of Gawd, as shown by his statement that "[Gawd] is *omnipotent*: he can do anything."[5] In a book devoted to arguments for the existence of Gawd, Swinburne added, to the list of the traditional arguments, an "argument from consciousness," which he introduced thus:

> I do not know of any classical philosopher who has developed the argument from consciousness with any rigor. But one sometimes hears theologians and ordinary men saying that conscious men could not have evolved from unconscious matter by natural processes. I believe that those who have said this have been hinting at a powerful argument to which philosophers have not given nearly enough attention.[6]

Believing, like Descartes, that most events in the world, including "brain-events," are purely physical (material) in the sense of being devoid of experience, Swinburne argued that there is "no natural connection between brain-events and correlated mental events." As a result, he said, this correlation can be explained only by the will of an omnipotent deity.[7] Swinburne summarizes the argument thus:

> [S]cience cannot explain the evolution of a mental life. That is to say, . . . there is nothing in the nature of certain physical events . . . to give rise to connections [to mental events]. . . . [Gawd], an omnipotent, omniscient, perfectly free and perfectly good source of all . . . [could] explain the otherwise mysterious mind-body connection. . . . [Gawd], being omnipotent, would have the power to produce a soul thus interacting, to produce intentionally those connections which, we have seen, have no natural connections.[8]

Swinburne claims that he was not thereby appealing to a "[Gawd] of the gaps."[9] But he clearly was.

The criticism of a gap-filling deity is often traced to Henry Drummond, a late 19th-century Scot who combined preaching with lecturing on natural science. Arguing that the scientific principle of continuity—one could say "uniformitarianism"—extends from the physical to the spiritual world, Drummond criticized the practice of some Christian thinkers who, pointing to "gaps" (phenomena that science cannot yet explain), which they "fill up with God."[10] Rejecting the "occasional wonder-worker, who is the [Gawd] of an old theology," Drummond advocated "an immanent God, which is the God of Evolution" and is "infinitely grander."

The phrase "God of the gaps" was evidently first used in a 1955 book entitled *Science and Christian Belief* by Charles Alfred Coulson, who was a mathematics professor at Oxford University, as well as a Methodist church leader. Rejecting, like Drummond, the practice of filling gaps with supernatural interventions, Coulson said: "Either God is in the whole of Nature, with no gaps, or He's not there at all."[11]

In rejecting only a gap-filling deity, neither Drummond nor Coulson was saying that the idea of God could not be used to understand anything about the universe. They were rejecting the idea of deity as miraculously intervening now and then.

Swinburne's use of Gawd to explain mind-brain interaction is, therefore, a perfect example of a "Gawd of the gaps"—especially because, as discussed below, recent microbiology has shown there to be no absolute dualism between the mind and the components of the brain.

COLIN MCGINN

Although philosopher Colin McGinn is a materialist and atheist, he declared the use of the mind-body problem to prove the existence of deity a good argument, even if false.

McGinn's discussion of the mind-body relation starts off from philosopher Thomas Nagel's distinction between a *pour soi*, meaning an entity that is something "for itself" (because it has experience), and an *en soi*, which is something that is merely "in itself," because it has no experience. If we assume that a neuron in the brain is merely "in itself," so that it is completely devoid of sentience or experience, Nagel said, the relation between the mind and the brain was impossible to understand. In his words:

> One cannot derive a *pour soi* from an *en soi*. . . . This gap is logically unbridgeable. If a bodiless god wanted to create a conscious being, he could not expect to do it by combining together in organic form a lot of particles with none but physical properties.[12]

In other words, unless a deity were a *deus ex machina* that, in Whitehead's words, is "capable of rising superior to the difficulties of metaphysics,"[13] it would not be able to form a mind out of entities completely devoid of experience, no matter how complexly they might be organized. In his book *The Problem of Consciousness*, McGinn began by asking:

> How is it possible for conscious states to depend upon brain states? . . . How could the aggregation of millions of individually insentient neurons generate subjective awareness?[14]

Then, answering his own question, he said that "our understanding of how consciousness develops from the organization of matter is non-existent."[15] Clarifying the reason for the impossibility of acquiring such an understanding, McGinn wrote:

> [T]he human sperm and ovum are not capable of consciousness, and it takes a few months before the human fetus is. So when consciousness finally dawns in a developing organism it does not stem from an immediately prior consciousness: it stems from oblivion, from insensate (though living) matter.[16]

Moreover, said McGinn, there is no hope for people ever to understand this sometime in the future:

> The difficulty here is one of principle: we have no understanding of how consciousness could emerge from an aggregation of non-conscious elements. . . . [I]t remains a mystery . . . how mere matter could form itself into the organ of consciousness.[17]

Discussing the difference between consciousness and matter in Descartes' terms, McGinn said:

> [T]he senses are geared to representing a spatial world; they essentially present things in space with spatially defined properties. But it is precisely *such* properties that seem inherently incapable of resolving the mind-body problem. . . . No property we can ascribe to the brain on the basis of how it strikes us perceptually . . . seems capable of rendering perspicuous how it is that damp grey tissue can be the crucible from which subjective consciousness emerges fully formed.[18]

On the basis of his conception of mind and body, McGinn declared the rise of consciousness to be a permanent *mystery*. Indeed, this idea was so central to McGinn that he came to be called the "New Mysterian."[19]

McGinn recognized, of course, that some people say that because "nothing merely natural could do the job," we have to appeal to supernatural power. Although he rejected this idea out of hand, he said that supernaturalist solutions "at least recognize that something pretty remarkable is needed if the mind-body relation is to be made sense of."[20]

Darwinism undermined the creationist argument that a supernatural creator was needed to explain our world, said McGinn, by showing how our world could have come about naturalistically. However, continued McGinn,

> In the case of consciousness the appearance of miracle might also tempt us in the 'creationist' direction, with [Gawd] required to perform the alchemy necessary to transform matter into

experience. . . . We cannot, I think, refute this argument in the way we can the original creationist argument, namely by actually producing a non-miraculous explanatory theory.[21]

McGinn repeatedly returned to this point—that the emergence of consciousness cannot be explained in a naturalistic way. For example, speaking of the rise of mollusks and fish, he said:

> [W]e do not know how consciousness might have arisen by natural processes from antecedently existing material things. Somehow or other sentience sprang from pulpy matter, giving matter an inner aspect, but we have no idea how this leap was propelled. . . . One is tempted, however reluctantly, to turn to divine assistance: for only a kind of miracle could produce *this* from *that*. It would take a supernatural magician to extract consciousness from matter, even living matter. Consciousness appears to introduce a sharp break in the natural order—a point at which scientific naturalism runs out of steam.[22]

Evidently not knowing the writings of his erstwhile Oxford colleague Richard Swinburne, McGinn even said:

> I do not know if anyone has ever tried to exploit consciousness to prove the existence of [Gawd]. . . . It is indeed difficult to see how consciousness could have arisen spontaneously from insentient matter; it seems to need an injection from outside the physical realm.[23]

Accordingly, the only difference between Swinburne and McGinn is that while Swinburne embraces the supernaturalist argument, McGinn rules it out, saying: "It is a condition of adequacy upon any account of the mind-body relation that it avoid [supernaturalistic] theism."[24]

SUMMARY

Descartes and Swinburne would be able, therefore, to argue that McGinn actually supports their argument—that he only rejects their conclusion because of anti-theistic prejudice. It could appear, therefore, that the existence of consciousness, whenever it arose during the evolutionary process, is a powerful argument for the existence of Gawd. But it is not.

2. THE EMERGING VIEW OF CELLS

According to the view of the brain held by Descartes, Swinburne, and McGinn, it is constituted of brain cells, called neurons, that are mere matter in Descartes' sense—that is, devoid of experience or sentience. In McGinn's words, the mystery is how "the aggregation of millions of individually insentient neurons generates subjective awareness." This truly is an unanswerable question, as Nagel had already pointed out. But what if the neurons are not insentient? What if they have their own experiences, only at a much lower level than ours?

As we saw, McGinn said, "when consciousness finally dawns in a developing organism it does not stem from an immediately prior consciousness: it stems from oblivion, from insensate (though living) matter." But what if living matter is not insensate, so human consciousness emerges not from oblivion, but from a complex organism composed of billions of interconnected sentient cells? Then human (or mollusk) experience would not emerge from oblivion, but from more elementary types of experience.

Swinburne's argument was based on the same view of the brain as McGinn's, saying that "conscious men could not have evolved from unconscious matter." On this basis, Swinburne argued that "science cannot explain the evolution of a mental life." This was why Swinburne concluded that only an omnipotent deity could "explain the otherwise mysterious mind-body connection." But what would be left of the argument if scientists had recently discovered the Descartes-Swinburne-McGinn view of the brain to be false?

DECISION-MAKING BACTERIA

That is exactly what has happened. In the 1970s, a few scientists started reporting that bacteria, the lowest form of life, make decisions on the basis of receiving information from their environments. For example, a 1974 article in *Science* was entitled "Decision-Making in Bacteria."[25]

By now, this then-startling idea has become commonplace, with many journal articles reporting experiments verifying the idea. For example, articles with the following titles appeared in recent years:

- "Bacteria Provide New Insights into Human Decision Making" (2009).

- "Bacteria Use Chat to Play the 'Prisoner's Dilemma' Game in Deciding Their Fate" (2012).

- "How Do Bacteria Make Decisions?" (2014).[26]

The last of these three articles began:

> Decision making is not limited to animals like humans or birds. Bacteria also make decisions with intricate precision. . . . Depending on the size of a bacterium's genome, these tiny organisms have the ability to sense hundreds to thousands of internal and external signals like carbon sources, nitrogen sources, and pH changes. If these bacteria are motile (able to move around), they can compare how conditions are for them now against how they were a few seconds ago. That's right, bacteria have a memory albeit short. If conditions are better, they can continue to move in a forward direction. If conditions are worse compared to a few seconds earlier, they can change direction and continue searching for better conditions in their environment to generate energy.[27]

The discovery that experience, memory, and decision-making occur in cells is a major development in recent microbiology. According to University of Chicago microbiologist James Shapiro, "Cells are capable of sophisticated information processing."[28] Shapiro used the word *cognition* to refer to regulatory processes of cells. In explaining his use of this term, he said that "cognitive actions are knowledge-based and involve decisions appropriate to acquired information." Even the smallest cells, he says, "use sophisticated sensory and intracellular communication processes to discriminate between alternative nutrients."[29]

In a book providing a "21st century" view of evolution, Shapiro rejected the neo-Darwinian belief that evolution proceeds entirely through natural selection of purely random mutations. On the basis of the neo-Darwinian view, according to which there is no intelligent guidance to evolution, Shapiro said that "less than one in a billion divisions of our own cells would be successful."[30] Intelligence must be involved.

However, rather than thinking of the intelligent guidance as that of a supernatural mind, as do proponents of Intelligent Design, Shapiro speaks of *cellular* intelligence.[31] "To a remarkable extent," Shapiro said, "contemporary biology has become a science of sensitivity, inter- and intra-cellular communication, and control."[32]

SENTIENT CELLS VS. MIND-BODY MYSTERY

Famous and once-controversial biologist Lynn Margulis,[33] who died in 2011, is best known for her theory of "symbiogenesis," which began with her discovery that the eukaryotic cell is a composite resulting from a symbiotic union of primitive prokaryotic cells. In other words, eukaryotes resulted when large prokaryotes absorbed smaller ones. Although her worldview differed radically from that of Richard Dawkins, who had long ridiculed her views, he eventually called her discovery "one of the great achievements of twentieth-century evolutionary biology." Likewise, Niles Eldredge wrote: "Lynn was put down as having had a really crazy idea. . . . Now it's taught in all the textbooks as the self-evident truth."[34]

Her theory of symbiogenesis was based on the idea that all living organisms are sentient. Saying that her worldview "recognizes the perceptive capacity of all live beings,"[35] she held that "consciousness is a property of all living cells," even the most elementary ones: "Bacteria are conscious. These bacterial beings have been around since the origin of life."[36]

Although some of us prefer to save the term "consciousness" for higher types of experience, the crucial point is that all cells have perceptive experience, rather than being, as Descartes, Swinburne, and McGinn believed, "insensate matter." Alluding to how this new view can dissolve the traditional mind-body problem, Margulis said:

> Thought and behavior in people are rendered far less mysterious when we realize that choice and sensitivity are already exquisitely developed in the microbial cells that became our ancestors.[37]

Indeed, a recent study revealed that, in the words of the study's lead author, "Just like the neurons in our brain, we found that bacteria use ion channels to communicate with each other through electrical signals. "[38]

PANEXPERIENTIALISM

Of course, one might suppose that a "mind-body problem" emerges with the rise of prokaryotic cells, such as bacteria, with their sentience. How could they have emerged out of insentient components? However, there is good reason to hold that the prokaryotic cell as such, with its level of experience, emerged from incorporating entities with still lower levels of sentience.

Relevant to this issue is the article, cited above, that speaks of "decision-making at a subcellular level." The most complex components of prokaryotic cells are their organelles, so the author's reference to "subcellular decision-making" would evidently refer to decisions made by organelles. We could then assume that organelles themselves emerged out of entities with lower-level experiences, and so on down.

Alfred North Whitehead and Charles Hartshorne: This view was developed in Alfred North Whitehead's "philosophy of organism," in which he spoke of complex organisms as "organisms of organisms." Electrons and hydrogen nuclei are, he said, quite elementary organisms; then "the atoms, and the molecules, are organisms of a higher type, which also represent a compact definite organic unity." Still more complex are "individual living beings."[39]

A term for this notion was provided by philosopher Charles Hartshorne in an essay entitled "The Compound Individual."[40] The basic idea was that one individual, such as an atom, can be present in a more complex individual, such as a molecule, which can in turn be present in a still more complex individual, such as a macromolecule, which can in turn be present in the still more complex individual that we call an organelle, which in turn is present in the prokaryotic call. Prokaryotic cells can then be compounded to form the more complex eukaryotic cells, which can then be compounded to form still more complex individuals, such as flies, squirrels, and humans.

Lynn Margulis: Realizing that "[l]ive small cells reside inside the larger cells,"[41] Margulis worked out a similar notion, saying:

[D]ifferent bacteria form consortia that, under ecological pressures, associate and undergo metabolic and genetic change such that their tightly integrated communities result in individuality at a more complex level of organization.

In such developments, she said, the joining together of individuals at one level can create "a new whole that was, in effect, far greater than the sum of its parts."[42] "The basic issue," she said, "is how independent, separate organisms fuse to form new individuals."[43] Although she did not speak of "compound individuals," she did use the term "composite individuality" to describe the "transition from bacterial to eukaryotic genomes."[44]

Although Margulis as a biologist evidently limited her discussion to living cells, the idea that the components of the cells must themselves have sentience would be consonant with her outlook, so that nature would contain compound individuals, in the Whiteheadian-Hartshornean sense, all the way down to the simplest entities discussed by physicists.

This view, that experience goes all the way down, is known as "pan-experientialism." Although this position, under the older name "pan-psychism," was long derided, it is now gaining adherents. According to the Wikipedia article on Panpsychism, "The recent interest in the hard problem of consciousness has once again made panpsychism a main-stream theory."[45] A look at the Internet, moreover, shows that during recent years the term "panexperientialism" has become quite common.[46]

Thomas Nagel: Among the contemporary philosophers who have moved it into mainstream thinking,[47] the most important so far has been Thomas Nagel. Having argued that the mind-body relation is impossible to understand on the assumption that the brain is composed of purely physical entities, devoid of experience, he also said, as quoted in Chapter 3, that he "reject[s] both supernaturalism and neo-Darwinism's explanation of the sources of evolutionary change."

Agreeing with neo-Darwinism that a theory of evolution must be naturalistic, he said that we need "a naturalistic expansion of evolutionary theory to account for consciousness."[48] This expansion involves rejecting "psychophysical reductionism," according to which the mind can be reduced to the brain understood in a Cartesian sense. Needing a way to understand how we "descended from bacteria," we must think of natural entities as "something more than physical all the way down." In other words, a fully naturalistic worldview requires some version of panpsychism, according to which "organisms with mental life are not miraculous anomalies but an integral part of nature."[49]

Besides affirming panpsychism in general, Nagel approvingly cited both Whitehead and Hartshorne. With regard to Whitehead, Nagel endorsed his idea that philosophers should not equate the "abstractions of physics with the whole of reality," but should regard "concrete entities, all the way down to the level of electrons," as "embodying a standpoint on the world"—that is, as having experience. With regard to Hartshorne, Nagel described an essay by him on "the place of mind in nature," in which Hartshorne affirmed panpsychism, as an "acute and historically informed discussion."[50]

Lying behind Whitehead's position on "concrete entities," incidentally, was William James. Speaking of "a concrete bit of personal experience," James said: "It is a *full* fact," being "of the *kind* to which all realities whatsoever must belong." Our *feeling*, said James, "is the one thing that fills up the measure of our concrete actuality." In support of this view, James wrote: "Lotze's doctrine that the only meaning we can attach to the notion of a thing as it is 'in itself' is by conceiving it as it is *for* itself; i.e., as a piece of full experience."[51]

Galen Strawson: Another major philosopher who has adopted a panexperientialist position is Galen Strawson (the son of the famous British philosopher P. F. Strawson), who now teaches at the University of Texas, Austin. Saying that the intractability of the mind-body problem has been due to the inadequacy of philosophers' concept of the physical, not the mental, he said: "The descriptive scheme of physics . . . will have to change dramatically," giving us "a qualitative-character-of-experience physics."[52] In a recent essay arguing for "the primacy of panpsychism," Strawson discussed "compelling reasons for favoring panpsychism above all other positive substantive proposals about the fundamental nature of concrete reality." Strawson added, incidentally, that he uses the terms "panpsychism" and "panexperientialism" interchangeably.[53]

3. DISTINCTIVELY HUMAN CONSCIOUSNESS

If experience goes all the way down, there is no problem in principle in understanding how the consciousness of primates evolved. But
what about distinctively *human* consciousness? Although the difference
between human consciousness and that of other primates is a matter of
degree, it is a difference in degree that is in effect a difference of kind.

Gorillas and chimpanzees have exhibited mental abilities far beyond
what scientists had previously assumed, but their differences from
humans are nevertheless enormous with regard to mathematics, logic,
science, history, religion, technology, music, and so on—the kinds of
differences that led Lyell to posit a supernatural injection into the evolutionary process. How could distinctively human consciousness have
emerged without supernatural assistance?

In a book discussing structures of existence, John Cobb, a philosophical theologian employing the ideas of Whitehead and Hartshorne,
sought to describe the transition from the pre-human primates' structure
of existence to the structure of human existence. The distinctiveness of
human beings, he suggested, involves "surplus psychic energy," meaning
energy beyond that needed for the well-being of the body. The thresh-
old dividing humans from other primates occurred when "the surplus
psychic energy became sufficient in quantity to enable the psychic life
to become its own end rather than primarily a means to the survival and
health of the body." This surplus psychic energy was the precondition
for religion and all those other activities in which the mind treats itself
as an end in itself, not simply as the director of its bodily activities.[54]

With regard to what is distinctive about human existence, Cobb
agreed with the standard evolutionary accounts, insofar as they make
symbolism central. But he did not agree with those who focus only on
the practical advantages for survival provided by symbolic language.
Rather, suggested Cobb—who was influenced by the Jungian historian of consciousness Erich Neumann—the evolutionary development
constituting human distinctiveness consisted of "the greatly increased
unconscious psychic activity organizing the whole of experience for its
own sake." Although the much greater supply of surplus psychic energy

exists primarily in what we call the unconscious portion of the mind, the unconscious psychic activity of symbolization resulted in "a new and incomparably richer mode of consciousness."[55]

Referring to the first stage of human existence as "primitive existence," Cobb then dealt with the emergence of "archaic existence" and then, about 500 years BCE, "axial existence." Moreover, he portrayed axial existence as taking various forms, which he discussed as Buddhist, Homeric, Socratic, Prophetic, and Christian existence.

Different scholars would surely describe the developments from primitive to axial existence differently. But Cobb's portrayal describes how the type of human existence we exemplify today could have gradually emerged from the earliest humans, which in turn emerged from less sophisticated hominids, and so on back.[56] No supernatural infusion was necessary.

However, the emergence of today's human experience did presuppose something distinctive rooted in God, namely, the ideal (non-physical) forms expressed in the distinctively human capacities for morality, mathematics, logic, and rationality, which will be discussed in Part II of this book.

CONCLUSION

The argument from consciousness to Gawd fails. There is certainly no proof that the mind is absolutely different in kind from the cells making up the brain, so there is no proof of a gap between the mind and the brain cells that could only be bridged by an omnipotent power. Moreover, leaving aside proof, there is not even any good reason anymore to consider it probable that the mind and the brain's components are different in kind, so that they would be unable to interact naturally. There is also no good reason to think that there was some place in the evolutionary process where experience arose suddenly—with *en soi* giving rise to *pour soi*.

If the evolutionary process involves *pour soi*, or experience, all the way down, then the rise of conscious minds could have occurred naturally. With panexperientialism, we can have what Darwin wanted:

an evolutionary process without a single interruption of the normal cause-effect relations.

Likewise, there is no reason to hold that the human mind is so different from pre-human psyches that the intervention of an omnipotent deity was needed to effect the transition.

ENDNOTES

1. Lyell's statements are quoted in R. Hooykaas, *Natural Law and Divine Miracle: A Historical-Critical Study of the Principle of Uniformity in Geology, Biology, and Theology* (E. J. Brill, 1959), 114.

2. Gordon Baker and Katherine J. Morris, *Descartes' Dualism* (Routledge, 1996), 153–54, 167–70.

3. Ibid., 167–70.

4. William James, *Some Problems of Philosophy* (Longman & Green, 1911), 195.

5. Richard Swinburne, *Is There a God?* (Oxford University Press, 1996), 7.

6. Richard Swinburne, *The Existence of God* (Clarendon, 1979), 161.

7. Ibid., 172–73.

8. Richard Swinburne, *The Evolution of the Soul* (Clarendon, 1986), 198–99.

9. Swinburne, *Is There a God?* 68.

10. Henry Drummond, *The Lowell Lectures on the Ascent of Man* (Hodder and Stoughton, 1904), 333.

11. Charles Alfred Coulson, *Science and Christian Belief* (1955; Fontana Books, 1958), 32.

12. Thomas Nagel, *Mortal Questions* (Cambridge University Press, 1979), 189.

13. Alfred North Whitehead, *Science and the Modern World* (1925; Free Press, 1967), 156.

14. Colin McGinn, *The Problem of Consciousness: Essays Toward a Resolution* (Basil Blackwell, 1991), 1.

15. Ibid., 19.

16. Ibid., 46.

17. Ibid., 213.

18. Ibid., 11, 27.

19. "Colin McGinn—Cognitive Closure," Conscious Entities (wwww. consciousentities.com).

20. McGinn, *The Problem of Consciousness*, 2.

21. Ibid., 17n.

22. Ibid., 45.

23. Ibid., 45n.

24. Ibid., 17n.

25. Julius Adler and Wung-Wai Tso, "Decision-Making in Bacteria," *Science* 184 (1974): 1292–94.

26. Kim McDonald, "Bacteria Provide New Insights into Human Decision Making," UC San Diego, 8 December 2009; "Bacteria Use Chat to Play the 'Prisoner's Dilemma' Game in Deciding Their Fate," *American Chemical Society*, 27 May 2012; Matthew Russell, "How Do Bacteria Make Decisions?" *Frontiers*, 23 January 2014.

27. Russell, "How Do Bacteria Make Decisions?" Additional articles include M. Gomelski and W. D. Hoff, "Light Helps Bacteria Make Important Lifestyle Decisions," *Trends in Microbiology*," 19 September 2011, and Daniel M. Cornfortha, et al., "Combinatorial Quorum Sensing Allows Bacteria to Resolve Their Social and Physical Environment," *Proceedings of the National Academy of Sciences*, 4 March 2014.

28. James A. Shapiro, "Transposable Elements as the Key to a 21st Century View of Evolution," *Genetica*, 107: 171–70 (1999).

29. James Shapiro, "Cell Cognition and Cell Decision-Making," Huffington Post, 19 March 2012.

30. Ibid.

31. Ibid.

32. James A. Shapiro, "A Third Way," *Boston Review*, 1997.

33. Widely recognized as the most gifted evolutionary biologist of her generation, Margulis was a Distinguished University Professor at the University of Massachusetts, Amherst. She was elected to the National

Academy of Sciences in 1983 and to the Russian Academy of Natural Sciences in 1997; awarded the National Medal of Science in 1999; and received the Darwin-Wallace Medal in 2008.

34. In John Brockman, *The Third Culture: Beyond the Scientific Revolution* (Simon & Schuster, 1995).

35. Lynn Margulis, "Gaia and Machines," in John B. Cobb, Jr., ed., *Back to Darwin: A Richer Account of Evolution* (Eerdmans, 2007), 167–75, at 172.

36. Dick Teresi, "Lynn Margulis Says She's Not Controversial, She's Right," *Discover Magazine*, April 2011.

37. Lynn Margulis, "Gaia Is a Tough Bitch," Chap. 7 of John Brockman, *The Third Culture: Beyond the Scientific Revolution* (Simon & Schuster, 1995).

38. "Bacteria Communicate Like Neurons in Human Brain, New Study Finds," Sci-News.com, 23 October 2015.

39. Whitehead, *Science and the Modern World*, 110.

40. Charles Hartshorne, "The Compound Individual," Otis Lee, ed., *Philosophical Essays for Alfred North Whitehead* (Longmans, Green & Co., 1936). Reprinted in Hartshorne, *Whitehead's Philosophy: Selected Essays, 1936–1970* (University of Nebraska Press, 1972).

41. Margulis, "Gaia Is a Tough Bitch."

42. Ibid.

43. Lynn Margulis and Dorion Sagan, *Acquiring Genomes: A Theory of the Origins of Species* (Basic Books, 2003), 97.

44. Lynn Margulis, "Serial Endosymbiotic Theory (SET) and Composite Individuality: Transition from Bacterial to Eukaryotic Genomes," *Microbiology Today* 31 (2004): 172–74.

45. "Panpsychism," Wikipedia, accessed January 2015. Philosophers who had made panpsychism a somewhat mainstream theory in earlier times included Wilhelm Gottfried Leibniz, Henri Bergson, Herman Lotze, William James, and Charles Peirce, while scientists included Charles Birch, David Bohm, Bernard Rensch, C. H. Waddington, and Sewall Wright (all of these scientists had essays in John B. Cobb, Jr., and David Ray Griffin, eds., *Mind in Nature: Essays on the Interface of Science and Philosophy* (Washington, D.C.: University Press of America, 1977).

46. See especially "Panexperientialism" (http://panexperientialism.blog-spot.com).

47. Aside from Thomas Nagel, these contemporary philosophers include Michael Blamauer of the University of Vienna (Blamauer ed., *The Mental as Fundamental: New Perspectives on Panpsychism* [Ontos Verlag, 2013]); David Chalmers of the University of California at Santa Cruz (*The Conscious Mind: In Search of a Fundamental Theory* [Oxford University Press, 1997], and *The Character of Consciousness* [Oxford University Press, 2010]); D. S. Clarke of Southern Illinois University at Carbondale (*Panpsychism and the Religious Attitude* [Albany: State University of New York Press, 2003]); Freya Matthews of Latrobe University (*For Love of Matter: A Contemporary Panpsychism* [State University of New York Press, 2003]); William Seager of the University of Toronto at Scarborough ("Whitehead and the Revival (?) of Panpsychism," Philosophical Papers, 2001; "Panpsychism, Aggregation and Combinatorial Infusion," *Mind and Matter,* 2010; and "Emergentist Panpsychism," *Journal of Consciousness Studies,* 2012); David Skrbina of the University of Michigan at Dearborn (*Panpsychism in the West* [Bradford Books, 2007], and *Mind That Abides: Panpsychism in the New Millennium* [John Benjamins, 2009]); Galen Strawson of the University of Texas at Austin (Strawson et al., *Consciousness and Its Place in Nature: Does Physicalism Entail Panpsychism?* [2006; Imprint Academic, 2010]).

48. Thomas Nagel, *Mind and Cosmos: Why the Materialist Neo-Darwinian Conception of Nature Is Almost Certainly False* (Oxford University Press, 2012), 48.

49. Ibid., 30, 34, 53, 57.

50. Ibid., 33, referring to Charles Hartshorne, "Physics and Psychics: The Place of Mind in Nature," in John B. Cobb, Jr., and David Ray Griffin, eds., *Mind in Nature: Essays on the Interface of Science and Philosophy* (University Press of America, 1977), 89–96.

51. William James, *The Varieties of Religious Experience* (Collier, 1961), 387.

52. Galen Strawson, *Mental Reality* (MIT Press, 1994), 89, 99, 104. See also a book devoted to Strawson's developing position: Galen Strawson et al., *Consciousness and Its Place in Nature: Does Physicalism Entail Panpsychism?* ed. Anthony Freeman (2006; Imprint Academic, 2010).

53. Strawson, "Mind and Being: The Primacy of Panpsychism," in

Panpsychism: Philosophical Essays, ed. G. Brunstup and L. Jaskolla (Oxford University Press, 2015).

54. John B. Cobb, Jr., *The Structure of Christian Existence* (Westminster Press, 1967), 39.

55. Ibid., 39, 41.

56. "The Emergence of Humans," *Understanding Evolution;* Dennis O'Neil "Humans," Behavioral Sciences Department, Palomar College, 2014.

5

Miracles

The main argument for the existence of an omnipotent deity had long been the argument from miracles. Although this argument started going out of fashion in the 18th century, some contemporary philosophers and theologians still argue that miracles add to the evidence for the existence of Gawd.

1. CONTEMPORARY DEFENDERS OF MIRACLES

Three of these defenders are Evangelical theologian Millard Erickson, Eastern Orthodox philosopher of religion Richard Swinburne, and Evangelical philosopher of religion William Lane Craig.

MILLARD ERICKSON

In Chapter 1, Millard Erickson's affirmation of omnipotence based on *creatio ex nihilo* was quoted. Stating that his theology is based on "a definite supernaturalism," Erickson spelled out the meaning of this supernaturalism thus: "[Gawd] resides outside the world and intervenes periodically within the natural processes through miracles."[1]

In explaining how miracles could occur, Erickson rejected the idea that they involve local suspensions of laws of nature. Rather, he suggested, "when miracles occur, natural forces are countered by super-natural force." Take, for example, the floating axhead reported in the Old Testament (2 Kings 6:6). Rather than holding that the law of gravity was momentarily suspended at that place, Erickson suggested that "the law of gravity continued to function in the vicinity of the axhead, but the unseen hand of [Gawd] was underneath it, bearing it up, just as if a human hand were lifting it."[2]

As to why the biblical miracles occurred, Erickson said that, in addition to meeting human needs and glorifying Gawd, they served to "establish the supernatural basis of the revelation which often accompanies them." The miracles also demonstrated "the power of [Gawd] over nature," as in the birth of Isaac, the plagues in Egypt, and Jesus' "nature miracles," such as stilling the storm and walking on water.[3]

RICHARD SWINBURNE

According to Richard Swinburne, as we saw in previous chapters, "[Gawd] is *omnipotent*: he can do anything"[4] (Chapter 2), and only an omnipotent deity can "explain the otherwise mysterious mind-body connection" (Chapter 4). It is not surprising, therefore, that Swinburne's long list of arguments for the existence of Gawd includes an argument from miracles.

Miracles, he said, would be events that "clearly would not have occurred as a result of natural laws, and which are also events of a kind that [Gawd] might be expected to bring about." Moreover, history "contains *reports* of many events which, *if* they occurred as reported," fit those conditions.[5] Given this situation, Swinburne asserted, the basic question is whether the affirmation of miracles is credible.

Hume, of course, said that it was not, because when we confront a miracle claim, we must evaluate it in terms of our background knowledge, and this background knowledge teaches us that events occur in terms of what we call the laws of nature. However, said Swinburne, Hume was wrong to assume that our knowledge of the laws of nature "is our main relevant background evidence." More important is all of our evidence "about whether there is or is not a [Gawd]," because "if there is a [Gawd], there exists a being with the power to set aside the laws of nature that he normally sustains."[6] In speaking of "all of our evidence," Swinburne meant his other arguments for the existence of Gawd.

Accordingly, Swinburne argued, given the occurrence of events that contradict natural laws and that are "of a kind that [Gawd] would have reason to bring about," such events provide evidence "of the existence of [Gawd]."[7]

WILLIAM LANE CRAIG

A similar view has been expressed by William Lane Craig, who has defended five arguments for the existence of Gawd.[8] A miracle, said Craig, should be defined not as a violation of a law of nature, but as an event that is logically possible but "naturally impossible." What makes miracles not only logically but also *historically* possible "is the personal [Gawd] of theism," meaning a deity "who is omnipotent" and "free to act as He wills." "Only an atheist," said Craig, "can deny the historical possibility of miracles."[9]

That is true, of course, if a "miracle" is by definition an event that is naturally impossible and if "an atheist" is by definition one who denies the existence of Gawd. But there are other possibilities.

2. NEWTON AND THE EARLY MODERN SCIENTIFIC WORLDVIEW

As discussed in Chapter 2, the early modern scientific worldview was created in reaction not only to Aristotelean philosophy but also to the Hermetic tradition, according to which causal influence could occur at a distance naturally. The mechanical philosophy of the early modern worldview declared that influence at a distance could happen only through supernatural agency.

Although the early modern worldview was created by various thinkers prior to Isaac Newton, especially Mersenne, Descartes, and Boyle, that worldview came to be called *Newtonian*. Nevertheless, although the Hermetic (or magical) and mechanical worldviews were radically opposed to each other, Newton himself was deeply influenced by both of them—by the former before he publicly adopted the latter. Because of the influence of both traditions on him, Hugh Kearney called Newton "the great amphibian."[10]

The Hermetic side of Newton has been known since economist John Maynard Keynes, having acquired Newton's manuscripts, concluded that he should be classified as "a magician." In the same vein, Frank Manuel argued that Newton saw more than a metaphorical affinity among all forms of action at a distance, such as magnetism, gravity, telepathy, and healing at a distance. In relation to Newton's discovery of the law of gravity, Manuel said: "Newton lived in an animistic world in which feelings of love and attraction could be assimilated to other forces."[11]

Newton's deep interest in alchemy, Manuel pointed out, was shown by the fact that his library contained 175 books on it, that he left 650,000 words on it, and that he performed alchemical experiments in his laboratory for many weeks a year, often working through the night.[12]

Newton's interest in the Hermetic tradition led mechanists on the Continent to be suspicious of him, partly because of his use of the term "attraction" in discussing the idea with which his name was most associated, gravity. This was problematic, explained Richard Westfall— who most fully discussed Newton from this point of view—because the mechanical philosophy had banished "attractions of any kind."

> From one end of the century to another, the idea of attractions, the action of one body upon another with which it is not in contact, was anathema to the dominant school of natural philosophy. Galileo could not sufficiently express his amazement that Kepler had been willing to entertain the puerile notion, as he called it, that the moon causes the tides by action upon the waters of the sea.[13]

Christiaan Huygens, who was the major Cartesian scientist after the death of Descartes himself, said in a letter about Newton: "I don't care that he's not a Cartesian as long as he doesn't serve us up conjectures such as attractions."[14]

In protecting himself from these suspicions, Newton declared that he used the word "attraction" only to refer to the "quantities and mathematical proportions" of the forces by which bodies approach each other. His account, he said, was neutral with regard to theories attempting to explain this force. He also ruled out the idea that matter has any internal powers that could explain attraction, saying that the creator of the world "form'd Matter in solid, massy, hard, impenetrable, moveable Particles."[15]

In her definitive study subtitled *The Concept of Action at a Distance in the History of Physics*, Mary Hesse said that the idea of action at a distance lost repute in physics after the introduction of the idea of matter as devoid of an inside.[16] In any case, stating his position more fully, Newton said:

> It is inconceivable that inanimate brute matter should without mediation of something else which is not material, operate upon and affect other matter without mutual contact. . . . That gravity should be innate, inherent, and essential to matter, so that one body may act upon another at a distance through a *vacuum,* without the mediation of anything else, . . . is to me so great an absurdity that I believe no man who has in philosophical matters a competent faculty of thinking can ever fall into it.[17]

Accordingly, Newton argued, "Gravity must be caused by an agent acting constantly according to certain laws," that is, "a Being incorporeal, living, intelligent, omnipresent."[18]

Although Newton himself employed the rejection of action at a distance simply as an argument for the existence of a divine agent in relation to gravity, others could use his authority to support the contention by Mersenne and Boyle that the Christian miracles could not be understood without reference to Gawd.

3. THE LATE MODERN SCIENTIFIC WORLDVIEW

Discussions of the "modern scientific worldview" have often been confusing because of a failure to recognize that this label has been applied to two radically different worldviews. The first version of the modern scientific worldview came about through the victory of the mechanical philosophy over Aristotelean and Hermetic traditions.

This version, for which miracles were central, had (i) a mechanistic view of nature, (ii) a dualistic view of human beings, and (iii) a supernaturalistic view of the universe. These three dimensions of this worldview presupposed each other: The mechanism, miracles, and dualism all required the supernatural creator, and evidence for the supernaturalistic view of the universe was provided by the dualism, mechanism, and miracles.

However, because of problems in this version of the scientific world-view, it began to unravel almost as soon as it was established. One problem was that supernaturalism seemed to be contradicted by the world's evils, especially natural evils, as discussed in Chapter 1. Whereas this problem had always created difficulties, the mechanistic doctrine of matter, with its portrayal of the natural world as having no capacity for self-movement, had made the problem even more obvious. This problem influenced many eighteenth-century thinkers, such as Voltaire, to reject supernaturalistic theism in favor of deism.

The move to deism was influenced by a growing distaste for the idea of supernatural interruptions of the laws of nature. Numerous thinkers influenced by science came to regard supernatural interventions as unseemly. One argument was that Gawd, being all-wise as well as all-powerful, would have ordered the world so well at the creation, as Leibniz had argued, that no interventions would be needed. Another factor was the growing sense that all events are so intertwined in the universal causal nexus that occasional interruptions of it are inconceivable. As Darwin said in his *Autobiography*, "the more we know of the fixed laws of nature the more incredible do miracles become."[19]

However, the deistic worldview itself soon came to be considered unsatisfactory: Deism was still a form of supernaturalism and, as such, still had a problem of evil, with which thinkers as different as Voltaire and Darwin struggled. Also, the appeal to a supernatural agent to explain mind-body interaction also came to seem unseemly.

Thus by the end of the 19th century, dualism had been replaced by materialism and the supernatural deity by atheism. All that was left of the three dimensions of the early scientific worldview was the mechanistic-materialistic view of nature. Whereas the early modern scientific worldview said, contrary to the Hermetic tradition, that miracles were impossible *naturally*, the late modern worldview said they were impossible *period*.

4. THE IMPORTANCE OF PSYCHICAL RESEARCH

In the latter part of the nineteenth century, when the late modern world-view was being established, a new science, "psychical research," emerged.

PSYCHICAL RESEARCH VS. MATERIALISM

The purpose of the Society for Psychical Research, said the charter when it was founded in 1882, was

> to investigate that large body of debatable phenomena designated by such terms as mesmeric, psychical and spiritualistic . . . in the same spirit of exact and unimpassioned enquiry which has enabled Science to solve so many problems.[20]

The founders of this society hoped to provide scientific grounding for a positive creed to undermine the materialistic worldview, which—partly through the influence of Darwinism—was increasingly thought to be scientifically validated.[21]

Put otherwise, the purpose of this new discipline was to engage in scientific studies of the kinds of phenomena that had generally been considered miracles. This meant that psychical research studied phenomena ostensibly involving influence at a distance—as indicated by several of the names for the phenomena, such as *telepathy* (which means "feeling at a distance") and *telekinesis* (the original name for what is now called psychokinesis).

The term "parapsychology" was coined to refer to the part of psychical research that employs experimental methods, usually in a laboratory. However, the two terms eventually came to be used interchangeably.

The discipline of psychical research or parapsychology is extremely controversial, which is not surprising, because it can be viewed as providing scientific evidence for central tenets of the Hermetic tradition. Accordingly, its data conflict with both of the dominant worldviews of the modern period. On the one hand, its data challenge the supernaturalistic dualism of early modernity, which is still the worldview of conservative-to-fundamentalist Christianity. On the other hand, its data challenge the materialistic atheism of late modernity, which in the latter half of the nineteenth century became the dominant worldview of the scientific community.

After the Society for Psychical Research was founded in England, where the first president was Henry Sidgwick (a Cambridge University professor of moral philosophy whose honesty was legendary), the

American Society for Psychical Research was formed in the United States, with William James as one of the founders. Although it is well known that James advocated a method he called "radical empiricism," it is less well known that this type of empiricism included, in his words, "the phenomena of psychic research so-called."[22]

SCIENCE OR PSEUDO-SCIENCE

Although the founders of the British and American societies established them to engage in scientific studies, most scientists and philosophers of science nowadays reject the idea that parapsychology could be considered a science, referring to it instead as a "pseudoscience." For example, in a book entitled *Parapsychology: Science or Magic?* psychologist James Alcock said: "Parapsychology is indistinguishable from pseudo-science."[23] Insofar as people accepted this classification, parapsychological evidence could be ignored without violating one's intellectual responsibility to take account of all relevant scientific evidence.

Some thinkers holding this view have been embarrassed by the fact that the Parapsychological Association has long been a member of the American Association for the Advancement of Science. For example, in an address entitled "Drive the Pseudos Out of the Workshop of Science," physicist John Wheeler launched a campaign to get the Parapsychological Association disaffiliated. However, during this event, Wheeler wrongly accused the best-known experimental parapsychologist, J. B. Rhine, of fraud, which Wheeler later had to retract.[24] Philosopher Antony Flew, also calling parapsychology a pseudoscience, argued that the Parapsychological Association should be "politely disaffiliated."[25]

However, many scholars in the sociology and philosophy of science have concluded that the attempt to formulate criteria for establishing a "line of demarcation" between science and pseudoscience—a line that would show all generally recognized sciences to be in the former category and all the disliked fields to be in the latter—has proved to be a failure.[26]

One reason for the failure is that the argument is often circular. For example, psychologist Ray Hyman, who had his own reasons to reject parapsychological beliefs, criticized the criteria used by Alcock, writing:

The categories of both science and pseudoscience are fuzzy. . . . It looks very much like the criteria themselves were chosen in order to exclude parapsychology.[27]

Although many reasons have been given for classifying parapsychology as a pseudoscience, the basic reason is the conviction that parapsychology's alleged phenomena conflict with science. For example, in an essay asking "Is Parapsychology a Science?" Paul Kurtz said that its findings "contradict the general conceptual framework of scientific knowledge." Alcock said that genuine parapsychological occurrences would imply a "relationship between consciousness and the physical world radically different from that held to be possible by contemporary science." In an essay entitled "Science and the Supernatural," George Price relegated the phenomena of parapsychology to the category of the "supernatural"—by which he meant the nonexistent—on the grounds that "parapsychology and modern science are incompatible."[28]

Moreover, the main ground for holding parapsychology and science to be incompatible is the belief that science is necessarily mechanistic.

- Making his most well-known claim—"The essence of science is mechanism. The essence of magic is animism"—Price argued that a scientific claim about some phenomenon requires the possibility of "a detailed mechanistic explanation."

- Flew likewise stated that the decisive objection to parapsychology's alleged phenomena is the lack of a "conceivable mechanism."

- Psychologist Donald Hebb, saying that parapsychologists have "offered enough evidence to have convinced us on almost any other issue," admitted that his reason for rejecting it "is—in a literal sense—prejudice," adding that he could have found the evidence convincing if he had "some guess as to the mechanics of the disputed process."[29]

This frame of mind is also illustrated by philosopher Jane Duran. A highly respected British philosopher named C. D. Broad had developed a list of "basic limiting principles," meaning ones that have been widely accepted as limiting what is credible. One of these principles, Broad pointed out, is that "any event that is said to cause another event (the second event being referred to as an 'effect') must be related to the effect through some causal chain."

Broad argued that the evidence for telepathy was strong enough that we should reject this principle. Duran, however, said:

> [T]he absence of a specifiable and recognizably causal chain seems to constitute a difficult, if not insurmountable, objection to our giving a coherent account of what it means to make such a claim [and hence] for concluding that telepathy [is] not possible.[30]

Accordingly, the main reason that most science-based thinkers consider parapsychological data impossible is that they think that science is necessarily mechanistic, not realizing that the mechanical worldview was adopted for other than empirical reasons, including, ironically, the desire to support supernatural miracles.

5. PARAPSYCHOLOGY VS. SUPERNATURAL MIRACLES

Defenders of supernatural miracles are generally Christian thinkers, who think primarily of miracles in relation to Jesus—that is, of the miracles reportedly performed by him and his reported "resurrection from the dead." However, scholars have shown that similar events have occurred elsewhere.

TELEPATHY AND CLAIRVOYANCE

In speaking of the "mental miracles" of Jesus, Roman Catholic New Testament theologian Raymond Brown wrote that the "Gospels attribute to Jesus the ability to know what is in others' minds [and] to know what is happening elsewhere."[31]

However, *telepathy*—the capacity of some people to become aware of other people's feelings and thoughts by means of extrasensory perception (ESP)—has been well documented in parapsychological and scientific literature.[32] The same is true of *clairvoyance*, the ability of some people, without any sensory-based information, to know facts about physical things. In some cases, the object is at some distance away, in which case the phenomenon may be called "remote viewing."[33]

Accordingly, it is problematic to use the reported telepathic and clairvoyance abilities of Jesus to attribute divine omniscience to him.

PSYCHOKINESIS

The other major category of Jesus' so-called miracles are the "physical miracles." Various types of these are reported in the gospels, such as healings, walking on water, feeding multitudes, and turning water into wine. In parapsychology, all such reported occurrences are classified as forms of psychokinesis, defined as the ability of the mind to bring about physical changes in the world without the normal physical means. There have been many documented cases of psychokinesis in the parapsychological literature.[34] These cases include the phenomenon known as levitation.

LEVITATION

The story about Jesus' walking on water has been widely taken as a supernatural miracle. For example, in his generally excellent historical study of the miracle stories, entitled *Jesus the Miracle Worker*, Graham Twelftree says that modern people can often agree that some of the stories, such as those about exorcisms and healings, may have natural explanations, but not other stories, such as the account of Jesus walking on water. It is generally agreed that walking on water would be an example of levitation, and Richard Swinburne expresses a widespread belief in saying that levitation would be a violation of "the laws of nature," hence a supernatural miracle.[35]

However, if we assume that Jesus really did this, it would not be proof of supernatural working in him. There are well-documented cases of levitations of Christian saints. Besides St. Teresa of Avila, there was also St. Joseph of Copertino, an extremely pious young man who became a Franciscan monk in 1625. While rapt in prayer—often in broad daylight—he reportedly would levitate several feet off the ground. Having heard of these levitations, Gottfried Leibniz's patron, John Frederick, the Duke of Braunschweig-Luneberg, journeyed to Italy in hopes of seeing them with his own eyes. After reportedly witnessing two of Joseph's levitations, he converted from Protestantism to Catholicism, having become convinced that this is the branch of Christianity that is approved by Gawd.[36]

Catholics can, of course, regard the levitations of the saints as supernatural miracles, but Protestants always considered the age of miracles to have lasted only through the lifetime of the original apostles. Protestants have inclined, therefore, to reject the levitation accounts as false. But some non-Catholics who have actually studied the evidence, such as Esalen founder Michael Murphy, have concluded that they were sometimes genuine, but non-miraculous, events.[37] Moreover, levitations have also reportedly occurred in non-Christian traditions.[38]

6. APPARITIONS AND THE RESURRECTION APPEARANCES OF JESUS

Many Christian thinkers put the "resurrection of Jesus" in a class by itself, or at least call it the *supreme* miracle. "The resurrection of Jesus," said Raymond Brown, "was the supreme intervention of [Gawd] in human existence, the supreme miracle." Likewise, Anglican theologian Austin Farrer said: "Christ's Resurrection, as faith conceives it, is unique in its kind; Christians will always resist the reduction of it to a level with any class of facts whatsoever."[39]

Farrer is certainly correct that this is the way that traditional Christianity has conceived it. But is it the best way? Given the fact that parapsychological research has shown the so-called miracles of Jesus to be analogous to other extraordinary but natural occurrences, could not the same be said about the so-called resurrection of Jesus?

Anglican priest and theologian Alan Richardson said no. "Against all modern attempts to explain the resurrection as something natural and comprehensible," as might be done by psychical researchers, said Richardson, "it is necessary to insist that the resurrection of Jesus is a *miracle*."[40]

However, some prominent New Testament scholars, while accepting the historicity of the event, have disagreed with the view of it as absolutely unique. This disagreement involves a difference in how the event called "the resurrection of Jesus" is understood.

Those who speak of the uniqueness of this event usually think in terms of the "bodily resurrection of Jesus." But those who think in terms of analogies speak of "the *appearances* of Jesus after his death"—as did St. Paul, who wrote nothing about an empty tomb, but instead spoke of life after physical death in a "spiritual body."[41]

A judgment as to the appropriateness of speaking of analogies requires an understanding of the standard features of apparitions.

APPARITIONS

In the early days of psychical research, the major interest was in evidence for life after death, so much of the research focused on apparitions. After these had been extensively studied, emphasis shifted to other phenomena, so much of the documented evidence about apparitions is many decades old. However, rather than making this evidence unreliable, this fact can increase its reliability, because in those days there was none of today's technology that could be used to fabricate apparitions.

A summary of the features of apparitions, as provided by psychical research, shows that they support the possibility that the post-mortem appearances of Jesus might have reflected the continuing reality of the personality of Jesus. Here are several features of apparitions that are important for this issue.

Veridical Apparitions: Some apparitions are veridical, meaning that the person(s) who saw the apparition acquired from it true information that would not have been knowable by normal means. The existence of veridical apparitions counts against the common assumption that all apparitions can be dismissed as pathological hallucinations.[42]

For example, there are well-documented cases in which family members of a deceased person have learned from an apparition the location of some money or important document. There are also some cases in which someone learns that and how "the apparent" had been injured or killed.[43]

During the American Civil War, for example, Captain Russell Colt and his eldest brother, Oliver, a lieutenant, had agreed that if the latter were to be killed in the upcoming offensive, he would let his brother know by appearing in his room. Shortly thereafter, Russell awoke at night and saw Oliver kneeling. Thinking the moonlight was playing a trick on him, Russell walked through the apparition but then looked back and saw that Oliver had a wound on his right temple, with blood streaming from it. He told other people in the house about this strange occurrence and then, two weeks later, learned that Oliver had been killed that night by a bullet that struck his right temple. He also learned that

Oliver, being propped up by other dead bodies, had been found "in a sort of kneeling posture."[44]

However, the fact that an apparition is veridical does not prove that it originated with the still-living soul of the apparent, because one could assume that the apparition was unconsciously created out of telepathic and/or clairvoyant perception. Nevertheless, veridical perceptions show that some apparitions have at least an element of objectivity, so that they cannot all be explained as purely subjective hallucinations.

Multiple Apparitions: Although most apparitions are seen by only one person, some of them are *multiple,* meaning that two or more persons at different locations see the apparition within roughly the same time period.

One famous case involved Eldred Bowyer-Bower, an airman who was shot down over France on the morning of March 19, 1917. Apparitions of him were seen that day by his three-year-old nephew in England, who came to his mother's room to tell her that "Uncle Alley Boy is downstairs," and by his half-sister in India, who did not learn that he was missing for two more weeks. (The fact that it occurred so many decades ago, before communication was so rapid, made it easier to be certain that the apparition was discussed before any word of the apparent's fate was known through normal channels.)[45]

Multiple cases strengthen the degree of objectivity that apparitions can have.

Collective Apparitions: Some apparitions are collective, meaning that two or more persons simultaneously see the apparition at the same place. Sometimes, moreover, the apparition is seen by at least one person who had never seen the apparent while he or she was alive.

For example, one night two years after a young woman had gotten married, she and her husband, Willie, were ready to turn out the light when she saw a man, dressed as a naval officer, at the foot of her bed. Willie, who had already turned toward the other direction, did not see the apparition until his wife called his attention to it. Astonished, Willie said "What on earth are you doing here, sir?" In a commanding and reproachful voice, the figure said, "Willie! Willie!" after which the figure walked away and "disappeared, as it were, into the wall." Willie then explained to his wife that his father, who had been dead 14 years, had been a naval officer as a young man. Later, Willie also told her that his father's apparition had led him not to take some financial advice, which would have led him to ruin. This case was of extra interest because of the fact that the apparition, unlike most apparitions, spoke.[46]

Collective apparitions count heavily against the assumption not only that all apparitions are purely subjective hallucinations, but also against the assumption that they result simply from projections based on telepathic and/or clairvoyant perceptions. That assumption would require that two or more people each had the same extrasensory perception at the same time, from which they simultaneously projected an image of the apparent at the same place. And this assumption would have a temporal problem: Sometimes an apparition will fade in, remain a while, and then fade out, and yet everyone seeing it agrees on when it became visible and when it faded away.

One attempt to explain collective apparitions involves a theory of "psychic contagion," according to which one person creates the apparition—whether from extrasensory perception or a subjective hallucination—and then induces a vision of it telepathically in others. But this theory has a spatial problem: how to explain why all the percipients see the apparition in the same place and from their own perspectives, so that, for example, one person may see it from the back, another from the front, a third from the left side, and so on. This feature of collective apparitions suggests that they are objective.

One more attempt to dismiss collective apparitions is to argue that, because reports of them are exceedingly rare, we can assume that they have been products of mistakes and lies. However, they are not so rare: In a 19th-century census of 1,087 cases of visual apparitions, 95 of them were collective. Moreover, according to that census plus a 1956 study of apparitions in which two or more persons were in position to see the apparition, the apparitions were collective from one third to one half of the time.[47]

Reciprocal Apparitions of the Living: Whereas the apparitions discussed thus far have all involved post-mortem apparitions, there have also been apparitions of people who were still alive. These "apparitions of the living" were of two types: those that occurred spontaneously and those in which one person intentionally created the apparition. Occasionally, the apparition is reciprocal, meaning that both people—the one who is there physically and the one who is not—are aware of each other.

One famous case involved S. R. Wilmot. He was returning from Europe by ship, sharing a cabin with his friend W. J. Tait. While sleeping one night, Wilmot dreamed that his wife had come to see him in her night-dress. According to his report, he said that she "advanced to my side, stooped down and kissed me and after gently caressing me for a few moments, quietly withdrew." Upon waking, Tait said: "You're a pretty fellow, to have a lady come and visit you in this way." It quickly became clear that his description of what he said corresponded with Wilmot's dream. And after returning home, Wilmot learned that his wife, having deliberately sought to reach him, reported that she did what Tait and Mr. Wilmot had seen her do, and that she had seen Tait looking at her.[48]

The major study of reciprocal apparitions concluded that apparitions of the dead and reciprocal apparitions of the living are so similar that, as the researcher Hornell Hart concluded, "the two types must be regarded as belonging to the same basic kind of phenomena."[49]

The major point of Hart's 1956 study of apparitions was, in fact, that some apparitions of the dead have been produced, at least partly, by the intentional activity of the still-conscious minds of the apparents.[50]

APPARITIONS AND THE RESURRECTION APPEARANCES

As the above examples of apparitions show, some of those reported by psychical researchers had features similar to the reported post-mortem appearances of Jesus. According the New Testament reports, the resurrection appearances of Jesus included these features:

- There were reportedly multiple appearances (e.g., Lk 24:34; Lk 24:36–38).

- There were reportedly collective appearances (e.g., Mt 28:9-10; 1 Cor 15:6; Acts 1:3).

- There were reportedly appearances in which Jesus spoke (e.g., Mt 28:9; Acts 1:3; Mt 23:16–18; Mk 16:14–16).

- Some appearances appeared to be entirely physical (e.g., Lk 24:36–43; Mt 28:9; Jn 20:20), while other reports indicated that, although they in some respects seemed physical, they in other respects did not, as the apparition was able, for example, to enter into houses with locked doors (Jn 20:26; Mk 16:12; Lk 24:30–36; Lk 24:5–53; Acts 1:1–11).

- By definition, of course, the apparitions of Jesus could not have been reciprocal. But most of them were *like* reciprocal apparitions, in that both parties were reportedly aware of each other and even talked to each other.

Being cognizant of these similarities, some New Testament scholars have treated the post-mortem appearances of Jesus as instances of apparitions:

- In 1907, Kirsopp Lake, who taught at the universities of both Leiden and Harvard, published a book entitled *The Historical Evidence for the Resurrection of Jesus Christ*, in which he said that "the phenomenon which we call the Resurrection cannot be isolated, but must be considered in connection with others which belong to the same class."[51]

- In 1912, B. H. Streeter published a book entitled *Foundations: A Statement of Christian Belief in Terms of Modern Thought*, in which he said that the resurrection appearances to the disciples were visions "directly caused by the Lord himself, veritably alive and personally in communication with them."[52]

- In 1941, C. J. Cadoux published a book called *The Historic Mission of Jesus*, in which he said that the appearances were "real manifestations given to his followers by Jesus himself, not by means of his physical body resuscitated from the empty tomb, but by way of those strange processes sufficiently attested to us by psychical research, but as yet very imperfectly understood."[53]

- In a 2007 book, Marcus Borg said that St. Paul, who wrote the first words in the New Testament about the resurrection, said four times in his statement in First Corinthians that Jesus "appeared" to various people. In the Bible, Borg pointed out, the word "appeared" is often "used in connection with 'apparitions' [and] an apparition is a paranormal kind of experience, not visible to everybody who happens to be there." That Paul thought of the resurrection appearances as apparitions, Borg continued, "is further suggested by his inclusion of himself in the list of people to whom the risen Christ appeared," which implied that Paul "regards his own experience of the risen Christ [his vision on the Damascus Road] as similar to the others." Borg added that "visions and apparitions can be true," so he did "not put them in the category of hallucinations." Borg also said that "apparitions do not involve a physical body, even though what is seen often includes seeing a person in bodily form."[54]

The fact that the "resurrection of Jesus," insofar as it is taken as a real event, need not be categorized as a supernatural miracle is also illustrated by the position of Pichas Lapide, an orthodox Jewish theologian, who believed in the resurrection of Jesus without thereby believing that Jesus was in any way absolutely unique. Although "the resurrection belongs to the category of the truly real and effective occurrences," Lapide held, it was not a "miracle" in the supernaturalist sense. Instead, he wrote:

> The works of our creator are altogether wonderful—but not miraculous. They do not arbitrarily skip the natural chain of cause and effect. . . . [A]t the beginning there was dead matter. Out of this matter arose life in a 'development' that lasted for billions of years. Out of life, consciousness gradually arose, and out of consciousness . . . love and self-knowledge. This can be called a global or comprehensive resurrection from that which was dead. . . . Why should the resurrection of the personal ego after passing through death be more miraculous than the gradual awakening of a human being out of the lifeless matter of a fertilized ovum?[55]

CONCLUSION

Conservative philosophers of religion argue that the miracles reported in the New Testament prove the existence of Gawd. Conservative Christian theologians argue that these miracles show that Christianity is the one religion approved by Gawd. In the late modern world, these claims are rejected out of hand on the basis of the belief that none of the "miracle stories" reported in the New Testament really happened, except perhaps those, such as the stories about exorcisms and faith healings, that can be explained in terms of suggestion.

These two views—(i) the New Testament miracles were supernatural, (ii) the New Testament miracles did not happen—reflect the early modern and late modern worldviews, respectively.

However, the Hermetic tradition provided a third alternative— that the New Testament's "miracles" were actual but not supernatural. The discipline called psychical research or parapsychology has provided empirical support for this third view. Thanks to this alternative, people need not hold that the only way to reject the idea of supernatural miracles is to reject the reality of all stories reporting the kinds of events that had long been considered miraculous.

In other words, even if we do not resort to the desperate method of denying the reality of every single reported "miracle," such so-called miracles do not prove the existence of Gawd.

ENDNOTES

1. Millard J. Erickson, *Christian Theology* (Baker Book House, 1985), 54.

2. Ibid., 408.

3. Ibid., 409, 277.

4. Richard Swinburne, *Is There a God?* (Oxford University Press, 1996), 7.

5. Ibid., 102.

6. Richard Swinburne, *The Existence of God* (1979; Oxford University Press, 2004), 284.

7. Ibid., 288, 292.

8. William Lane Craig, "The New Atheism and Five Arguments for God," Reasonable Faith, 2010.

9. William Lane Craig, "The Problem of Miracles: A Historical and Philosophical Perspective," in David Wenham and Craig Blomberg, eds.,

Gospel Perspectives VI (JSOT Press, 1986), 9–40.

10. Hugh Kearney, *Science and Change 1500-1700* (McGraw-Hill, 1971), 313.

11. John Maynard Keynes, *Essays in Biography,* ed. Geoffrey Keynes, 2nd ed. (R. Hart-Davis, 1951), 313; Frank Manuel, *A Portrait of Isaac Newton* (Harvard University Press, 1968), 85.

12. Manuel, *A Portrait of Isaac Newton*, 162–63, 170–72.

13. Richard J. Westfall, "The Influence of Alchemy on Newton," in Marsha P. Hanen et al., eds., *Science, Pseudo-Science, and Society* (Wilfrid Laurier University Press, 1980), 145–70.

14. Richard J. Westfall, *Never at Rest: A Biography of Isaac Newton* (Cambridge University Press, 1980), 464.

15. Alexandre Koyré, *From the Closed World to the Infinite Universe* (The Johns Hopkins Press, 1957), 217–19.

16. Mary Hesse, *Forces and Fields: The Concept of Action at a Distance in the History of Physics* (Littlefield, Adams, and Co., 1965), 118, 125, 291.

17. Koyré, *From the Closed World*, 173–74, 178–79.

18. Ibid., 178–79, 208–09.

19. John Hedley Brooke, *Science and Religion: Some Historical Perspectives* (Cambridge University Press, 1991), 271.

20. Alan Gauld, *The Founders of Psychical Research* (Shocken Books, 1978), 138.

21. Ibid., 141–42.

22. William James, *Essays in Radical Empiricism,* ed. Ralph Barton Perry, published in one volume with James's *A Pluralistic Universe* (E. P. Dutton, 1971), 270, 271.

23. James E. Alcock, *Parapsychology: Science or Magic? A Psychological Perspective* (Pergamon Press, 1981), 196.

24. *New York Review of Books,* April 13, 1979; Richard S. Broughton, *Parapsychology: The Controversial Science* (Ballantine Books, 1991), 75n.; *Science,* July 13, 1979: 144.

25. Antony Flew, "Parapsychology: Science or Pseudoscience?" Paul Kurtz, ed., *A Skeptic's Handbook of Parapsychology* (Prometheus Press, 1985), 519–36, at 529.

26. Rachel Laudan, ed., *The Demarcation between Science and Pseudo-Science* (Center for the Study of Science & Society, 1983); Patrick Grim, ed., *Philosophy of Science and the Occult* (State University of New York Press, 1982).

27. Ray Hyman, *The Elusive Quarry: A Scientific Appraisal of Psychical Research* (Prometheus Books, 1989), 176.

28. Paul Kurtz, "Is Parapsychology a Science?" Paul Kurtz, ed., *A Skeptic's Handbook of Parapsychology* (Prometheus Press, 1985), 503–18, at 510; James E. Alcock, *Science and Supernature: A Critical Appraisal of Parapsychology* (Prometheus Books, 1990), 19; George Price, "Science and the Supernatural," Jan Ludwig, ed., *Philosophy and Parapsychology* (Prometheus Books, 1978), 145–71.

29. Price, "Science and the Supernatural," 152–53; Flew, "Parapsychology: Science or Pseudoscience?" 532; D. O. Hebb, "The Role of Neurological Ideas in Psychology," *Journal of Personality* 20/1 (September 1951): 39–55, at 45.

30. C. D. Broad, *Religion, Philosophy and Psychical Research* (Humanities Press, 1969), 9; Jane Duran, "Philosophical Difficulties with Paranormal Knowledge Claims," Patrick Grim, ed., *Philosophy of Science and the Occult* (State University of New York Press, 1982), 196–206, at 202.

31. Raymond E. Brown, *An Introduction to New Testament Christology* (Paulist Press, 1994).

32. See, for example, Ian Stevenson, *Telepathic Impressions* (University Press of Virginia, 1970); Richard S. Broughton, *Parapsychology: The Controversial Science* (Ballantine Books, 1991); Carles Grau et al., "Conscious Brain-to-Brain Communication in Humans Using Non-Invasive Technologies," PLOS One, 19 August 2014; Patrizio E. Tressoldi et al., "Extrasensory Perception and Quantum Models of Cognition," *Neuro-Quantology*, 8/4 (December 2010), Suppl. 1: 81-87; Russell Targ, *The Reality of ESP: A Physicist's Proof of Psychic Abilities* (Quest Books, 2012).

33. Broughton, *Parapsychology*; Stephen E. Braude, *The Limits of Influence: Psychokinesis and the Philosophy of Science* (New York: Routledge & Kegan Paul, 1986); Stanley Krippner, ed., *Psychokinesis: Advances in Parapsychological Research*, Vol. 1 (Springer Science, 1977).

34. Broughton, *Parapsychology*; Stephen E. Braude, *The Limits of Influence: Psychokinesis and the Philosophy of Science* (Routledge & Kegan Paul, 1986); Stanley Krippner, ed., *Psychokinesis: Advances in Parapsychological*

Research, Vol. 1 (Springer Science, 1977).

35. Graham H. Twelftree, *Jesus the Miracle Worker: A Historical and Theological Study* (InterVarsity Press, 1999), 38; Richard Swinburne, "For the Possibility of Miracles," *Philosophical Quarterly* 18 (1968).

36. Herbert Thurston, *The Physical Phenomena of Mysticism* (Henry Regnery, 1952), 16. For recent discussions of levitation in general and Joseph in particular by a serious scholar, see Michael Grosso, "Why Levitation?" Rhine Magazine, 4/1, 2013, and *The Man Who Could Fly: St. Joseph of Copertino and the Mystery of Levitation* (Rowman and Littlefield, 2015).

37. A great account is provided in Michael Murphy, *The Future of the Body: Explorations into the Further Evolution of Human Nature* (Penguin Putnam, 1991), Chap. 22, "The Charisms of Catholic Saints and Mystics."

38. See *The Autobiography of a Yogi* (New York: The Philosophical Library, 1946).

39. Brown, *An Introduction to New Testament Christology*, 162; Austin Farrer, "Introduction" to Michael C. Perry, *The Easter Enigma: An Essay on the Resurrection with Special Reference to the Data of Psychical Research* (Faber & Faber, 1959), 11.

40. Alan Richardson, ed., *A Theological Word-Book of the Bible* (SCM Press, 1950), 194.

41. First Corinthians, 15:44; William Witt, "Against a Subjectivist Interpretation of 1 Cor. 15: Contemporary Discussions of the Resurrection of Christ and the Apostle Paul," William G. Will (Blog), 11 February 2009.

42. George Tyrrell, *Apparitions* (University Books, 1961), 22.

43. Frederick W. H. Myers, *Human Personality and Its Survival of Bodily Death*, abridged by Susy Smith (University Books, 1961), 228–29; Curt J. Ducasse, *A Critical Examination of the Belief in a Life After Death* (Charles C. Thomas, 1961), 157–58; Myers, *Human Personality*, 230–31.

44. Myers, *Human* Personality, 230–31.

45. Tyrrell, *Apparitions,* 36.

46. Myers, *Human Personality*, 218–19.

47. Hornell Hart, "Six Theories about Apparitions," *Proceedings of the Society for Psychical Research*, 50 (May 1956), 153–249; Alan Gauld,

Mediumship and Survival (Granada, 1983), 240.

48. Tyrrell, *Apparitions*, 116–17.

49. Carl B. Becker, *Paranormal Experiences and Survival of Death* (State University of New York Press, 1993), 52.

50. Hart, "Six Theories."

51. Kirsopp Lake, *The Historical Evidence for the Resurrection of Jesus Christ* (Williams & Norgate, 1907), 275–76.

52. B. H. Streeter, *Foundations: A Statement of Christian Belief in Terms of Modern Thought* (Macmillan, 1912), 136.

53. C. J. Cadoux, *The Historic Mission of Jesus* (Lutterworth, 1941), 166.

54. Marcus J. Borg and N. T. Wright, *The Meaning of Jesus: Two Visions,* 2nd ed. (HarperOne, 2007), 132–33.

55. Pichas Lapide, *The Resurrection of Jesus* (Augsburg Fortress, 1983), 92, 151.

6

Immoral Effects

It has long been argued that atheism promotes immorality. Even thinkers who have personally given up theism have argued that public belief in a deity is needed to prevent the masses of people from descending into immoral anarchy.

Some critics of traditional theism, however, have argued that its moral effects are more destructive than helpful. In the 18th century, Voltaire argued that people concerned with morality should "crush the infamous thing," meaning the Christian religion. Although Voltaire retained a deistic belief, he mercilessly attacked Christian theism. In his *Heavenly City of the Eighteenth-Century Philosophers*, Carl Becker, referring to Voltaire and many others, wrote that "God was on trial."[1]

The trial continued in the nineteenth century. Ludwig Feuerbach argued that belief in a deity outside ourselves alienated us from our own deepest nature. Karl Marx argued that theism is "the opium of the people," because it prevents people from throwing off the chains of their capitalist oppressors. And Friedrich Nietzsche, stating that "God is dead," argued that although this death has traumatic consequences, it allows for a better morality.[2]

In the twentieth century, there were dozens of writers promoting atheism—from Sigmund Freud to Jean-Paul Sartre to the "Death of God" theologians—saying that the rejection of theism will improve the morality of society and individuals.

More recently, the case for the moral superiority of atheism has been presented by a movement that came to be called the New Atheism, which has been discussed primarily in terms of books by three men: Richard Dawkins (*The God Delusion*, 2006); Sam Harris (*The End of Faith*, 2005, and *Letter to a Christian Nation*, 2008); and Christopher Hitchens (*God is Not Great: How Religion Poisons Everything*, 2007).

During the same years, Daniel Dennett published an argument against theism entitled *Breaking the Spell: Religion as a Natural Phenomenon* (2006). As a result of this timing, Dennett was categorized as one of the New Atheists, and he and the other three writers were dubbed the "four horsemen of the anti-religious apocalypse."[3] However, Dennett's approach was very different from that of the other three, so if New Atheism is to be considered a school of thought, it should be limited to Dawkins, Harris, and Hitchens, who have been called "The Unholy Trinity."[4]

Some critics have considered the term New Atheism a misnomer because, in the words of one writer, it is "difficult to identify anything philosophically unprecedented in their positions and arguments."[5] Another critic pointed out that, except for Dawkins, they have little to say about arguments for Gawd's existence but instead "tend to focus on the social effects of religion, arguing that religious belief is not good for society," a view that Dawkins also expressed.[6]

The so-called New Atheists, in other words, have provided a restatement of the claim that theistic religion promotes immorality, so that atheism would improve morality.

I. THE CLAIM THAT THEISM PROMOTES IMMORALITY

This observation about the New Atheists—that their primary focus was on the moral issue— is reinforced by the fact that this movement could also have been called "post-9/11 atheism." Astute critic Jackson Lears said of these men: "In the shadow of 9/11, they were ready to press the case against religion with renewed determination."[7] Referring in particular to Harris's 2005 book—the subtitle of which is "Religion, Terror, and the Future of Reason"—Lears wrote:

> *The End of Faith*, written in the wake of 9/11, bears all the marks of that awful time: hysteria, intolerance, paranoia; cankered demands for unity and the demonization of dissent. The argument is simple: the attacks on the World Trade Center awakened us to the mortal danger posed by dogmatic religion. Enlightened atheists must take up Voltaire's challenge and crush the infamous thing at last—with the weight of scientific arguments if possible, with the force of military might if necessary.[8]

Although Harris' book was published four years after the 9/11 attacks, Christopher Hitchens' book contained a statement written only months after them. Reflecting about his own reaction to 9/11, Hitchens wrote:

> On examination, and to my own surprise and pleasure, it turned out to be exhilaration. Here was the most frightful enemy—theocratic barbarism—in plain view. . . . I realized that if the battle went on until the last day of my life, I would never get bored in prosecuting it to the utmost.[9]

In any case, although the New Atheists claimed that theism promotes immorality, their criticisms were not directed at theism in general but at theism understood as belief in Gawd—a deity that could support theocratic barbarism.

SAM HARRIS

As Lears observed, Sam Harris was writing about "dogmatic religion." To be sure, Harris did not call for the end of only dogmatic religion. Rather, he said that all religions, with their defense of the right to faith, are "in large part, responsible for the religious conflict in our world." Although many nonsensical things held by religious people are in themselves innocuous, said Harris, they open the space for unjustified beliefs that lead to "the most monstrous crimes against humanity."[10]

Nevertheless, Harris focused primarily on the moral destructiveness of supernatural, dogmatic religion. Besides saying that "[Gawd] has given us far many more reasons to kill one another than to turn the other cheek," Harris said:

> We all know that human beings are capable of incredible brutality, but we should do well to ask, What sort of ideology will make us *most* capable of it? . . . It has long been obvious that the dogma of faith—particularly in a scheme in which the faithful are promised eternal salvation and doubters are damned—is nothing less than their perfect solution.[11]

CHRISTOPHER HITCHENS

As shown by the 2001 statement of Hitchens quoted above, the New Atheism began with him. In a review of Hitchens' book, *God Is Not Great*, Ross Douthat said:

> For years now, [Hitchens] has supplemented his prolific punditry and criticism with a stream of anti-theistic diatribes, and now these rivers of vituperation have pooled into a single volume. . . . The book has been written with two main purposes in mind: to show that all religions are false, and to prove that their effects are near-universally pernicious.[12]

However, although Hitchens spoke about "all religions," he treated only Gawd-based religion, as illustrated by the fact that, as Douthat pointed out, Hitchens' book "includes exactly two quotations from religious intellectuals born since 1800." Both of these quotations, moreover, were from C. S. Lewis, who famously defended the existence and goodness of Gawd.[13]

RICHARD DAWKINS

That Richard Dawkins criticizes Gawd-based theism is suggested by his well-known statement about the Bible's first testament:

> The God of the Old Testament is arguably the most unpleasant character in all fiction: jealous and proud of it; a petty, unjust, unforgiving control freak; a vindictive, bloodthirsty ethnic

cleanser; a misogynistic, homophobic, racist, infanticidal, geno-
cidal, filicidal, pestilential, megalomaniacal, sadomasochistic,
capriciously malevolent bully.[14]

The fact that Dawkins' case was against supernaturalism is shown by
his rejection of the "God Hypothesis," which holds that "there exists a
superhuman, supernatural intelligence who deliberately designed and
created the universe and everything in it." The fact that supernaturalism
is the target is made even clearer by his statement that, according to the
God Hypothesis,

> The reality we inhabit also contains a supernatural agent who
> designed the universe and—at least in many versions of the
> hypothesis—maintains it and even intervenes in it with mir-
> acles, which are temporary violations of his own otherwise
> grandly immutable laws.

Dawkins illustrated this supernatural interventionism by quoting
Richard Swinburne's statement, "[Gawd] is not limited by the laws of
nature: he makes them and he can change or suspend them—if he
chooses."[15]

Moreover, in a chapter entitled "What's Wrong with Religion? Why
Be So Hostile?" Dawkins answered—to repeat a statement quoted in
Chapter 2: "As a scientist, I am hostile to fundamentalist religion because
it actively debauches the scientific enterprise."[16]

Dawkins added that he was also against "non-fundamentalist"
religion, because it "is making the world safe for fundamentalism by
teaching children, from their earliest years, that unquestioning faith is
a virtue."[17] But this is a poorly thought-out claim: It is obviously not
true of Unitarians, Quakers, and many present-day Congregationalists,
Disciples of Christ, Episcopalians, Lutherans, Methodists, and
Presbyterians, among others. Dawkins' main objection is to fundamentalist religion and hence Gawd.

Because Dawkins' book is directed against the existence of a supernaturalistic deity, the title of his book, *The God Delusion*, is misleading,
suggesting that all belief in God—not simply in Gawd—is delusory. The
nature of the target was clearly stated in his first chapter: After a brief

discussion of the "pantheistic God" of Einsteinian religion, Dawkins said: "I am calling only *supernatural* gods delusional. . . . In the rest of this book I am talking only about *supernatural* gods."[18]

And yet Dawkins knew that supernaturalism—by which he primarily meant a deity that "intervenes in the world by performing miracles"—and pantheism do not exhaust the possible meanings of the term "God." Dawkins was also not hostile towards (in addition to pantheism) deism, which affirms a "supernatural intelligence, but one whose activities were confined to setting up the laws that govern the universe." Dawkins even spoke kindly of one type of theism: In response to a question of why he speaks only of fundamentalists, "rather than sophisticated theologians like Tillich or Bonhoeffer," Dawkins replied:

> The melancholy truth is that this kind of understated, decent, revisionist religion is numerically negligible. To the vast majority of believers around the world, religion all too closely resembles what you hear from the likes of [Pat] Robertson, [Jerry] Falwell, or [Ted] Haggard, Osama bin Laden or the Ayatollah Khomeini.[19]

However, regardless of how many people hold a non-fundamentalist version of theism, it was misleading of Dawkins to use objections to Gawd to criticize all belief in God. Although Dawkins said that his "central question [is] whether God exists,"[20] his moral argument was directed only against the existence of Gawd.

To be sure, although Dawkins spoke more favorably of a deity that creates but does not intervene in the universe, he rejected belief in a divine creator in every sense. This complete rejection was made clear by his endorsement of "philosophical naturalism," according to which "there is nothing beyond the natural, physical world."[21] But rather than giving an argument for this type of naturalism Dawkins simply presupposed it.

Dawkins did, however, offer an idiosyncratic argument for the impossibility of a divine creator. A deistic designer could not have existed prior to the creation of our world, Dawkins argued, because very complex beings can come about only by evolution from simpler things, and a cosmic designing mind would be even more complex than a Boeing 747.[22]

But the fact that complex entities can come about only through evolution is a statement about *material* entities. To argue that this would also be true of a divine *mind* would be simply to presuppose, as Alvin Plantinga pointed out, "the premise that materialism is true."[23]

Accordingly, insofar as Dawkins had a valid argument against theism, it was his argument that science necessarily presupposes naturalism, in the sense that there can be no interruptions of the world's causal relations. Dawkins had a good argument, therefore, only against the existence of Gawd. It was also his opposition to Gawd that provided the basis for his moral argument against theism.

2. THE CLAIM THAT ATHEISM PROMOTES MORALITY

Besides saying that theism promotes immorality, the New Atheists claimed that atheism is more likely than theism to produce morality. Dawkins told an interviewer: "I'm quite keen on the politics of persuading people of the virtues of atheism."[24] It seems, however, that for Dawkins the main virtue of atheism was atheism—that is, not believing in theism, because it is false, childish, and evil.

INTOLERANCE OF THE TOLERANCE FOR RELIGION

In his book *God and the New Atheism*, John Haught said that, although in most respects there is nothing *new* in the so-called New Atheism, there is one new element: the view that the liberal tolerance of faith should no longer be tolerated, because the hope for a better world rests upon getting rid of religion. This is, in fact, a view held by all three of the New Atheists.[25]

Actually, however, even this element is not really new. The term "antitheism" has been used since at least 1883 to refer to the belief that theism is destructive.[26] Indeed, Hitchens in 2001 said:

> I'm not even an atheist so much as I am an antitheist; I not only maintain that all religions are versions of the same untruth, but I hold that the influence of churches, and the effect of religious belief, is positively harmful.[27]

In any case, besides holding that atheism is a virtue, Dawkins argued, like Sam Harris, that toleration of religion is a vice. We should be intolerant not only of extremist faiths, Dawkins said, but also of "the teachings of 'moderate' religion," because such religion is "an open invitation to extremism." Dawkins thereby reflected the above-quoted statement by Harris about the responsibility of moderates for religious conflict.[28]

But is the intolerance of religion really a way to promote more ethical views? In the view of millions of religious people, one of the great moral steps of modernity is religious pluralism, according to which people of one faith should be tolerant of the people of other faiths, that those with religious faith should be tolerant of those who completely reject religion, and that those who reject all religion should be tolerant of the religious. The rejection of the tolerance of faith by the New Atheists is a moral regression, not an advance.

ISLAMOPHOBIA

There is, moreover, an even stronger reason for saying that the atheism of these men has not promoted morality, namely, that all of them have embodied, and strongly expressed, Islamophobia. This point has been made by Nathan Lean, who in 2012 published a well-received book entitled *The Islamophobia Industry*.[29] In 2013, Lean wrote:

> [I]n the wave of the [9/11] terrorist attacks, the New Atheists joined a growing chorus of Muslim-haters, mixing their abhorrence of religion in general with a specific distaste for Islam, [thereby] rebrand[ing] atheism into a popular, cerebral and more bellicose version of its former self.

Indeed, wrote Lean:

> The New Atheists became the new Islamophobes, their invectives against Muslims resembling the rowdy, uneducated ramblings of backwoods racists rather than appraisals based on intellect, rationality and reason.[30]

In addition, the full extent of the immorality of the New Atheists is realized only, as Murtaza Hussain argued, in the context of the conflict of the United States and Great Britain "with Muslim-majority nations." In that context, the New Atheists "stepped in to give a veneer of scientific respectability to today's politically useful bigotry."[31] This politically useful Islamophobia was endorsed by all three of the New Atheists.

Sam Harris: Glenn Greenwald, one of our most astute commentators on public policy, has written that Harris "spout[s] and promote[s] Islamophobia under the guise of rational atheism." As to the meaning of "Islamophobia," Greenwald pointed out that it is as clear as the meaning of anti-semitism and racism:

> It signifies (1) irrational condemnations of all members of a group or the group itself based on the bad acts of specific individuals in that group; (2) a disproportionate fixation on that group for sins committed at least to an equal extent by many other groups, especially one's own; and/or (3) sweeping claims about the members of that group unjustified by their actual individual acts and beliefs.[32]

Harris' Islamophobia was shown, said Greenwald, by the fact that, rather than criticizing Islam in a general critique of religion, Harris presented Islam as *uniquely* threatening. Greenwald supported this characterization of Harris' position by quoting several of his statements:

- "At this point in human history, Islam simply is different from other faiths."[33]

- "While the other major world religions have been fertile sources of intolerance, it is clear that the doctrine of Islam poses unique problems for the emergence of a global civilization."[34]

- "All civilized nations must unite in condemnation of a theology that now threatens to destabilize much of the earth."[35]

- "Islam, more than any other religion human beings have devised, has all the makings of a thoroughgoing cult of death."[36]

- Islam presents "a special problem for nuclear deterrence."[37]

- "[W]e are not at war with terrorism. We are at war with Islam. . . . [T]his is not to say that we are at war with all Muslims, but we are absolutely at war with millions more than have any direct affiliation with Al Qaeda."[38]

- "We should profile Muslims, or anyone who looks like he or she could conceivably be Muslim."[39]

- "I am one of the few people I know of who has argued in print that torture may be an ethical necessity in our war on terror."[40]

- "The idea that Islam is a 'peaceful religion hijacked by extremists' is a fantasy, and is now a particularly dangerous fantasy for Muslims to indulge."[41]

Besides considering Harris' Islamophobia immoral, Greenwald disapproves more generally of the behavior of westerners like Harris, "who spend the bulk of their time condemning the sins of other, distant peoples rather than the bulk of their time working against the sins of their own country." On this point, Greenwald shared the view of Noam Chomsky, who wrote:

> My own concern is primarily the terror and violence carried out by my own state. . . . [T]he ethical value of one's actions depends on their anticipated and predictable consequences. It is very easy to denounce the atrocities of someone else. That has about as much ethical value as denouncing atrocities that took place in the 18th century.[42]

But Harris, rather than criticizing sins of his own country, praised it as moral compared with Muslim countries, saying in 2008 of the U.S.-led war in Iraq: "[C]ivilized human beings are now attempting, at considerable cost to themselves, to improve life for the Iraqi people."[43]

Harris illustrated his jingoism during a long exchange with Chomsky. In one passage, describing Arundhati Roy as "a great admirer of Chomsky," Harris said that she "summed up his [Chomsky's] position very well" in this statement:

> [T]he U.S. government refuses to judge itself by the same moral standards by which it judges others. . . . Its technique is to position itself as the well-intentioned giant whose good deeds are confounded in strange countries by their scheming natives, whose markets it's trying to free, whose societies it's trying to modernize, whose women it's trying to liberate, whose souls it's trying to save.

In response, Harris said:

> But we are, in many respects, just such a "well-intentioned
> giant." And it is rather astonishing that intelligent people, like
> Chomsky and Roy, fail to see this.[44]

What is *really* astonishing is that Harris believes that his moral sense is
superior to that of Chomsky and Roy. In any case, speaking of Muslims,
Harris said:

> Unless liberals realize that there are tens of millions of people
> in the Muslim world who are far scarier than Dick Cheney,
> they will be unable to protect civilization from its genuine
> enemies.[45]

Greenwald commented:

> Just ponder that. To Harris, there are "tens of millions" of
> Muslims "far scarier" then the US political leader who aggres-
> sively invaded and destroyed a nation of 26 million people,
> constructed a worldwide regime of torture, oversaw a network
> of secret prisons beyond the reach of human rights groups, and
> generally imposed on the world his "Dark Side." *That* is the
> Harris worldview: obsessed with bad acts of foreign Muslims,
> almost entirely blind to—if not supportive of—the far worse
> acts of westerners like himself.[46]

In perhaps the statement that best illustrated Harris' post-9/11 state
of mind, he said that "the people who speak most sensibly about the
threat that Islam poses to Europe are actually fascists."[47] Amazingly,
Harris' denunciation of Islam as immoral led him to praise fascists.

Christopher Hitchens: The portrayal by Hitchens of Islam as an especially evil religion was manifested in his above-quoted statement about
the 9/11 attacks—that they showed Islam to be "theocratic barbarism,"
which he would be "prosecuting" the rest of his life. That Hitchens'
attack on religion was especially directed at Islam was also shown by his
common reference to Muslims as "Islamofascists," along with the title
of his book, *God Is Not Great*, which ridicules the Arabic refrain *Allah
Akbar*, meaning "God is great."[48]

After Hitchens died in 2011, he was praised by many well-known people. This praise was based primarily upon his early writings, when he was a highly entertaining, incisive, left-leaning critic of imperialists, such as his 1999 book on Bill Clinton and his 2001 book on Henry Kissinger.[49]

But after 9/11, Hitchens became supportive of U.S. imperialism, portraying the American attack on Iraq as, in the words of John Cook, "the opening maneuver in a grand, imagined clash of western civilization against the Islamofascist hordes." How, asked Cook, "can someone who devoted so much of his life to as noble a cause as destroying the reputation of Henry Kissinger blithely stand shoulder to shoulder with Rumsfeld?" Although people do make mistakes, Cook added, Hitchens continued to support the war after it was clear it was an imperialist misadventure, as shown by his article in September 2005 entitled "A War to Be Proud Of."[50]

The post-9/11 Hitchens was also found appalling by Glenn Greenwald. "Subordinating his brave and intellectually rigorous defense of atheism," said Greenwald, "Hitchens' glee over violence, bloodshed, and perpetual war dominated the last decade of his life." While being "more urbane and well-written than the average neocon *faux*-warrior," Greenwald added, Hitchens "was also often more vindictive and barbaric about his war cheerleading."[51]

Richard Dawkins: Islamophobia also infected Dawkins, whom the world had known as a best-selling author defending neo-Darwinian evolution. People who have read only Dawkins' pre-9/11 writings would likely consider him a brilliant writer and speaker; or they might be critical, regarding him a dogmatic neo-Darwinist; they might even say that he often pontificated about things he knew little about. But they would probably not believe that Dawkins could have, like Harris and Hitchens, become an Islamophobe. But he did.

In a tweet of February 2013, Dawkins proclaimed: "[I] often say Islam [is the] greatest force for evil today." The fact that Dawkins took an unscholarly approach on this issue was illustrated by his admission that he had never read the Koran.[52]

Dawkins' Islamophobia was blatantly expressed in his praise for far-right Dutch politician Geert Wilders, who announced that he "hates

Islam." Wilders produced a short film entitled "Fitna," which has an image of Muslims with Nazis and another with a ticking time bomb attached to Mohammad's head. "On the strength of 'Fitna' alone," Dawkins said to Wilders, "I salute you as a man of courage who has the balls to stand up to a monstrous enemy."[53]

The following month, Lean wrote an article headed "Richard Dawkins Does It Again," with "it" meaning "simple-minded anti-Muslim Twitter trolling." In this case, the tweet by Dawkins said, "All the world's Muslims have fewer Nobel Prizes than Trinity College, Cambridge." This comment has no relevance to Dawkins' supposed agendas—defending atheism and showing Islam to be evil. It seemed to be simply something negative to say about Muslims—which was, incidentally, an unfortunate comparison for Dawkins to make, given the fact that, as Lean pointed out, the score is: "Muslim Nobel Prizes to date: 10. Dawkins Nobel Prizes to date: zero."

In any case, having stated that Dawkins "use[s] rational atheism as a cover for anti-Muslim prejudice," Lean concluded by saying: "It's about time that the ugly underbelly of his rational atheistic disguise is exposed for what it really is."[54]

This statement is partly wrong, because Dawkins continues to take his atheism, which he considers rational, seriously. But his Islamophobia, combined with that of Harris and Hitchens, undermines the claim that atheism promotes more ethical attitudes than does theism. In fact, their arguments are so poor that readers may conclude that they have undermined the first claim, namely, that the acceptance of supernaturalistic theism tends to foster immoral attitudes.

But this claim is valid and has been better stated by other critics of Gawd-belief, including some theistic philosophers.

3. WHITEHEAD'S CRITICISM OF GAWD-BASED RELIGION

One of these philosophers was Alfred North Whitehead. In expressing his moral objection to the deity of traditional theism, Whitehead said:

> He stood in the same relation to the whole World as early Egyptian or Mesopotamian kings stood to their subject populations. Also the moral characters were very analogous.[55]

This problem with the "moral character" of Gawd involves the problem of evil, as discussed in Chapter 1. Writing sardonically, Whitehead said:

> If we mean by [Gawd's] goodness that He is the one self-existent, complete entity, then He is good. But such goodness must not be confused with the ordinary goodness of daily life.[56]

In other words, if the meaning of terms when applied to the deity is equivocal, being completely different from their meaning when applied to humans, calling the deity "good" is meaningless: If the terms "good" and "evil" when applied to the deity mean something completely different from their meaning in reference to human beings, calling the deity "good" does not necessarily contradict the claim that the deity is evil.

Whitehead considered this conclusion disastrous, because in an ethically purified religion, he said, the emphasis is on the "concept of the goodness of God," with one studying God's "goodness in order to be like him."[57] Whitehead was here, of course, referring to the *imitatio dei*—the human desire to imitate deity. If we become convinced that the divine goodness has nothing in common with what we normally mean by "goodness," then the concept of deity provides no model for morality.

Even more important: Besides failing to support the moral life, traditional theism, by subordinating divine goodness to divine power, promotes an immoral use of human power. Referring to the "glorification of power" in portions of the Bible—which appalled him no less than it does Dawkins—Whitehead complained:

> This worship of glory arising from power is not only dangerous: it arises from a barbaric conception of God. I suppose that even the world itself could not contain the bones of those slaughtered because of men intoxicated by its attraction.[58]

By a "barbaric conception," Whitehead meant one in which the "final good is conceived as one will imposing itself upon other wills."[59] Whitehead thereby anticipated Sam Harris' critique of "theocratic barbarism."

Given humanity's desire to imitate deity, the barbaric conception of deity has promoted war. If people believe that the most fundamental attribute of deity is power—rather than love, wisdom, goodness, or compassion—then the *imitatio dei* will lead them to want to exercise power over others. This is especially dangerous when the deity is portrayed as employing power violently.

One condition for overcoming the barbaric morality that infects civilization will be the overcoming of a barbaric conception of deity. This is one of the reasons that Whitehead emphasized his view of the power of God as persuasion, not coercion.[60]

CONCLUSION

Atheists have been right in charging that religion based on the worship of an omnipotent creator tends to promote the immoral use of power. Hitchens was correct insofar as his book's title meant *Gawd Is Not Great*. Belief in Gawd can easily be used to justify slaughter and many other evils. But atheists, both new and old, have been wrong to claim that the best cure for belligerent theism is atheism. More helpful would be a different type of theism—a type that, besides avoiding the problem of evil and the violation of scientific naturalism, also fits with the fact that our world was created by a very slow process, inspired by a deity with persuasive, rather than coercive, power.

In that connection, a new label may become important. Whereas we have distinguished between theism, pantheism, and atheism, Rupert Sheldrake has coined a new term, *anatheism*, meaning "returning to a belief in God after passing through the purifying fires of atheism."[61] Of course, it will seldom be returning to traditional theism. For people who have rejected Gawd, Part II of this book provides several reasons for returning to belief in a divine reality, but of another type, sometimes called *panentheism*.

ENDNOTES

1. Carl Becker, *The Heavenly City of the Eighteenth-Century Philosophers* (Yale University Press, 1932), 73–74.

2. While pointing out that Nietzsche had some similarities with the New Atheists, scholars have said that the New Atheists do not have Nietzsche's depth. David Bentley Hart wrote: "The only really effective antidote to

the dreariness of reading the New Atheists . . . is rereading Nietzsche," because he "understood how immense the consequences of the rise of Christianity had been, and how immense the consequences of its decline would be as well" ("Believe It or Not," *First Things*, May 2010). Thomas Howe has supported Hart's comparison. Whereas Dawkins conveys a naive optimism according to which "human beings, educated in science and purged of religion, will find lives of easy peace and comfortable wonder," Howe says, Nietzsche had "a deep sense of the seriousness of atheism and the challenges for living well that it presents" (J. Thomas Howe, "Affirmations after God: Friedrich Nietzsche and Richard Dawkins on Atheism," *Zygon*, March 2012, 140–55).

3. Bryan Appleyard, review of A. C. Grayling, *The God Argument: The Case Against Religion and for Humanism* (*New Statesman*, 13 February 2013).

4. Jerome Taylor, "Atheists Richard Dawkins, Christopher Hitchens and Sam Harris Face Islamophobia Backlash," *Independent*, 12 April 2013. Unlike these three men (see section 2), Dennett did not demonize Islam.

5. James E. Taylor, "The New Atheists," Internet Encyclopedia of Philosophy, 2010.

6. William Lane Craig, "The New Atheism and Five Arguments for God," Reasonable Faith, 2010.

7. Jackson Lears, "Same Old New Atheism: On Sam Harris," *The Nation*, April 27, 2011.

8. Ibid.

9. Christopher Hitchens, "Images in a Rearview Mirror," 3 December 2001; quoted in Lears, "Same Old New Atheism."

10. Sam Harris, *The End of Faith* (Norton, 2005), 45, 78–79.

11. Ibid., 35, 44.

12. Ross Douthat, "Lord Have Mercy: A Review of *God is Not Great: How Religion Poisons Everything*, by Christopher Hitchens," *Claremont Review of Books*, 15 December 2007.

13. Ibid. On C. S. Lewis, see his *The Problem of Pain* (1940) and his *Mere Christianity* (1952).

14. Richard Dawkins, *The God Delusion* (Houghton Mifflin, 2006), 51.

15. Ibid., 52, 81–82.

16. Ibid., 321.

17. Ibid., 321.

18. Ibid., 36, 41.

19. Ibid., 14, 15.

20. Ibid., 14.

21. Ibid., 15.

22. Ibid., 137-38. The use of "Boeing 747" refers to astrophysicist Fred Hoyle's argument that evolution, based on chance, could not possibly have produced a Boeing 747.

23. Alvin Plantinga, "The Dawkins Confusion: Naturalism ad Absurdum," Books and Culture: A Christian Review, March/April 2007.

24. Gary Wolf, "The Church of the Non-Believers," *Wired,* November 2006.

25. John F. Haught, *God and the New Atheism: A Critical Response to Dawkins, Harris, and Hitchens* (Westminster John Knox, 2008), 8.

26. "Antitheism," The Shorter Oxford English Dictionary (1970), 78. See also Robert Flint, *Anti-Theistic* Theories (London: William Blackwood and Sons, 1994); Christopher New, "Antitheism—A Reflection," *Ratio* 6/1 (June 1993), 36–43; Wallace A. Murphree, "Natural Theology: Theism or Antitheism," *Sophia* 36/1 (1997), 75–83.

27. Christopher Hitchens, *Letters to a Young Contrarian* (Basic Books, 2001), 55.

28. Dawkins, *The God Delusion*, 346; Harris, *The End of Faith*, 45.

29. Nathan Lean, *The Islamophobia Industry: How the Right Manufactures Fear of Muslims* (Pluto Press, 2012).

30. Nathan Lean, "Dawkins, Harris, Hitchens: New Atheists Flirt with Islamophobia," *Salon*, 30 March 2013.

31. Murtaza Hussain, "Scientific Racism, Militarism, and the New Atheists," Al Jazeera, 2 April 2013.

32. Glenn Greenwald, "Sam Harris, the New Atheists, and Anti-Muslim Animus," *Guardian*, 3 April 2013.

33. Sam Harris, "What Obama Got Wrong about the Mosque," Daily Beast, 13 August 2010.

34. Harris, "Bombing Our Illusions," Huffington Post, 25 May 2011.

35. Ibid.

36. Harris, *The End of Faith*, 123.

37. Ibid., 128.

38. Ibid., 110.

39. Sam Harris, "In Defense of Profiling" (blog), 28 April 2012.

40. Harris, "In Defense of Torture," Huffington Post, 25 May 2011.

41. Sam Harris, *Letter to a Christian Nation* (Vintage, 2008), 85.

42. Greenwald, "Sam Harris, the New Atheists, and Anti-Muslim Animus," quoting Noam Chomsky, *On Power and Ideology: The Managua Lectures* (South End Press, 1999), 51.

43. Sam Harris, *Letter to a Christian Nation* (Vintage, 2008), 85.

44. Sam Harris, "Noam Chomsky's Heated Debate With Sam Harris," Sam Harris' Blog, 15 May 2004.

45. Harris, *Letter to a Christian Nation*, 85.

46. Greenwald, "Sam Harris, the New Atheists, and Anti-Muslim Animus."

47. Harris, "The End of Liberalism," Sam Harris' Blog, 19 September 2006.

48. Christopher Hitchens, *God Is Not Great: How Religion Poisons Everything* (Twelve, 2009).

49. Christopher Hitchens, *No One Left to Lie To: The Triangulations of William Jefferson Clinton* (Verso, 1999); *The Trial of Henry Kissinger* (Verso, 2001).

50. John Cook, "Christopher Hitchens' Unforgivable Mistake," Gawker, 16 December 2011.

51. Glenn Greenwald, "Christopher Hitchens and the Protocol for Public Figure Deaths," Salon, 17 December 2011.

52. Lean, "Dawkins, Harris, Hitchens." Dawkins' statement, which was tweeted 1 March 2013, was also quoted in Taylor, "Atheists Richard Dawkins, Christopher Hitchens and Sam Harris Face Islamophobia Backlash."

53. Quoted in Lean, "Dawkins, Harris, Hitchens."

54. Nathan Lean, "Richard Dawkins Does It Again: New Atheism's Islamophobia Problem," *Salon*, 10 August 2013.

55. Alfred North Whitehead, *Adventures of Ideas* (1933; Free Press, 1967), 169.

56. Alfred North Whitehead, *Religion in the Making* (1926; Fordham University Press, 1996), 59.

57. Ibid., 30.

58. Ibid., 44.

59. Whitehead, *Adventures of Ideas,* 51.

60. Ibid., 25, 42, 68, 83, 160, 166.

61. Rupert Sheldrake, "News Release from Rupert Sheldrake Online," 14 February 2014, referring to an audio-taped lecture, "Finding God Again: The Rise of Anatheism."

Part II

Why God
Does Exist

7

Mathematics

Having looked in Part I at six reasons for denying the existence of Gawd, the present part examines eight reasons for affirming the existence of God, beginning with the reality of mathematics and mathematical truth.

Mathematics has been a problem for the philosophy of science. On the one hand, the objects of mathematics,[1] such as the number 2 and the truth that 2 and 2 are 4, appear to exist objectively. On the other hand, modern philosophy, since the rise of sensate empiricism in the 17th century, has assumed that all knowledge about what is real beyond our own minds is based upon sensory perception. Whereas *empiricism as such* is the doctrine that all knowledge is rooted in perceptual experience, *sensate* empiricism is the doctrine that all perception is by means of our physical senses. For example, Harvard philosopher Willard Van Quine said that the "stimulation of his sensory receptors is all the evidence anybody has to go on, ultimately, in arriving at his picture of the world."[2]

One of the central issues in the philosophy of mathematics over the past century has been how, given sensate empiricism, how could one understand the objectivity of mathematical truths.

1. PLATONIC REALISM AND SENSATE EMPIRICISM

The traditional view of the objectivity of mathematics is often called "Platonic realism," or simply "Platonism," because "ideas" or "forms"—held to be real although they cannot be perceived by means of our physical senses—were central to Plato's philosophy. Surely because of the influence on him of Pythagoreanism, mathematical objects were central to Plato's discussion of "ideas."

The central role of Pythagoras was mentioned in Alfred North Whitehead's first book, *Science and the Modern World*. He said of Pythagoras:

> He started a discussion which has agitated thinkers ever since. He asked, 'What is the status of mathematical entities, such as numbers for example, in the realm of things?' The number 'two,' for example is in some sense exempt from the flux of time and the necessity of positions in space. Yet it is involved in the real world.[3]

In dealing with this issue, Platonic realists say that, in the words of a recent writer, "mathematical entities exist outside space and time, outside thought and matter, in an abstract realm"—with "abstract" meaning that they are not concrete, physical things that activate our physical senses.[4]

However, the rise of sensate empiricism has led many philosophers to conclude that mathematics cannot be objective. Not all philosophers and mathematicians, to be sure, have accepted the sensate empiricism on which this conclusion is based. For example, famous mathematician and logician Kurt Gödel said:

> [D]espite their remoteness from sense experience, we do have something like a perception also of the objects of set theory, as is seen from the fact that the axioms force themselves upon us as being true. I don't see any reason why we should have less confidence in this kind of perception, i.e., in mathematical intuition, than in sense perception.[5]

However, many philosophers of mathematics, presupposing sensate empiricism, have strongly rejected Gödel's thesis. For example, in an essay with a very long title—"A Gödelian Thesis Regarding Mathematical Objects: Do They Exist? And Can We Perceive Them?"—Charles Chihara asked rhetorically: "What empirical scientist would be impressed by an explanation this flabby?"[6] Also in reaction to Gödel's view, Hilary Putnam declared:

> The trouble with this sort of Platonism is that it seems flatly incompatible with the simple fact that we think with our brains, and not with immaterial souls. . . . We cannot envisage *any* kind of neural process that could even correspond to the 'perception of a mathematical object.'[7]

In the same vein, Reuben Hersh, in a book entitled *What is Mathematics, Really?* charged mathematicians who accept the Platonic view with being "unscientific." Asking rhetorically, "How does this [alleged] immaterial realm . . . make contact with flesh and blood mathematicians?" Hersh added: "Ideal entities independent of human consciousness violate the empiricism of modern science."[8] (Hersh thereby equated empiricism with the sensate form of empiricism.)

This problem, of how mathematical entities can exist, and in such a way that they can be known by us, can be called the "Platonic problem," because it was in relation to Plato's affirmation of the real existence of numbers and other forms that this issue was first discussed in Western philosophy. Plato's affirmation seemed to imply that numbers (and other ideal forms) somehow existed on their own—in the void, as it were. Aristotle rejected this view on the grounds that abstract, non-actual things can exist only in actual things (which he called "substances").

REALISM AND FORMALISM

Because sensate empiricism is so widespread, there has been strong pressure to reject the Platonic, realistic conception of mathematical truth. One result has been that philosophers and mathematicians have tended to endorse the position known as "formalism," according to which mathematics is just a game with meaningless symbols, because numbers do not really exist. This pressure sometimes leads mathematicians to contradict their own working presupposition. In a book entitled *The Mathematical Experience*, Hersh and two co-authors wrote:

Most writers on the subject seem to agree that the typical work-ing mathematician is a Platonist on weekdays and a formalist on Sundays. That is, when he is doing mathematics he is convinced that he is dealing with an objective reality whose properties he is attempting to determine. But then, when challenged to give a philosophical account of this reality, he finds it easiest to pretend that he does not believe in it after all.[9]

Mathematical realism is also rejected by some philosophers. For example, William Lycan, who had appealed to mathematical sets, realized that this appeal is "an embarrassment to physicalism, since sets et al. are nonspatiotemporal, acausal items." Accordingly, he said, he had only two options: either to "naturalize" mathematical objects or to reject set theory and the existence of numbers.[10] Both options have been taken by philosophers.

Although avoiding a conflict with physicalism by adopting formal-ism, hence rejecting numbers, is extreme, philosophers of mathematics have written entire books defending formalism, as illustrated by ones entitled *Science without Numbers* and *Mathematics without Numbers*.[11] Adopting formalism is an extreme solution because it, in the words of Y. N. Moschovakis, violates "the instinctive certainty of most everybody who has ever tried to solve a [mathematical] problem that he is think-ing about 'real objects,' whether they are sets, numbers, or whatever."[12] (Many other philosophers and mathematicians agree.[13])

Famous mathematical physicist Roger Penrose has provided an illus-tration of the certainty that mathematical objects are really objective. Speaking of the mathematical structure called the Mandelbrot Set—which was described in 1980 by Benoit Mandelbrot—Penrose said: "The Mandelbrot Set is not an invention of the human mind: it was a discov-ery. Like Mount Everest, the Mandelbrot Set is just *there*!"[14]

The denial of realism involves a contradiction between what mathematicians espouse verbally and what they believe in practice. In Moschovakis' words, "most mathematicians claim to be formalists (when pressed) while they spend their working hours behaving as if they were unabashed realists."[15] As Whitehead said, we should not espouse ideas that involve "negations of what in practice is presupposed."[16]

Another unsatisfactory approach would be simply to ignore the problem. And yet this was the solution of Willard Quine, one of the most influential philosophers of the 20ᵗʰ century.

The problem of mathematical knowledge was especially serious in Quine's philosophy, because of his equal emphasis on (1) "physicalism," by which he meant that our ontology should be settled by the discipline of physics, and (2) the "tribunal of sense experience," according to which "whatever evidence there *is* for science *is* sensory evidence." In speaking of this "tribunal," Quine meant that everything that really exists is material, because sensory perception by definition is activated only by material objects.[17]

However, given Quine's definition of physicalism—according to which ontology is to be based on physics—his ontology had to include what he called "the abstract objects of mathematics," with the result that his ontology was, in his words, "materialism, bluntly monistic except for the abstract objects of mathematics."[18] But this exception meant that he violated his "tribunal of sensory experience." Besides the fact that mathematical objects are not sensorily perceived, they are also not located anywhere in space or time, instead somehow existing "over and above the physical objects."[19]

Quine justified this exception on the grounds of his "indispensability argument"—that mathematical objects are indispensable for physics. But Quine's acceptance of mathematical objects contradicted his dictum that sense experience is to settle what can be affirmed to exist. How did Quine deal with this contradiction? He simply, in Putnam's words, "ignore[d] the problem as to how we can know that [these] abstract entities exist unless we can interact with them in some way."[20]

That procedure, of course, is irrational, violating the very spirit of philosophy. Philosophers have usually maintained that a particular worldview is not to be held on the basis of authority, whether it be the authority of theologians or that of physicists. A worldview has no authority beyond that of its ability to deal with all the indubitable facts of experience in a self-consistent way. For Quine to refuse to deal with the main problems raised by his position—how mathematical objects can be affirmed while holding sense experience to be the criterion of existence, and how mathematical objects can exist in an otherwise wholly materialistic universe—was to admit that his position was inconsistent.

In any case, whatever Quine himself may have said, most philosophers hold that, insofar as a position is inconsistent, it must *ipso facto* be considered false.

THE BENACERRAF PROBLEM

In addition to the Platonic problem of how mathematical objects can exist, another problem was formulated in Paul Benacerraf's 1983 essay, "Mathematical Truth." He began by endorsing the so-called causal theory of truth, according to which true beliefs can be considered knowledge only if that which makes the belief true is *causally* responsible for the belief in an appropriate way.[21] In other words, the belief and the truth of its propositional content must be, in Bernard Williams' words, "non-accidentally linked."[22] For example, my belief that there is a tree in my garden can be considered knowledge only if causation from the tree is partly responsible for my belief.

Summarizing the resulting problem for the Platonic view of mathematical entities, which can be called the "Benacerraf problem," Penelope Maddy asked:

> But how can entities that don't even inhabit the physical universe take part in any causal interaction whatsoever? Surely to be abstract is also to be causally inert. Thus if Platonism is true, we can have no mathematical knowledge.[23]

NATURALIZING MATHEMATICAL OBJECTS

Maddy herself, who argued in her book *Realism in Mathematics* that the reality of mathematical objects could not be plausibly rejected, tried the other way, mentioned by Lycan, of avoiding conflict with physicalism: to "naturalize" mathematical objects, meaning redefining them as aspects of material things. Seeking to develop a materialistic version of Platonic realism, Maddy said that the problem of "unobservable Platonic entities" could be avoided by "bringing [mathematical] sets into the physical world," so that they are no longer "abstract" but have "spatio-temporal location." In this way, she said, we could bring "mathematical ontology and epistemology into line with our overall scientific world-view."[24]

But this solution is clearly desperate. What could it mean to say that the entire realm of mathematics explored by pure mathematicians is embodied in the physical world? Maddy says that her view allows us to say that mathematical perception, which some have tried to explain by positing a nonsensory form of perception, is simply a type of *sensory* perception.[25] This would seem to imply that mathematicians discover all mathematical truths, including the most esoteric proofs, many of which have no relevance to our universe, by perceiving the physical world. But this is implausible. Eugene Wigner, the great Nobel Prize-winning mathematician, said:

> [Although] the concepts of elementary mathematics and particularly elementary geometry were formulated to describe entities which are directly suggested by the actual world, the same does not seem to be true of the more advanced concepts, in particular the concepts which play such an important role in physics.

"The complex numbers," he added, "provide a particularly striking example. . . . Certainly, nothing in our experience suggests the introduction of these quantities."[26]

Even if Maddy were to ignore Wigner's point, we must ask—with apologies to Hume—What kind of sensory perception would this be: Do we perceive numbers and mathematical truths with our eyes? Do we hear them with our hears? Do we touch them with our hands? Do we smell them with our noses? Do we taste them with our palates?

In any case, being explicit about her attempt, Maddy says: "Of course, my motivation for bringing sets into the physical world and for tying mathematical intuition so closely to ordinary perception is naturalism," by which she means materialism. This approach seemed to her, she said, "the most promising approach for bringing mathematical ontology and epistemology into line with our overall scientific world-view."[27]

As Maddy's statement shows, she equates our "scientific worldview" with "naturalism," which she equates with physicalism in the sense of materialism. But this is an arbitrary conception of "naturalism." Lycan made the same equation, saying that to naturalize mathematical objects would be to materialize them, that is, redefining them as aspects of material things.

Historically, naturalism meant merely the rejection of supernaturalism, according to which the normal cause-effect relations can be interrupted. Holding mathematical objects to be real has nothing to do with supernaturalism. One could not reasonably call Gödel a supernaturalist because he believed mathematical objects to be real.

The scientific worldview is rightfully naturalistic, in the sense of rejecting supernatural interventions. But this worldview provides no reason to consider mathematical objects supernatural. Accordingly, there is no need to "naturalize" mathematical objects by materializing them, in order for them to belong to a naturalistic ontology.

ENLARGING NATURALISM

Two other proponents of scientific naturalism, Bernard Linsky and Edward N. Zalta, reject Maddy's "naturalized Platonism" in favor of a view they call "Platonized naturalism," which holds that "a more traditional kind of Platonism is consistent with naturalism." They endorse, in other words, traditional Platonism, according to which abstract objects are causally inert, outside of spacetime, and not discovered by means of natural science. This Platonism is "consistent with naturalism because such a Platonism is required," they argue, "for our very understanding of scientific theories."[28]

While agreeing with Quine that naturalism must include the existence of numbers, because they are indispensable for physics, Linsky and Zalta consider inadequate Quine's "limited Platonism," which arbitrarily limits the realm of abstract objects to mathematical objects. For example, a realistic ontology must, as Frege said, speak of logical as well as mathematical objects. Indeed, Linsky and Zalta say, arbitrary limits should be avoided by including "the existence of all the abstract objects there could possibly be."

By affirming a plenitude of abstract objects, they argue, they can meet the Benacerraf problem of how we can know mathematical objects. They agree with Benacerraf that naturalism is incompatible with Gödel's idea of "some perception-like intuition of those objects that guides our choice of axioms." By saying that all possible abstract objects exist, they say, there is no need for a special argument for the existence of mathematical objects.

However, while Linsky and Zalta provide a more adequate version of naturalism than did Quine, there are at least three problems with their proposal. First, they still fail to answer the Platonic problem of the location of Platonic objects: How can they exist in a universe otherwise limited to physical (material) things?

Second, Linsky and Zalta provide an unsatisfactory answer to the Benacerraf problem. Their overcoming of Quine's limitation of the Platonic realm to mathematical objects is an improvement. But a naturalistic worldview includes *empiricism*, according to which we should not affirm the existence of entities beyond all possible experience. So a naturalistic worldview needs to explain how *any* abstract objects can be experienced—which was Maddy's reason for trying to materialize mathematical objects.

A third problem with Linsky and Zalta's position is their own limited conception of naturalism, defining it as "the realist ontology that recognizes only those objects required by the explanations of the natural sciences."[29] The limitation to the natural sciences presupposes a Cartesian dualism between physical things, on the one hand, and non-physical but actual things, such as human minds, as studied by psychological and sociological sciences, on the other. A central feature of Darwin's work was to overcome this dualism by showing that human beings, with our minds, are fully natural. A non-arbitrary view of the Platonic realm would also include all abstract objects needed for the social sciences and the humanities, including ethics, as discussed in the following chapter.

2. MATHEMATICS AND THEISM

As the chapter has shown thus far, philosophers who accept materialism and sensate empiricism have been unable to explain the reality of mathematical objects, as presupposed by mathematicians and physicists—a reality that Quine and others rightly called indispensable. But this "Platonic problem" had not always been a problem.

MIDDLE PLATONISM AND THE PLATONIC PROBLEM

Prior to the age of materialism and sensate empiricism, the Platonic problem did not exist, insofar as philosophers were theists. Pathbreaking was Middle Platonism, with its doctrine that Plato's eternal forms exist in the divine logos, the mind of God.[30]

To be sure, Platonism, with its doctrine that Platonic forms (such as mathematical truths) exist eternally and independently, contradicted traditional Christian theism, according to which—in the words of the Nicene Creed—Gawd was the maker of "all things visible and invisible." But Augustine and other theologians effected a reconciliation similar to that of the Middle Platonists by holding that the eternal ideas exist in the divine intellect.[31]

Some version of this Middle Platonic reconciliation was retained by early modern philosophers such as Leibniz and Berkeley. The Platonic problem arose only with the growth of atheism (including merely *methodological* atheism, according to which phenomena cannot be explained by reference to the notion of deity). In the words of Reuben Hersh:

> For Leibniz and Berkeley, abstractions like numbers are thoughts in the mind of God, but Heaven and the Mind of God are no longer heard of in academic discourse. Yet most mathematicians and philosophers of mathematics continue to believe in an independent, immaterial abstract world—a remnant of Plato's Heaven . . . , with all entities but the mathematical expelled. Platonism without God is like the grin on Lewis Carroll's Cheshire cat. . . . The grin remained without the cat.[32]

One reason to affirm theism, therefore, would be so that the grin would again be embodied in the cat.

MIDDLE PLATONISM AND THE BENACERRAF PROBLEM

Middle Platonism's solution to the Platonic problem also provided, in advance, a solution to the Benacerraf problem: Mathematical objects, which in themselves are inert, can be given agency by virtue of being in the divine mind, so that they can exert causal efficacy upon our minds. This approach was taken again in the 20th century by Alfred North Whitehead. Having long worked on both mathematics and logic,

Whitehead needed, when he developed his philosophical position, to deal with the question of their status in the universe and how they, as Platonic forms, can be influential.

Whitehead's term for Platonic forms was "eternal objects." They are *objects* because they have no subjectivity—they are merely objects of experience, rather than also being subjects with their own experience. (An eternal object is, in Thomas Nagel's terms, an *en soi*, not a *pour soi*.) Eternal objects are *eternal* because they are unchanging and outside of time: the passage of time makes no difference to them.

Eternal objects of two types exist. Eternal objects of the *objective species* are ones that can inform only the objects of experience (not also the experiences themselves). Whitehead called them "mathematical Platonic forms."[33] Eternal objects of the *subjective species*, by contrast, can inform experiences.

In saying that both species exist, Whitehead reaffirmed the equal reality of what early modern philosophers distinguished as "primary" and "secondary" qualities, according to which only the primary qualities—Whitehead's eternal objects of the objective species—really exist. In Hersh's words, these philosophers believe in "an immaterial abstract world—a remnant of Plato's Heaven . . . with all entities but the mathematical expelled."[34]

SOLVING PROBLEMS

Whitehead's treatment of eternal objects also dealt with Hersh's problem of the how the cat's grin could remain "without the cat." When Whitehead first introduced eternal objects into his philosophy, he portrayed them as existing in an "envisagement" by the "underlying eternal energy."[35] Later naming this underlying eternal energy "creativity," he soon saw that he could not attribute any kind of activity, even "envisagement," to creativity, because of what he called the "ontological principle." According to this principle, only *actual* things can *act*, and creativity is not an actuality, but only that which is embodied in all actual things.

Whitehead referred to this notion as the "ontological principle," because the most fundamental distinction for an ontology is that between, on the one hand, things that are real in the fullest sense (called "substances" in traditional philosophy), because they can exert and receive influence, and, on the other hand, things that cannot be influenced or do anything on their own.

Given this distinction, the ontological principle also says that "everything must be somewhere." Actual things, being in space and time, are already somewhere. But non-actual things, such as Platonic forms, are not, so they can exist only in something actual. Whitehead thereby had agreed in advance with the insistence of Maddy and Hersh, that agency cannot be attributed to things that do not exist in space and time. In a statement that expresses both dimensions of the ontological principle (which he also called the "Aristotelian principle"), Whitehead said that, "apart from things that are actual, there is nothing—nothing either in fact or in efficacy."[36]

The ontological principle led Whitehead to affirm the existence of an actuality that could be called "God." He said:

> Everything must be somewhere; and here 'somewhere' means 'some actual entity.' Accordingly the general potentiality of the universe must be somewhere. . . . The notion of 'subsistence' is merely the notion of how eternal objects can be components of the primordial nature of God.[37]

In saying that the mathematical Platonic forms are *in God,* Whitehead was agreeing with everyone who holds that mathematical objects are real while adding that, if they are real, they must exist somewhere. On the basis of this twofold agreement, he then addressed the question of how and where they exist. His answer was that they can exist by virtue of "subsisting" in something actual.

PANENTHEISM

Many people assume, to be sure, that mathematical objects simply exist in the universe. But merely saying that would bring us back to the problem raised in Plato's time: Was one supposed to believe that the forms simply exist "in the void"? By the ontological principle, the idea that the mathematical objects exist "in the universe" would make sense only if the universe as a whole is itself actual, so that it can cause and receive effects.

This is, in fact, what Whitehead said. When asked whether it is "possible to indicate God's locus," Whitehead reportedly replied that, "in respect to the world, God is everywhere. Yet he is a distinct entity. . . . God and the world have the same locus."[38]

This position has come to be called "panentheism."[39] It differs from pantheism, according to which the "universe"—understood as the totality of all finite existents—and "God" are simply two words for the same reality. That this was *not* Whitehead's doctrine was indicated by his statement that God is "a distinct entity." According to panentheism, the universe, in the sense of the totality of all finite existents, exists in God.

By analogy, one could say that the brain and the mind have the same locus, because the brain exists in the mind. This view does not make them identical (as the doctrine of "identism" holds): The brain is the totality of the cells making up the brain, while the mind is the overarching experience that unifies all the particular experiences that it derives from the brain. In a similar way, the universe is the totality of finite experiences, whereas God is the mind of the universe—the universe as an experiencing whole.

For those who dislike the word "God"—perhaps because they find it hard to avoid thinking of a reality called "God" in terms of the attributes of Gawd—there is no need to use the word. Whitehead sometimes spoke of the "unity of the Universe" and the "deity of the universe." Charles Hartshorne referred to God as the "soul of the universe." Schubert Ogden, a theologian heavily influenced by Hartshorne, spoke of "the one all-inclusive whole of reality." And Jeremy Hayward, a Whiteheadian Buddhist, spoke of the "wholeness of the universe" and the "universe considered in its unity."[40]

In referring to God understood as the unity of the universe, Whitehead distinguished between the "primordial nature" and the "consequent nature" of God. In speaking of the *primordial* nature of God, Whitehead meant that, because the Platonic forms are eternal, they must exist in something that is both eternal and actual. God has, of course, traditionally been called "eternal," so why speak of "the primordial nature of God"? Because God as a whole is not eternal, that is, unaffected by temporal processes. Rather, as the term "consequent nature" indicates, God is affected by the world, and in this respect God is "everlasting," rather than eternal. So God's embodiment of the eternal objects is merely one aspect of God.

In any case, by portraying the Platonic mathematical forms as subsisting in God, Whitehead answered the Platonic problem, which asks where and how mathematical objects exist, along with the Benacerraf problem, which is how these objects can have any influence in the world.

Although it seems to be generally thought that Plato himself did not give this position, so that the Platonic forms were first placed into God by Middle Platonism, Whitehead believed that this idea had already been expressed by Plato—that "the agency whereby ideas obtain efficiency in the creative advance" was for Plato "a basic Psyche whose active grasp of ideas conditions impartially the whole process of the Universe."[41]

GOD, NOT GAWD

However, this idea—that the mathematical objects are in, and given efficacy by, God—could be misunderstood to mean that God is responsible for the truths of arithmetic, so that, in Nagel's words, "it could have been false that twice four is eight."[42] In referring to mathematical forms as "eternal objects," Whitehead excluded this possibility, saying: "[God] does not create eternal objects, for his nature requires them in the same degree that they require him. This is an exemplification of the coherence of the categoreal types of existence"—namely, that they presuppose each other.[43]

It should be clear that we are here talking about God, not Gawd. Traditional theists, who say that the world was created *ex nihilo,* do not allow for the existence of uncreated eternal objects, such as numbers and logical truths, as these would be "restrictions" on Gawd's omnipotence. For example, William Lane Craig, who in Chapter 5 was used as an example of a defender of divine omnipotence, made the point stated earlier—that belief in the eternal existence of numbers would be inconsistent with the Nicene Creed's affirmation that Gawd made "all things visible and invisible."[44]

Accordingly, Nagel's concern—that "it could have been false that twice four is eight"—is a concern about Gawd, not God.

A MYSTERY: WHY IS THE UNIVERSE MATHEMATICAL?

The fact that the universe is mathematical, leading physicists and mathematicians have admitted, is a mystery. For example:

- Roger Penrose said that for him and many other physicists, the fact that "somehow the structure of the physical world is rooted in mathematics" is "a very great mystery."[45]

- One of those other physicists was Richard Feynman, who won a Nobel Prize for work in quantum electrodynamics. "Why nature is mathematical is a mystery," said Feynman. "The fact that there are rules at all is a kind of miracle."[46]

- In a book on this issue, astrophysicist Mario Livio entitled the first chapter "A Mystery," referring to the mystery as the omnipresence of mathematics.[47]

Part of the mystery is why, given the enormous size of the universe, these same laws of physics seem to apply everywhere. According to the principle of *universality,* said physicist and science writer James Trefil, "the laws of nature we discover here and now in our laboratories are true everywhere in the universe and have been in force for all time." Calling this fact "astonishing," Trefil, in explaining why, said:

> [The Earth] is an insignificant ball of rock circling a very ordinary star located about two-thirds of the way out in the spiral arms of a very ordinary galaxy. This galaxy is one of hundreds in a supercluster of galaxies, and even the supercluster is only one of many in a universe that stretches billions of light-years in every direction. And yet [humans] are able to discover the laws that make the whole marvelous machine work. If that's not astonishing, I don't know what is![48]

This principle of universality has recently been given new empirical support. In an article entitled "Earth's Laws Still Apply in Distant Universe," Dr. Emily Baldwin wrote:

> One of the most important numbers in physics, the proton-electron mass ratio, is the same in a galaxy six billion light years

away as it is here on Earth, according to new research, laying to rest debate about whether the laws of nature vary in different places in the Universe.[49]

By saying that mathematical objects could influence the world because of their presence in a "basic Psyche," Plato—or at least Whitehead—provided in a statement quoted above an explanation of why the same mathematical principles apply to all parts of the universe, namely, that "a basic Psyche whose active grasp of ideas conditions impartially the whole process of the Universe."[50]

It seems that, if the mystery of why the universe is mathematical is to be dispelled, at least partly, philosophers and scientists will need to overcome their conviction that every question about the universe can be satisfactorily answered without appeal to a reality that could be considered divine.

3. NONSENSORY PERCEPTION

Modern thought has raised another problem: Even if there be a "Psyche whose active grasp of [Platonic mathematical forms] conditions impartially the whole process of the Universe," how can we human beings be aware of these forms?

GÖDEL'S SOLUTION

This is not a problem insofar as people are assumed to have nonsensory as well as sensory perception. As we saw above, Kurt Gödel suggested this solution, saying that he did not know of "any reason why we should have less confidence in this kind of perception, i.e., in mathematical intuition, than in sense perception."[51]

However, in spite of the fact that Gödel was held in high esteem—being "[c]onsidered with Aristotle and Gottlob Frege to be one of the most significant logicians in history"[52]—this suggestion by him was treated with disdain by most contemporary mathematicians, scientists, and philosophers.

PREJUDICE AGAINST NONSENSORY PERCEPTION

Behind this disdain, there was a long history that created a strong prejudice against the idea of any kind of nonsensory perception. This prejudice stemmed primarily, as discussed in Chapters 2 and 5, from early modern philosophers such as Mersenne, Descartes, Boyle, and Newton, who supported the conservative Christian desire to protect the supernaturalist nature of the "miracles of Jesus." They meant to protect them by denying that causal influence at a distance—which extrasensory perception would involve—could happen naturally. All natural causation was declared to occur *by contact.*

In the *late* modern worldview, explaining anything by reference to divine agency became *verboten.* Everything had to be explained by means of contact between finite entities. However, while accepting the idea that there is no physical action at a distance, some thinkers contended that telepathy, being the direct influence of one mind on another, was possible. This idea became ruled out, however, when Descartes' mind-body dualism was rejected in favor of identism, according to which the mind is in some sense identical with the brain. So the endorsement of even telepathy became heretical.

The animus against nonsensory perception was first directed against telepathy and clairvoyance, which are phenomena to which the term "extrasensory perception" usually refers. As discussed in Chapter 5, psychical research, which set out to study it, has been almost entirely rejected within scientific and philosophical circles. But although the original reason for rejecting nonsensory perception was to rule out telepathy and clairvoyance, the doctrines developed in the modern worldview to rule them out led to the rejection of nonsensory perception of every type.

According to the late modern worldview, therefore, nonsensory perception is impossible *naturally*, and because there cannot be any supernatural assistance for it, it is impossible *period.*

4. TESTIMONIES TO EXTRASENSORY PERCEPTION

Nevertheless, a significant number of philosophers and scientists have expressed their acceptance of the reality of telepathy, along with other types of extrasensory perception, on the basis of various types of evidence: anecdotal, sustained studies of apparently exceptional individuals, and laboratory experiments. For open minds—at least sufficiently open to examine the evidence—these types of evidence have provided strong evidence of the reality of extrasensory perception.[53]

Among the first major philosophers who studied and affirmed the reality of extrasensory perception, the two most important were philosophers mentioned in Chapter 5: Henry Sidgwick and William James.

HENRY SIDGWICK

Professor of Moral Philosophy at Trinity College of the University of Cambridge, Sidgwick was the first president of the Society for Psychical Research, which was established in 1882. With regard to the choice of Sidgwick as president, philosopher C. D. Broad said:

> [T]he fact that Sidgwick, whose reputation for sanity, truthfulness, and fairness was well known to everyone who mattered in England, was at the head of the Society gave it an intellectual and moral status which was invaluable at the time. It was hardly possible to maintain, without writing oneself down as an ass, that a society over which Sidgwick presided and in whose work he was actively interested consisted of knaves and fools concealing superstition under the cloak of scientific verbiage.[54]

Sidgwick's integrity was illustrated by his resignation as a Fellow at Trinity, which brought amenities and a significant income. A condition for such fellowships was for the holder to declare to be a "*bona fide* member of the Church of England." This obligation was usually not taken seriously, but Sidgwick decided to resign, because he did not accept some features of orthodox dogma, especially the miraculous origins of Christianity.[55]

Also, although Sidgwick was very interested in evidence for personal survival after death, which was one of the Society's major emphases, he wrote a few years before his own death: "I am drifting to the conclusion that we have not and are not likely to have empirical evidence of the existence of the individual after death." However, Sidgwick did come to the conclusion that there was sufficient evidence to affirm the reality of extrasensory perception.[56] Speaking about the areas studied by psychical research, Sidgwick said:

[T]he divided state of public opinion on all these matters was a scandal to science, absolute disdain on *a priori* grounds characterizing what may be called professional opinion, whilst completely uncritical and indiscriminate credulity was too often found amongst those who pretended to have a first-hand acquaintance with the facts.[57]

WILLIAM JAMES

Although James began his career at Harvard University as a professor of psychology, he eventually switched to the philosophy department. Easily America's most widely read philosopher, James was referred to by Alfred North Whitehead as "that adorable genius."[58] Although most biographers do not deal with this fact, James helped found the American Society of Psychical Research and spent much of his time investigating and writing about it, as evidenced by *Essays in Psychical Research*, which is a volume in *The Works of William James*, published by Harvard University.[59]

Against sensate empiricism, James affirmed a "thicker and more radical empiricism," which included an examination of "the phenomena of psychic research so-called."[60] We need a scientific worldview, he argued, that would allow these phenomena to be regarded as fully natural, albeit exceptional, occurrences. He said, for example: "Science, so far as science denies such exceptional occurrences, lies prostrate in the dust for me; and the most urgent intellectual need which I feel at present is that science be built up again in a form in which such things may have a positive place."[61]

With regard to life after death, James reached a conclusion similar to that of Sidgwick, saying, "I confess that at times I have been tempted to believe that the Creator has eternally intended this department of nature to remain *baffling.*" Like Sidgwick, however, James ended up with no doubts about telepathy.[62]

OTHER PHILOSOPHERS AND SCIENTISTS

Still other important philosophers who affirmed the reality of extrasensory perception include Henri Bergson, C. D. Broad, Curt Ducasse, Gabriel Marcel, H. H. Price. F. S. C. Schiller, and Michael Scriven.

In addition, the reality of nonsensory perception has also been affirmed by a significant number of scientists, including:

- *Psychologists* Carl Jung, William McDougall, and (after long rejecting it) Sigmund Freud.

- *Physicists* Sir William Barrett, David Bohm, Sir William Crookes, Thomas Edison, Pascual Jordan, Nobel laureate Brian Josephson, Sir Oliver Lodge, Lord Rayleigh (John William Strutt, who received a Nobel prize for isolating argon), and perhaps Albert Einstein.[63]

- *Biologists* Hans Driesch, Alfred Wallace (who came up with the natural-selection theory of evolution simultaneously with Darwin), and Nobel laureates Charles Richet and Alexis Carrel.

CONTINUING PREJUDICE

Nevertheless, the prejudice against extrasensory perception has remained so strong that even the considered judgment of these scientists and philosophers has not been able to overcome it. It is still "the orthodox belief," as William James put it, "that there can be nothing in any one's intellect that has not come in through ordinary experiences of sense."[64] James rejected this orthodox belief on the basis of the occurrence of telepathic influence, which he came to consider undeniable.

However, this orthodox belief rules out not only extrasensory perception in the sense of telepathy and clairvoyance, but also other types of nonsensory perception. One of these types is the "mathematical intuition" affirmed by Gödel. But there are still other types.

5. WHITEHEAD ON VARIOUS EXAMPLES OF NONSENSORY PERCEPTION

Alfred North Whitehead endorsed empiricism, saying that "all knowledge is grounded on perception."[65] However, he rejected *sensate* empiricism, according to which "all perception is by the mediation of our bodily sense-organs, such as eyes, palates, noses, ears, and the diffused bodily organization furnishing touches, aches, and other bodily sensations."[66] Indeed, he said, "science conceived as resting on mere sense perception, with no other source of observation, is bankrupt."[67] In reality, Whitehead pointed out, there are several types of nonsensory perception.

TELEPATHY

Whitehead was heavily influenced by William James, including his "radical empiricism," and Whitehead also taught at the University of Cambridge's Trinity College while Henry Sidgwick was there, and where Whitehead, like Sidgwick twenty years before him, belonged to the debating society known as the Cambridge Apostles. In Whitehead's *Science and the Modern World*, moreover, Whitehead quoted Sidgwick's *Memoirs*, suggesting that he had read this book.[68] It is not surprising, therefore, that Whitehead endorsed the reality of telepathy, which he did in at least four places.[69]

However, while mentioning telepathy as an example of nonsensory perception, Whitehead focused on other types of nonsensory perception, which he saw as important not only for science, as stated above, but also for philosophy, because the acceptance of sensate empiricism makes an adequate philosophy impossible: If we know of instances of nonsensory perception, he wrote, "then the tacit identification of perception with sense-perception must be a fatal error barring the advance of systematic metaphysics."[70] Whitehead provided, beyond telepathy, several more examples of nonsensory perception, all important for philosophy.

THE EXTERNAL WORLD

"The belief in an external world independent of the perceiving subject," declared Einstein, "is the basis of all natural science."[71] Besides being presupposed by science, the belief in a world beyond our own minds is also presupposed by all people. And yet, as David Hume pointed out, sensory perception by itself provides us knowledge only of sense data, not of an actual world that lies behind these data. According to Hume, "the mind [cannot] go beyond what is immediately present to the senses . . . to discover the real existence . . . of objects."[72] (Whitehead referred to perception in this sense as "perception in the mode of presentational immediacy.")

Hume's analysis led, therefore, to solipsism—the doctrine that we have no knowledge of the existence of a real world beyond our own minds, our own experiences. Hume acknowledged, however, that in our everyday living we have to presuppose the existence of an actual world—which he categorized as one of our "natural beliefs," which we must presuppose *in practice* even though we cannot justify them *in theory.*

This failure of sensory perception to account for this inevitable presupposition was illustrated more recently by Willard Quine. Having insisted, as stated earlier, that "whatever evidence there *is* for science *is* sensory evidence," Quine agreed with Hume that sensory perception provides no knowledge of physical objects, so they are in the same boat as Homer's gods. But he nevertheless, Quine said, "believe[d] in physical objects and not in Homer's gods."[73] Quine's Harvard colleague Hilary Putnam said, critically, that Quine sounded "like Hume saying that when he is in his study he sees that total skepticism is correct, but whenever he leaves his study he is a 'robust realist.'"[74]

In insisting on sensate empiricism, Quine also said, as we saw above, that "our statements about the external world [must] face the tribunal of sense experience"[75]—although sense experience itself, as Hume pointed out, does not provide knowledge of "the external world" (but only sensory data).

In summary, Hume and Quine both recognized that, although sensate empiricism implies solipsism, they in their daily living necessarily presupposed the existence of an actual world. The way to overcome this tension, said Whitehead, is to recognize that we have a mode of perception deeper than sense perception, through which we perceive the actual world beyond our own minds—which Whitehead called "perception in the mode of causal efficacy."

CAUSATION

Hume showed that sensory perception as well provides no basis for affirming causation, in the sense of the real influence of one thing on another. In the statement partially quoted above, Hume said that "the mind [cannot] go beyond what is immediately present to the senses . . . to discover . . . the [causal] relations of objects." Based entirely on our sense experience, Hume said, our belief in causation consists of nothing but "constant conjunction"—meaning that the kinds of events that we call "causes" are constantly conjoined with the kinds of events that we call "effects." In other words, according to Hume, there is no necessary connection between these types of events: There is, for example, only an accidental connection between putting one's hand in a fire and getting burned, or drinking a bottle of whisky and becoming drunk.

The idea that there is a necessary connection, because causes actually bring about the effects, is the basis of induction, on which science is based. If there were no necessary connection between causes and effects, then scientific induction would be baseless. Indeed, said Whitehead, "since the time of Hume, the fashionable scientific philosophy has been such as to deny the rationality of science." One famous philosopher of science who protested was Hans Reichenbach, saying that, on the basis of Hume's philosophy, science "is nothing but a ridiculous self-delusion."[76]

According to Whitehead, scientific induction is rational, because we have a nonsensory mode of perception, deeper than sensory perception. Through this deeper perception, he said, we learn about causation, in the sense that the "effects" are actually brought about, at least partly, by the "causes." This deeper, nonsensory perception is what Whitehead called "perception in the mode of causal efficacy." It is because of this mode of perception that we in practice have no doubts about either the existence of the actual world or of causation as real influence.

ONE'S OWN BODY

Behind our knowledge of causation and the external world is our non-sensory perception of our own bodies. In articulating his theoretical solipsism, as quoted above, Hume said that "the mind [cannot] go beyond what is immediately present to the senses." But in that statement, Hume showed that he was aware of something actual beyond his mind: his body. In asking where we get the idea of substances—that is, of actual things, as distinct from mere sense impressions—Hume asked which of our senses could have provided this idea:

> If it be perceived by the eyes, it must be a colour; if by the ears, a sound; if by the palate, a taste; and so of the other senses. But I believe none will assert that substance is either a colour, or sound, or a taste. . . . We have, therefore, no idea of substance, distinct from that of a collection of particular qualities.[77]

In response, Whitehead pointed out that Hume, in asserting the lack of any perception of anything beyond our own minds, implicitly presupposed it.

> For what is the meaning of '*by*' in '*by* the eyes,' '*by* the ears,' '*by* the palate'? His argument presupposes that sense-data, functioning in presentational immediacy, are 'given' by reason of 'eyes,' 'ears,' 'palates' functioning in causal efficacy. . . . Hume [stated] that sense-data functioning in an act of experience demonstrate that they are given *by* the causal efficacy of actual bodily organs.[78]

Our awareness of our body's causal efficacy for our experience is due to our nonsensory perception of this efficacy. This perception is obviously not itself a form of sensory perception: I do not see my eyes or hear my ears. My capacity to enjoy sights and sounds through my eyes and ears depends upon my more basic perception of my body, through which I receive the information that its sensory organs have brought in from the world beyond my body.

THE PAST AND TIME

George Santayana, a philosopher at Harvard in the early part of the twentieth century, pointed out that sensate empiricism is even more inadequate for our inescapable presuppositions than Hume acknowledged. Besides not informing us about the external world and causation, sense perception by itself also provides no knowledge of the existence of a past. Accordingly, Santayana said, sensate empiricism implies "solipsism of the present moment."[79]

If we had no knowledge of the past, we would have no knowledge of the distinction between past and present and hence no knowledge of time. We do, however, know the reality of time, because we know the difference between the past, the present, and the future. We know this, Whitehead said, because we perceive the world most fundamentally in the mode of causal efficacy: The separation of the world "into past and future lies with the mode of causal efficacy." Our knowledge of time comes from this distinction with regard to our own experiences: "Time is known to us as the succession of our acts of experience," said Whitehead, "and thence derivatively as the succession of events objectively perceived in those acts."[80]

MEMORY

The statement about "the succession of our acts of experience," through which we know about the past and time, points to another example of nonsensory perception. This is memory. Indeed, Whitehead suggested that "the most compelling example of non-sensuous perception is our knowledge of our own immediate past."[81]

Of course, memory is generally not considered an example of perception: It is not perception, it is assumed, but simply memory. However, Whitehead pointed out, "The mere word 'memory' explains nothing."[82] The question is: *How* do we remember past experiences? Whitehead's answer was that, just as we perceive our bodies and, through them, things outside our bodies, we perceive our previous experiences.

Another reason why people normally do not think of memories as perceptions is the tendency to think of memory in relatively long-range terms. But in speaking of "our knowledge of our own immediate past" as "the most compelling example of non-sensuous perception," Whitehead really meant *immediate*. He said: "I am not referring to our memories of a day past, or of an hour past, or of a minute past [but instead to] that portion of our past lying between a tenth of a second and half a second ago."[83]

In thinking of the way in which one's present experience is related to one's experience a tenth of a second ago, it is not so strange to see that memory is based on a type of (nonsensory) perception, in which my present occasion of experience perceives a previous occasion of experience, just as I perceive (pre-sensorily) my bodily organs.

SUMMARY

The idea that we cannot know mathematical objects by means of intuition, understood as nonsensory perception, is based entirely on the acceptance of sensate empiricism, which implies that, in developing a description of the world, as Quine put it, the "stimulation of his sensory receptors is all the evidence anybody has to go on."[84]

However, there are many things we know about the world that come from nonsensory, rather than sensory, perception. If we were to hold strictly to Quine's "tribunal of sense experience," we would need to eliminate knowledge of the external world, causation, our own bodies, memory, the past, and time. It would be insane, therefore, to regard sensory perception as a tribunal for deciding what exists.

6. BACK TO MATHEMATICAL OBJECTS

Given the fact that so much of our knowledge comes from nonsensory perception, there is no good reason to deny that we know the existence of the realm of mathematics by nonsensory perception, which Kurt Gödel called "mathematical intuition."

If mathematical intuition were the only alleged example of nonsensory perception, it might be reasonable to ask whether we really have a capacity for nonsensory, as well as sensory, perception. But we have looked at several examples, and in later chapters we will discuss still more examples, of knowledge that can be explained only on the assumption that we perceive things in a nonsensory way.

Our knowledge of logical truths and moral norms, moreover, shows that mathematical objects cannot be rejected on the grounds that nothing exists except physical things. We can hold, therefore, that we know mathematical objects by means of a nonsensory type of perception. This would certainly be more rational than insisting on sensate empiricism and then, like Quine, making an *ad hoc* exception for mathematics.

7. MATHEMATICS, NONSENSORY PERCEPTION, AND GOD

By combining the ideas expressed in this chapter—that we need a way to explain the reality and efficacy of mathematical objects; that this can be done by regarding these objects as present in, and given efficacy by, a universal mind; that nonsensory perception, at least telepathy, occurs; that telepathy is not unique by virtue of involving nonsensory perception—we can see that mathematics provides an argument for the existence of, in Whitehead's words, "a basic Psyche whose active grasp of ideas conditions impartially the whole process of the Universe."[85]

ANALOGY WITH TELEPATHY

With regard to the reality of telepathy in particular: If a human mind can get information received from another mind by means of nonsensory perception, thereby being influenced by that mind, there is no reason why human minds could not be directly influenced by the mind of the universe, if such there be. This position could handle both the Platonic problem, as to where the mathematical forms could be, and the Benacerraf problem, as to how they could exert influence on our minds.

Adopting this solution would, to be sure, be difficult for many science-based thinkers, not only because of the prejudice against non-sensory perception, but also because of the prejudice against any type of universal mind playing a role in scientific explanation. This prejudice was primarily created by the previous talk of Gawd, according to which the universal mind was omnipotent and hence capable of interventions in the normal natural processes. However, the idea of influence from a non-omnipotent but universal mind, understood as the soul of the universe, should not be rejected because of the rejection of Gawd.

GOD OF THE GAPS?

There is another possible objection to the idea that a divine mind explains where mathematical objects exist and how they can exert influence: The idea that this would be an example of the discredited "God of the gaps." But this would be a misplaced objection.

As discussed in Chapter 4, the "God of the gaps" refers to the appeal to an omnipotent deity to explain some gap in the present scientific knowledge of the world, which in principle could, with scientific advance, be explained by reference to finite causes. The classic example was Newton's appeal to deity to provide an adjustment of the planetary orbits required by his faulty calculations, a blunder immortalized by the (perhaps apocryphal) quip of the astronomer Pierre Laplace to Napoleon, that he had "no need of that hypothesis."

But the question of the existence of mathematical objects and their efficacy throughout the universe is not a question that could in principle be explained by reference to finite causation, so there is no possible scientific advance that could show the theistic answer to be unnecessary. The need for an answer to the reality and efficacy of mathematics points not to a Gawd of the gaps but to a God-shaped hole that is, arguably, in any worldview both coherent and adequate.

THE SHERLOCK HOLMES PRINCIPLE

Nevertheless, many people will likely find improbable the idea that something as commonplace as mathematics could point to the reality of a universal mind, understood as God. However, one should follow Sherlock Holmes's famous principle—that "when you have eliminated the impossible, whatever remains, *however improbable*, must be the truth." So however improbable this may seem to many people, the reality of mathematics appears to provide a strong argument for the existence of God.

8. MATHEMATICS IN THE NATURAL SCIENCES

There is another feature of mathematics that suggests the reality and efficacy of an all-inclusive mind. As we saw above, some of the world's leading mathematical physicists have spoken of the "great mystery," in Roger Penrose's words, that "somehow the structure of the physical world is rooted in mathematics."[86]

THE UNREASONABLE EFFECTIVENESS OF MATHEMATICS

This mystery had been discussed in a famous paper, "The Unreasonable Effectiveness of Mathematics in the Natural Sciences," by the aforementioned Eugene Wigner, who was both a pure and applied mathematician. (It was as an applied mathematician, dealing with elementary particles and the atomic nucleus, that he won a Nobel Prize.) Speaking of "the enormous usefulness of mathematics in the natural sciences," Wigner called this influence "something bordering on the mysterious," he said, because "there is no rational explanation for it."

One reason it is so mysterious is that, except for elementary mathematics—especially elementary geometry, which is suggested by the actual world—mathematics is pursued because "it is interesting," giving "many beautiful theorems." But advanced mathematics has nevertheless turned out to be extremely useful in physics. In fact, Wigner said, "the mathematical formulation of the physicist's often crude experience leads in an uncanny number of cases to an amazingly accurate description of a large class of phenomena."[87]

Expanding on Wigner's description of this mysterious fact, Mario Livio wrote:

> Concepts and relations explored by mathematicians only for pure reasons—with absolutely no application in mind—turn out decades (or sometimes centuries) later to be the unexpected solutions to problems grounded in physical reality![88]

For example, Livio said: "Kepler and Newton discovered that the planets in our solar system follow orbits in the shape of ellipses—the very curves studied by the Greek mathematician Menaechmus . . . two millennia earlier."[89]

For another example, Livio and Wigner both refer to Newton's law of gravity. In Livio's words:

> Newton took the laws of falling bodies discovered by Galileo, combined them with the laws of planetary motion determined by Kepler, and used this unified scheme to put forth a universal, mathematical law of gravitation. . . . The accuracy to which Newton himself could verify his law of gravity . . . was no better than about 4 percent. Yet the law proved to be accurate beyond all reasonable expectations. By the 1950s, the experimental accuracy was better than one ten-thousandth of a percent.[90]

How can this be explained? "It is difficult to avoid the impression," continued Wigner's article, "that a miracle confronts us here."

Still another example of this apparent miracle, he said, is provided by elementary quantum physics, which began when Max Born noticed that some of Heisenberg's rules of computation "were formally identical with the rules of computation with matrices, established a long time before by mathematicians." Born and Heisenberg then tried replacing the position and momentum variables of the equations of classical mechanics with matrix mechanics. Amazingly, when applied to the hydrogen atom by Wolfgang Pauli, matrix mechanics agreed with experience.

Although this was surprising, continued Wigner, "The miracle occurred only when matrix mechanics was applied to problems for which Heisenberg's calculating rules were meaningless." For example, these rules could not be applied to the two electrons of the helium atom. And yet, "the calculation of the lowest energy level of helium," reported Wigner, "agrees with the experimental data within the accuracy of . . . one part in ten million."

The miracle, explained Wigner, is the "[a]greement of the rules derived from quantum mechanical theory and the rules established by empirical research." Moreover, he added, "physics as we know it today would not be possible without a constant recurrence of miracles similar to the one of the helium atom."

An equally surprising agreement, added Livio, involves quantum electrodynamics, which seeks to describe all phenomena involving electrically charged particles and light. In 2006, Harvard physicists determined the strength of an electron's interaction with a magnetic field to a precision of eight parts in a trillion. And then theoretical calculations reached similar precision. When Freeman Dyson, one of the originators of quantum electrodynamics, learned about this, he said: "I'm amazed at how precisely nature dances to the tune we scribbled so carelessly fifty-seven years ago, and at how the experimenters and the theorists can measure and calculate her dance to a part in a trillion."[91]

This kind of agreement is what Wigner meant by "the unreasonable effectiveness of mathematics in the natural sciences." It is unreasonable, Wigner said, because "there is no rational explanation for it."[92]

EXPLAINING THE MYSTERY

In saying that there is "no rational explanation," Wigner meant an explanation that would be accepted within the prevailing worldview. That he had in mind an explanation of another type was suggested by his statement that the miracles on which he has focused are comparable "to the two miracles of the existence of laws of nature and of the human mind's capacity to divine them."

Roger Penrose, incidentally, had the same view. Saying that there are three worlds—"the world of our conscious perceptions, the physical world, and the Platonic world of mathematical forms"—Penrose spoke of a "triple mystery," namely:

- the world of physical reality seems to obey laws that actually reside in the world of mathematical forms;

- the perceiving minds somehow managed to emerge from the physical world;

- those perceiving minds were miraculously able to gain access to the mathematical world.[93]

All three of these "mysteries" are indeed inexplicable from a neo-Darwinian perspective, according to which the world was not created by a divine mind and, in Wigner's words, "our reasoning power was brought [about] by Darwin's process of natural selection."[94]

But Wigner knew, of course, that early modern scientists had an explanation, as suggested by his reference to Galileo's assertion, "Mathematics is the language with which God wrote the Universe." Livio dealt with this issue more explicitly, even taking as the title of his book the question, *Is God a Mathematician?* With reference to Galileo's statement, Livio said that for Galileo, "God is indeed a mathematician."[95]

In addition, Livio pointed out that this answer to the mystery did not originate in early modern science, but went all the way back to Plato and Archimedes. Mentioning that in Plato's dialogue *Timaeus,* "the creator god uses mathematics to fashion the world," he added: "The perception of mathematics being the language of the universe, and therefore the concept of God as a mathematician, was born in Archimedes' work."[96]

In early modern thought, moreover, Galileo's view of God as a mathematician was also expressed by Newton, for whom, in Livio's words, "the Creator God brought into existence a physical world that was governed by mathematical laws." One of Newton's big achievements, of course, was his demonstration that the earth and celestial bodies were governed by the same principles, and he regarded, Livio said, "the fact that the entire cosmos is governed by the same law and appears to be stable as further evidence for God's guiding hand."[97]

More recently, Livio pointed out that British astronomer and physicist James Jeans said in a 1930 book, entitled *The Mysterious Universe*, that "the Great Architect of the Universe begins to appear as a pure mathematician."[98] From such a perspective, according to which mathematics, the physical world, and human consciousness are all rooted in the same divine mind, it is less miraculous that mathematical concepts formulated by human minds so often apply to the empirically discovered laws of nature with uncanny accuracy.

CONCLUSION

Mathematics points to the existence of God, understood as the mind or soul of the universe, in four ways.

- The reality of God provides a place where Platonic mathematical forms can exist.

- The idea that these forms are actively prehended by God can explain the causality behind them that allows human beings to perceive them.

- God as the unity of the universe, "condition[ing] impartially the whole process of the Universe," can explain, as Newton had emphasized, the universality of the laws of nature.

- By saying that the laws of nature and the human mind are rooted in the same divine mind, we render less mysterious the fact that mathematical ideas formulated for their interest and beauty often turn out to be uncannily useful in physics.

Of course, Newton attributed the laws of nature to a divine mind that is omnipotent as well as omnipresent—that is, to Gawd. But as Whitehead indicated, they can also be explained in terms of God, as discussed below in Chapters 13 and 14.

ENDNOTES

1. Some people, on the assumption that the term "objects" refers exclusively to physical things that are objects of sensory perception, may consider it strange to refer to "mathematical objects." But there are objects of thought as well as objects of perception. Gottlob Frege, widely regarded as "the greatest logician since Aristotle [and] one of the most profound philosophers of mathematics of all times" ("Frege, Gottlob [1848–1925]," Encyclopedia.com), was emphatic about the reality of both logical and mathematical objects; see Edward N. Zalta, "Gottlob Frege," Stanford Encyclopedia of Philosophy, 2012, and "Natural Numbers and Natural Cardinals as Abstract Objects: A Partial Reconstruction of Frege's *Grundgesetze* in Object Theory," *Journal of Philosophical Logic,* 28/6 (1999), 619–60.

2. W. V. Quine, *Ontological Relativity and Other Essays* (Columbia University Press, 1969), 76.

3. Alfred North Whitehead, *Science and the Modern World* (1925; Free Press, 1967), 27–28.

4 Reuben Hersh, *What is Mathematics, Really?* (Oxford University Press 1997), 9.

5. Kurt Gödel, "What is Cantor's Continuum Problem? Supplement to the Second [1964] Edition," in *Collected Works,* Vol. II, ed. Solomon Feferman et al. (Oxford University Press, 1990): 266–69, at 268.

6. Charles Chihara, "A Gödelian Thesis Regarding Mathematical Objects: Do They Exist? And Can We Perceive Them?" *Philosophical Review* 91 (1982), 211–17, at 217.

7. Hilary Putnam, *Words and Life*, ed. James Conant (Harvard University Press, 1994), 503. The quotation comes from an essay originally published in 1979, when Putnam still held a materialist worldview, with a functionalist, cybernetic view of the mind, according to which there could be no nonsensory perception.

8. Hersh, *What is Mathematics, Really?* 11, 12.

9. Philip J. Davis, Reuben Hersh, and Elena Anne Marchisotto, *The Mathematical Experience* (Boston: Mariner Books, 1988), 359.

10. William G. Lycan, *Consciousness* (Cambridge: MIT Press, 1987), 90.

11. Hartry Field, *Science without Numbers* (Princeton: Princeton University Press, 1980); G. Hellman, *Mathematics without Numbers* (Oxford: Oxford University Press, 1989).

12. Y. N. Moschovakis, *Descriptive Set Theory* (Amsterdam: North Holland, 1980), 605–06.

13. For quotations from several other philosophers and mathematicians who agree, see Hersh, *What is Mathematics, Really?* 7, and Penelope Maddy, *Realism in Mathematics* (Oxford: Clarendon Press, 1990), 2–3.

14. Roger Penrose, *The Emperor's New Mind: Concerning Computers, Minds, and the Laws of Physics* (Oxford University Press, 1989), 123.

15. Moschovakis, *Descriptive Set Theory*, 320.

16. John Passmore, *Philosophical Reasoning* (Basic Books, 1961), 60; Alfred North Whitehead, *Process and Reality,* corrected edition, ed. David Ray Griffin and Donald W. Sherburne (1929; Free Press, 1978), 13.

17. Quine, *Ontological Relativity and Other Essays*, 75.

18. W. V. Quine, *From Stimulus to Science* (Harvard University Press, 1995), 14.

19. W. V. Quine, *Theories and Things* (Cambridge: Harvard University Press, 1981), 14–15.

20. Ibid., 14–15; Putnam, *Words and Life*, 153.

21. Paul Benacerraf, "Mathematical Truth" (originally 1973), ed. Paul Benacerraf and Hilary Putnam, *Philosophy of Mathematics,* 2nd ed. (Cambridge University Press, 1983), 402-20. The causal theory of knowledge is usually attributed to Alvin I. Goldman, "A Causal Theory of Knowing," *Journal of Philosophy* 64/12 (22 June 1967), 357–72. Some philosophers say that the causal theory of knowledge is dead (Mark Balaguer, "Fictionalism in the Philosophy of Mathematics," Stanford Encyclopedia of Philosophy, September 2011; Adam Morton and Stephen P. Stich, eds., *Benacerraf and his Critics* [Oxford: Blackwell, 1996]). However, the objections can be easily overcome. Mainly, the objections argue that the causal theory of knowledge, even with needed refinements made since Goldman's article, fails to provide conditions sufficient to call an idea true. But these problems disappear if we understand the Benacerraf contention to be only that causal responsibility is a necessary condition—even if not a sufficient condition—to call a belief knowledge. So the Benacerraf challenge cannot be ignored.

22. Bernard Williams, *Ethics and the Limits of Philosophy* (Harvard University Press, 1985), 142.

23. Maddy, *Realism in Mathematics*, 37.

24. Ibid., 44, 59, 78.

25. Ibid., 178.

26. Eugene Wigner, "The Unreasonable Effectiveness of Mathematics in the Natural Sciences," in *Communications in Pure and Applied Mathematics* (John Wiley & Sons 1980), 13 (February): 1–14.

27. Maddy, *Realism in Mathematics*, 178.

28. Bernard Linsky and Edward N. Zalta, "Naturalized Platonism vs. Platonized Naturalism," *Journal of Philosophy*, 92/10 (October 1995), 525–55.

29. Ibid.

30. Richard Hooker, "Renaissance Neo-Platonism," The Hermetic Library.

31. Eddy Carder, "Platonism and Theism," Internet Encyclopedia of Philosophy.

32. Hersh, *What is Mathematics, Really?* 12.

33. Whitehead, *Process and Reality: An Essay in Cosmology,* corrected edition, ed. David Ray Griffin and Donald W. Sherburne (1929; Free Press, 1978), 291.

34. Hersh, *What is Mathematics, Really?* 12.

35. Alfred North Whitehead, *Science and the Modern World* (1925; Free Press, 1967), 105.

36. Whitehead, *Process and Reality,* 40.

37. Ibid., 46.

38. A. H. Johnson, "Whitehead as Teacher and Philosopher," *Philosophy and Phenomenological Research,* 1969: 351–76, at 372.

39. See David Ray Griffin, *Panentheism and Scientific Naturalism: Rethinking Evil, Morality, Religious Experience, Religious Pluralism, and the Academic Study of Religion* (Claremont: Process Century Press, 2014).

40. Alfred North Whitehead, *Modes of Thought* (1938; Free Press, 1968), 8, 103; Charles Hartshorne, *Omnipotence and Other Theological Mistakes* (State University of New York Press, 1984), 52–62; Schubert M. Ogden, "The Experience of God: Critical Reflections on Hartshorne's Theory of Analogy," in John B. Cobb, Jr., and Franklin I. Gamwell, eds., *Existence and Actuality: Conversations with Charles Hartshorne* (University

of Chicago Press, 1984), 16–37, at 21; Jeremy W. Hayward, *Perceiving Ordinary Magic: Science and Intuitive Wisdom* (Shambhala, 1984), 241.

41. Whitehead, *Adventures of Ideas* (1933; Free Press, 1967), 147.

42. Thomas Nagel, *The Last Word* (Oxford University Press, 1997), 61.

43. Whitehead, *Process and Reality*, 257.

44. William Lane Craig (interviewed by Kevin Harris), "God, Abstract Objects, Platonism and Logic," Reasonable Faith, 2 August 2011.

45. Roger Penrose, "Interview with Jane Clark," *Journal of Consciousness Studies* 1/1 (1994): 17–24, at 23.

46. Richard Feynman, *The Meaning of It All: Thoughts of a Citizen-Scientist* (Basic Books, 1998), 43.

47. Mario Livio, *Is God a Mathematician?* (Simon & Schuster, 2009), 1.

48. James Trefil, *Reading the Mind of God: In Search of the Principle of Universality* (Scribner's, 1989), 1.

49. Dr. Emily Baldwin, "Earth's Laws Still Apply in Distant Universe," AstronomyNow.com, June 2008.

50. Whitehead, *Adventures of Ideas*, 147.

51. Gödel, "What is Cantor's Continuum Problem?" 268.

52. Kurt Gödel, *Wikipedia*, accessed August 15, 2014.

53. See, for example, Richard S. Broughton, *Parapsychology: The Controversial Science* (Ballantine Books, 1991); Benjamin Wolman, ed., *Handbook of Parapsychology* (Van Nostrand Reinhold, 1977); David Ray Griffin, *Parapsychology, Philosophy, and Spirituality: A Postmodern Exploration* (State University of New York Press, 1997).

54. C. D. Broad, *Religion, Philosophy, and Psychical Research: Selected Essays* (1953; Humanities Press, 1969), 86.

55. Ibid., 87, 108–09.

56. Ibid., 97, 114.

57. Paraphrase by William James in "What Psychical Research Has Accomplished," in William James, *Essays in Psychical Research*, ed. Robert A. McDermott (Harvard University Press, 1987), 89–106, at 90.

58. Whitehead, *Science and the Modern World*, 2.

59. James, *Essays in Psychical Research*. There was an earlier volume,

William James on Psychical Research, ed. Gardner Murphy and Robert O. Ballou (Viking Press, 1960).

60. William James, *Essays in Radical Empiricism* and *A Pluralistic Universe*, ed. Ralph Barton Perry; introduction by Richard J. Bernstein (E. P. Dutton, 1971), 270–71.

61. *William James on Psychical Research*, ed. Murphy and Ballou, 42.

62. Ibid., 310, 40.

63. Einstein had written a preface in 1939 for a projected German edition of Upton Sinclair's *Mental Radio*, in which Sinclair reported successful experiments with his wife. Although the publisher went out of business before the book could be published, Einstein's preface was included in the second American edition (Charles C. Thomas, 1962). Although Einstein said that the results of the experiments "stand surely far beyond those which a nature investigator holds to be thinkable," he said that Sinclair's "good faith and dependability are not to be doubted" (ix).

64. James, *Essays in Psychical Research*, 131.

65. Whitehead, *Process and Reality*, 158.

66. Whitehead, *Adventures of Ideas*, 177–78.

67. Whitehead, *Modes of Thought*, 154.

68. Whitehead, *Science and the Modern World*, 142.

69. Ibid., 150; *Process and Reality*, 308; *Adventures of Ideas*, 248; A. H. Johnson, "Whitehead as Teacher and Philosopher," 364.

70. Whitehead, *Adventures of Ideas*, 180.

71. Albert Einstein, "Maxwell's Influence on the Development of the Conception of Physical Reality," in J. J. Thomson et al., *James Clerk Maxwell: A Commemorative Volume* (Cambridge University Press, 1931), 66–73, at 66.

72. David Hume, *A Treatise of Human Nature*, *The Philosophical Works of David Hume* (1739), Bk. III, Sect. II.

73. W. V. Quine, *From A Logical Point of View: Nine Logico-Philosophical Essays* (Harvard University Press, 1953), 44.

74. Putnam, *Words and Life*, 347.

75. Quine, *Ontological Relativity and Other Essays*, 75; *From A Logical Point of View*, 41.

76. Whitehead, *Science and the Modern World,* 4; Hans Reichenbach, *Experience & Prediction* (University of Chicago Press), 346.

77. Hume, *A Treatise of Human Nature*, Bk. I, Sect. VI.

78. Alfred North Whitehead, *Symbolism: Its Meaning and Effect* (1927; Capricorn, 1959), 51.

79. George Santayana, *Scepticism and Animal Faith* (Dover, 1955), 14–15.

80. Whitehead, *Process and Reality,* 170; *Symbolism*, 35.

81. Whitehead, *Adventures of Ideas*, 181.

82. Ibid., 183.

83. Ibid., 181.

84. Quine, *Ontological Relativity and Other Essays*, 75.

85. Whitehead, *Adventures of Ideas*, 147.

86. Roger Penrose, "Interview [with Jane Clark]," *Journal of Consciousness Studies* 1/1 (1994): 17–24, at 23.

87. Wigner, "The Unreasonable Effectiveness of Mathematics in the Natural Sciences."

88. Livio, *Is God a Mathematician?* 4.

89. Ibid., 5.

90. Ibid., 218.

91. Ibid., 223.

92. Wigner, "The Unreasonable Effectiveness of Mathematics in the Natural Sciences."

93. Quoted in Livio, *Is God a Mathematician?* 2–3.

94. Wigner, "The Unreasonable Effectiveness." A year later, mathematician R. W. Hamming in "The Unreasonable Effectiveness of Mathematics" (*American Mathematical Monthly*, 87/2 [February 1980]) discussed Wigner's article. Hamming suggested four ways in which the effectiveness of mathematics might be explained. He concluded, however, that these four ways "added together simply are not enough to explain what I set out to account for." More recently, by contrast, engineer Derek Abbott published an anti-Platonist article entitled "The Reasonable Ineffectiveness of Mathematics" (*Proceedings of the IEEE*, 101/10 [October

2013], 2147–53), in which he sought to debunk Wigner's view that the effectiveness of mathematics in the natural sciences is a miracle of sorts. His approach was to "question the presupposition that mathematics is as effective as claimed and thus remove the quandary of Wigner's 'miracle,' leading to a non-Platonist viewpoint." But Abbott simply discussed the four reasons treated by Hamming; he did not discuss any of the examples that led to Wigner's amazement.

95. Livio, *Is God a Mathematician?* 77.

96. Ibid., 36, 59.

97. Ibid., 114–15.

98. James Jeans, *The Mysterious Universe* (Macmillan, 1929), 1930.

8

Morality

People invariably make value judgments with regard to human behavior, holding that some ways of acting are better than other ways, even if they try to avoid doing so: "[O]ur moral and aesthetic judgments," said Alfred North Whitehead, "involve the ultimate notions of 'better' and 'worse.'"[1] In making these judgments, we imply the position known as *moral realism*, according to which moral norms, like mathematical principles, exist objectively, so that moral judgments can be either true or false.

A philosophical worldview cannot be considered adequate unless it includes a treatment of morality. In the words of Henry Sidgwick:

> It is the primary aim of philosophy to unify completely, bring into clear coherence, all departments of rational thought, and this aim cannot be realised by any philosophy that leaves out of its view the important body of judgments and reasonings which form the subject matter of ethics.[2]

This treatment, moreover, cannot be one that dismisses the importance of moral judgments by declaring them to be non-cognitive—that is, as incapable of being either true or false. The cognition of facts cannot be limited to mere "matter-of-fact" issues, because "the impact," said Whitehead, of "moral notions is inescapable."[3]

As pointed out earlier, we cannot have a rational, self-consistent philosophical position unless we avoid "negations of what in practice is presupposed."[4] Given the fact that in practice moral judgments that presuppose moral realism are inevitable, we cannot have a consistent philosophical while denying this type of realism. And affirming moral realism, this chapter argues, finally implies theism.

I. MORAL PHILOSOPHERS AGAINST MORAL REALISM

In recent times, several of our best-known moral philosophers, teaching in our major universities, have denied moral realism, thereby rejecting the objectivity of moral values. For examples, I will use John Mackie, Gilbert Harman, Bernard Williams, and Richard Rorty. In each case, the rejection of moral realism was based on a rejection of theism.

JOHN MACKIE

John Mackie, who taught at Oxford University, subtitled his book on ethics *Inventing Right and Wrong* and bluntly said: "There are no objective values."[5] Making this abstract point concrete, the idea "that actions which are cruel," said Mackie, "are to be condemned" is not a "hard fact" about the universe. With regard to the idea that "if someone is writhing in agony before your eyes" you should "do something about it if you can," Mackie said that it is not an "objective [requirement] of the nature of things."[6]

It is not an objective requirement because moral principles, Mackie famously said, are not "part of the fabric of the world." In explaining why he made this claim, Mackie referred to the Platonic problem: "The difficulty of seeing how values could be objective is a fairly strong reason for thinking that they are not."[7]

He could not see how moral values could exist objectively, he said, because they would be too "queer" to be plausible—queer both ontologically and epistemologically. They would be *ontologically* queer, because they "would be entities," Mackie said, "of a very strange sort, utterly different from anything else in the universe." Explaining, Mackie said that, if Plato's "Form of the Good" existed, it would be utterly different from everything else by virtue of being inherently *prescriptive*—by having "has to-be-pursuedness somehow built into it."[8]

In explaining why they would be *epistemologically* queer, Mackie said—without any explicit reference to the Benacerraf problem—because we would have to know them by means of "some special faculty of moral perception or intuition, utterly different from our ordinary ways of thinking everything else," because we know everything else through "sensory perception or introspection."[9] So, just as most philosophers rejected Kurt Gödel's idea that we know the reality of mathematical objects by mathematical intuition, Mackie rejected the idea of *moral* intuition on the assumption that the only way to know things beyond our own minds is by sensory perception.

However, having said that his book was "a discussion of what we can make of morality without recourse to God," he conceded that, "if the requisite theological doctrine could be defended," then "a kind of objective ethical prescriptivity could be defended."[10] Mackie dismissed this possibility, however, by pointing to his earlier book, *The Miracle of Theism*, in which he argued that theism is *not* defensible, primarily because of the problem of evil.

However, Mackie in that book dealt only with *traditional* theism, according to which one of the divine attributes is "able to do everything (i.e. omnipotent)." Mackie, in other words, was equating theism with belief in Gawd. The problem of evil would cause no problem, Mackie conceded, for forms of theism that do not accept the view of divine power as omnipotence.[11] Accordingly, if the discussion were about God, rather than Gawd, Mackie's argument that moral values would be onto-logically queer would not apply: They could have to-be-pursuedness built into them by virtue of being rooted in God.

In fact, Hilary Putnam, without any appeal to deity, refuted this part of Mackie's claim. Pointing out that we take for granted the exis-tence of various cognitive values, such as the prohibition against self-contradictory statements, Putnam said: "There are 'ought-implying facts' in the realm of belief fixation, and that is an excellent reason not to accept the view that there cannot be 'ought-implying facts' anywhere."[12]

However, even if Mackie would have given up his argument about ontological queerness, he likely would have continued to deny objective values on the grounds they would be *epistemically* queer. They would be queer, he said, because we can have no sensory perception of them, or of a deity that would be prescribing them. So even if moral values were divinely prescribed, Mackie held, we would have no way of knowing anything about them.

GILBERT HARMAN

Princeton's Gilbert Harman has presented a similar view, saying that "there are no absolute facts of right or wrong."[13] Harman thereby articulated the view that he himself called nihilism—"the doctrine that there are no moral facts, no moral truths, and no moral knowledge."[14] However, Harman also claimed that he retained our ordinary view, according to which we "speak of moral judgments as true or false," rather than "endorsing some form of nihilism."[15]

Harman tried to reconcile these two views by saying that there are "no absolute facts of right or wrong, *apart from one or another set of conventions.*"[16] But this view, according to which morality does not exist in the fabric of the world but only because of social conventions, is precisely what moral nihilism holds.

Harman's reason for accepting nihilism was made clear in a chapter entitled "Nihilism and Naturalism." By naturalism, he meant not merely the idea that there are no supernatural interruptions of the laws of nature, but also the "thesis that *all* facts are facts of nature," with "nature" understood as the totality of material things making up the universe.[17] Accordingly, with reference to moral norms, Harman said that "our scientific conception of the world has no place for entities of this sort." Likewise, he said, our scientific view of the world has "no place for gods."[18]

Besides making the claim about ontology—that the world has no place for moral norms or anything divine—he also, like Mackie, provided an epistemological argument, saying that moral beliefs could not result from the impact of moral norms on our experience. The fact that ethics has no observational evidence, Harman argued, makes ethics completely different from science:

> Facts about protons can affect what you observe, since a proton passing through the cloud chamber can cause a vapor trail that

> reflects light to your eye. . . . But there does not seem to be any way in which the actual rightness or wrongness of a given situation can have any effect on your perceptual apparatus.

Harman was thereby equating, of course, perception with *sensory* perception. On this basis, Harman concluded that if there were such a thing as moral knowledge, it "would have to be a kind of knowledge that can be acquired other than by observation."[19]

At this point, however, Harman's argument encountered a difficulty. With reference to Benacerraf, Harman said:

> We do not and cannot perceive numbers. . . . Relations among numbers cannot have any more of an effect on our perceptual apparatus than moral facts can.[20]

Like Quine, Harman knew that mathematical knowledge is indispensable for physics. Having recognized that moral norms and mathematical objects are both in the same boat epistemically, how could Harman hold on to mathematical realism while dismissing moral realism?

He solved this problem by resorting to special pleading, saying that mathematics is different because there is "indirect observational evidence" for it.[21] This is clearly special pleading, because the same kind of argument could be made for morality. As quoted earlier, Whitehead pointed out that "the impact of . . . moral notions is inescapable."[22] This impact of inescapable moral notions could be called "indirect observational evidence."

Accordingly, Harman indulged in the same inconsistency as did Willard Quine. The "tribunal of sense experience," according to Quine, excluded moral judgments from the realm of cognitive assertions.[23] And yet Quine allowed "the abstract objects of mathematics" into his ontology, even though his tribunal should have kept them out.

In summary, Harman gave essentially the same three-fold argument against moral realism as that provided by John Mackie: First, there is no divine reality; second, there are no objective moral values; third, even if there were a divine reality and moral values, "there is no way in which we could become aware of such entities."[24]

BERNARD WILLIAMS

Bernard Williams, who taught moral philosophy at Cambridge University, entitled his major book *Ethics and the Limits of Philosophy*, by which he meant that morality "can[not] be justified by philosophy."[25]

Like Harman, Williams portrayed ethics as completely different from science: In scientific inquiry, we expect convergence of opinion, because the thinking of scientists is guided by the way the world really is. But in ethical thinking, Williams contended, there is no basis for expecting convergence, because we cannot perceive moral norms, so there is no way for the world to guide the thinking of moral philosophers.[26]

Although Williams recognized that some philosophers have claimed that "something like perception"—sometimes called moral intuition—accounts for our ethical concepts, Williams said that "the appeal to intuition as a faculty . . . seemed to say that these truths were known, but there was no way in which they were known." Therefore, Williams said, "intuition in ethics, as a faculty, is no more."[27] Williams had to deny moral intuition, of course, because he accepted the idea that all perception is by means of our physical senses.

In an essay on Mackie's position, Williams agreed that morality is not part of "the fabric of the world." With regard to what it "could mean to say that a requirement or demand was 'part of the fabric of the world,'" Williams said that it "might possibly mean that some agency which made the demand or imposed the requirement was part of the fabric." But Williams, like Mackie, believed that no such agency exists. Holding that "our values are not 'in the world,'" Williams said this "realization" followed upon the death of the teleological world-view, from which "ought" could be derived from "is." This death came with the demise of assumptions derived from theism, and "[n]o one has yet," Williams said, "found a good way of doing without those assumptions."[28]

Accordingly, because the rejection of theism is the reason why Williams considered philosophy unable to justify morality, he should have entitled his book, more modestly, "Ethics and the Limits of Atheistic Philosophy."

RICHARD RORTY

Although Richard Rorty was not a moral philosopher at a major university, he was certainly one of the best-known philosophers in the world, and he wrote a lot about morality. Like the previous philosophers, he grounded his denial of objective moral truths on the rejection of theism. Rorty, however, made this rejection so much more central that his writings could be read as a hermeneutic of the death of God.

According to Martin Heidegger, Nietzsche's slogan, "God is dead," meant the denial of the efficacy and even existence of a realm of supersensuous values.[29] Similarly, "to say, with Nietzsche, that God is dead," wrote Rorty, "is to say that we serve no higher purposes."[30] Rorty also, with Nietzsche, connected atheism with the rejection of Platonic forms. Using Whitehead's term for such forms, Rorty said that there are "no eternal relations between eternal objects."[31]

Because there are no Platonic forms, Rorty continued, all causal forces are "material, spatiotemporal causes." There are no nonmaterial entities—whether mathematical, divine, or moral—to exert causal influence on our minds.[32] We should hence not think of morality "as the voice of the divine part of ourselves," but as "the voice of ourselves as members of a community."[33]

Like Mackie, accordingly, Rorty held that moral truths are made, not discovered.[34] Hoping for a culture free of any "trace of divinity" or "idea of holiness," Rorty said that, in this culture, the idea of "objective moral values" would seem "merely quaint."[35]

Given this view, Rorty, like Mackie, could not say that anything is morally wrong objectively. For example, although Rorty was personally *against* cruelty, he could not provide any answer to the question, "Why not be cruel?" Likewise, although Rorty personally liked liberal democracy, he could not provide any defense of the moral superiority of liberal democracy to Nazi tyranny.[36]

Moreover, although Rorty was personally in favor of the rhetoric of "human solidarity," he said that a de-divinized cosmos provides no basis for the universalist attitude—which secular humanism, he acknowledged, had taken over from Christianity—that we should feel obligations to all human beings.[37]

As to whether Rorty's philosophy would have bad effects, he himself said that it should not be taught to young people until their consciences had been formed.[38] More generally, admitting that his position, if taken as a public philosophy, would be "at best useless and at worst dangerous," he said that, in his liberal utopia, only the intellectuals would share his views—"the nonintellectuals would not."[39]

SUMMARY

These examinations have shown that all four of these philosophers rejected the objectivity of morality because of their rejection of theism, which led them to reject Platonic realism about moral norms. But could moral realism be affirmed while rejecting theism? Two major philosophers, Charles Larmore and Ronald Dworkin, have suggested that it could.

2. LARMORE: MORAL REALISM WITHOUT THEISM

In a book entitled *The Morals of Modernity*, Charles Larmore of Brown University affirmed Platonic realism about moral norms while rejecting theism.

LARMORE'S DEFENSE OF MORAL REALISM

If "naturalism" is the view that the world contains nothing except matter and minds (with minds perhaps understood as "a complex system of matter in motion"), Larmore argued that we cannot do justice to human experience unless we say, with Plato, that the world also contains value, in the sense of a normative dimension.[40]

The obvious reason why affirming a normative realm is indispensable, said Larmore, is that it is necessary to do justice to our moral experience, which assumes that moral judgments presuppose moral truths that exist independently of our preferences.[41] Accordingly, just as Quine (followed by Harman) used his indispensability argument for mathematical realism, Larmore employed an indispensability argument for moral realism.

But a more general reason is that the affirmation of a normative realm is necessary to do justice to *any* of our normative beliefs about values, including cognitive values about "the way we ought to think."[42]

The reasons for doubting that there are moral values, such as the claim that they would be epistemically and metaphysically "queer," would apply equally to cognitive values, observed Larmore (as did Putnam). However, to deny that there are any objective cognitive values, he added, would mean that the idea that we *ought* to avoid self-contradiction is merely a preference, with no inherent authority.[43]

In another important point, Larmore said that although those who reject Platonic values generally portray this rejection as dictated by science (this was especially true of Harman), it is not. "[T]he belief that the achievements of modern science ought to command our assent," said Larmore, puts us beyond an anti-Platonic worldview, for "this belief makes reference to a truth about what we ought to believe."[44]

A still more general point made by Larmore is that anti-Platonic naturalism, if carried through consistently, "would destroy the very idea of rationality." It would thereby lead to *irrationalism*, according to which all norms about how to reason and what to believe would have no authority except the decision to abide by them.[45]

However, while Larmore showed persuasively that a realm of normative values is indispensable, he failed to portray the existence of such a realm persuasively, because of his positions on perception and theism.

LARMORE ON PERCEPTION

With regard to perception, Larmore's affirmation of Platonic forms might seem to imply that their existence is known through some type of nonsensory perception. But he did not challenge the modern doctrine that perception is to be entirely equated with sensory perception.

His position does not involve, said Larmore, "some obscure faculty of 'intuition.'" To speak of moral views as "intuitions" can be misleading, he added, by virtue of suggesting "that we arrived at them in some immediate, untheoretical way." Larmore also held that moral knowledge is not analogous to mathematical knowledge. He declared, accordingly, that if all knowledge had to be based on perceptual experience, moral knowledge would be impossible.[46]

Larmore's alternative proposal was that the "organ" or "faculty" of moral knowledge is reason or reflection.[47] But reason is always historically conditioned, he said: Rejecting the Kantian idea that reason can "take over the function of grounding morality, now that God has been dispensed from the task," Larmore said, "reason becomes capable of moral argumentation only with an already existing morality."[48]

As a result, Larmore was hardly less relativistic than Rorty, saying that our conscience is the voice not of eternity but of merely "our form of life."[49] If we cannot think that our conscience is even partly influenced by eternal principles, it is hard to see why the affirmation of their existence makes any difference.

LARMORE ON THEISM

If Larmore's position, with its Platonic affirmation of "abstract object[s]" and "ideal entities,"[50] is made difficult by his acceptance of a sensationist view perception, it is increased by his acceptance of atheism. In affirming atheism, he did not insist that no deity exists, but only that a deity would have no function:

> [R]eligion can no longer fulfill certain functions that belonged to it in premodern societies. We can no longer expect religion to provide ultimate explanations of nature or ultimate justifications of morality. . . . It is in this development that the so-called death of God consists. . . . We no longer need God to explain the world and to ground the rules of our common life.

This conclusion, claimed Larmore, is "already settled."[51]

However, given the widespread intuition that ideal entities can exist only in actual ones, the rejection of a divine actuality left Larmore with the Platonic problem of how and where these entities could exist. Larmore, surprisingly, seemed unaware of this problem.

Likewise, given the even more widespread intuition that only *actual* entities can exert agency, the rejection of any form of theism means that Larmore had no answer to the Benacerraf problem of how ideal entities could exert agency. Larmore did allude to this problem, pointing out that some thinkers have rejected the existence of moral facts because of their difficulty in understanding how such facts could be causally responsible for beliefs about them.[52]

Larmore, however, was unable to supply a satisfactory answer. He argued that, besides causal explanations, there are also normative explanations, which are known through reflection. But Larmore admitted there to be "great difficulties in this conception of normative knowledge, particularly in understanding how reasons, as something non-natural, can become the object of reflection (which is a psychological, natural process)."[53]

Larmore thereby enunciated a position similar to that of Willard Quine. Saying that his ontology was "materialism, bluntly monistic except for the abstract objects of mathematics," Quine made no attempt to explain how these abstract objects could exist in an otherwise materialistic universe. The two positions differed only in that, whereas Quine's abstract objects were limited to *mathematical* forms, Larmore's worldview also included *normative* principles. Both Quine and Larmore accepted these Platonic forms solely on the grounds of their indispensability for human thinking (for thinking in physics, in Quine's case; for normative thinking, in Larmore's case). Neither one sought to show how ideal forms could conceivably exist, in Quine's words, "over and above the physical objects."[54]

Besides leaving him with the Platonic and Benacerraf problems, Larmore's acceptance of sensate empiricism and atheism forced him to deny that moral conscience is even partly shaped by direct perceptual access to the normative realm, so that we must consider conscience to be wholly shaped by one's historical tradition. This conclusion created difficulties for his endorsement of a modern "ethics of the right" with its "imperative morality," which results in "categorical" obligations.[55]

While conceding that "Christian theology, both in its image of God as moral legislator and in its ideal of disinterested love, played an indispensable role in the rise of an ethics of the right," Larmore claimed that moral convictions resulting in categorical obligations can "stand on their own," with their source being "not God, nor practical reason, but rather the way of life expressed in these convictions."[56] However, Larmore candidly acknowledged, this position may give us an understanding of imperative morality that is "so meager an understanding as to be none at all." Larmore also confessed to a "nagging worry" that, if our ancestors had rejected "the metaphysical aspiration to eternity," thereby reasoning "as we think they should," they would never have developed a universalist morality.[57]

In calling it "already settled" that "[w]e no longer need God to explain the world and to ground the rules of our common life," Larmore was wrong, as illustrated by the problems in his position that resulted from his endorsement of this claim. In spite of his insistence on the importance of a Platonic realm of normative values, Larmore ended up with a position little different from that of Rorty and Quine.

3. DWORKIN: RELIGION AND MORAL REALISM WITHOUT GOD

Ronald Dworkin, who was a professor of law and philosophy at New York University, wrote a book entitled *Religion without God,* which was published after his death in 2013. His book argued that atheism provides no impediment to the affirmation of moral realism.

RELIGIOUS ATHEISM AND OBJECTIVE VALUE

Like Larmore, Dworkin affirmed moral realism while rejecting theism. But whereas Larmore held that atheism entails a non-religious view of the universe, Dworkin held that the rejection of theism does nothing to prevent a robust religious worldview. Arguing that "religious atheism" is not an oxymoron, Dworkin said that "religion is not restricted to theism."[58]

Religion does not need theism, said Dworkin, because of the nature of religion: Religion is a "comprehensive worldview," which "holds that inherent, objective value permeates everything."[59] Stating what he called "the metaphysical core" of the religious attitude, Dworkin wrote:

> The religious attitude accepts the full independent reality of value. It accepts the objective truth of two central judgments about value. The first holds that human life has objective meaning or importance. . . . The second holds that what we call "nature"—the universe as a whole and in all its parts—is not just a matter of fact but is itself sublime: something of intrinsic value and wonder.[60]

MORAL REALISM

According to the religious attitude, as articulated by Dworkin, it is the opposite of *naturalism*, which he defined as the "metaphysical theory that nothing is real except what can be studied by the natural sciences," so that there is "no such thing as a good life or justice or cruelty or beauty." Dworkin thereby equated naturalism with *scientistic* naturalism, as shown by this summary statement: "The religious attitude rejects all forms of naturalism. It insists that values are real and fundamental, not just manifestations of something else; they are as real as trees or pain."[61]

WAS DWORKIN REALLY AN ATHEIST?

In saying that moral realism did not require theism, Dworkin contrasted his religious attitude with what he called "conventional theistic religion."[62] In characterizing this conventional theism, Dworkin portrayed it as centered around "a supernatural person," an "all-powerful and all-knowing god," a "supernatural, all-powerful, omniscient, and living being."[63] He called this deity "the Sistine God, the bearded figure creating life on the ceiling and, in the person of his son, sending people to heaven and hell on the back wall. . . . [H]e is omniscient and all-powerful."[64]

As this description shows, Dworkin's Sistine God is a version of the deity called "Gawd" in the present book. In light of the fact that Dworkin's rejection of deity was a rejection of Gawd, one could ask: Would Dworkin's "religious attitude" really make sense apart belief in a reality that could be called "God"? Perhaps his "religious atheism" was not as atheistic as he suggested.

Insofar as atheism is understood as the rejection of Gawd, a.k.a. the Sistine God, Dworkin was an atheist. But by the same criterion, Whitehead, Hartshorne, and I are atheists. And Dworkin, after having defined his atheism primarily in terms of the rejection of the Sistine God, he admitted that "the idea of a god is anything but clear," so "the distinction between theism and atheism is therefore itself indistinct." Although Dworkin clearly rejected "conventional theism," there are features of his position that suggest a type of non-conventional theism. For example, Dworkin seemed to endorse the view that there is "a 'force' in the universe, 'greater than we are.'" And although "Percy Bysshe Shelley declared himself an atheist," Dworkin added, Shelley felt, he said, "The awful shadow of some unseen Power/Floats though unseen among us."[65]

Likewise, insofar as Dworkin accepted a label, he called himself a pantheist, and pantheism is not atheism. In opposition to Richard Dawkins' claim that pantheism is merely "sexed-up atheism," Dworkin said that this claim misses the crucial point—the religious attitude that "most of the people who call themselves pantheists take toward the nature they say is identical to God."[66]

As these statements show, although Dworkin named his book *Religion without God,* he had a deity of sorts—nature as a whole. Moreover, he said that the religious attitude of pantheists toward the universe is rooted in what some people call a "'numinous' experience— an experience of sensing something nonrational and emotionally deeply moving." Expanding his point, Dworkin said:

> [F]or pantheists a numinous experience is an experience of something they take to be *real.* . . . Pantheists believe there is wonder or beauty or moral truth or meaning or something else of value *in* what they experience.[67]

Accordingly, although the title of his book might suggest that Dworkin belonged to the category of writers who think that morality can get along perfectly well without belief in God, he meant only that it could get along without Gawd. Far from being similar to the atheism of Mackie, Harman, Rorty, and Williams, the "religious atheism" espoused by Dworkin insists on the objective truth of moral realism.

In a statement that was apparently meant to justify his book's title, *Religion without God,* Dworkin, after acknowledging that "the idea of a god is anything but clear," said: "It is the Sistine God [Gawd] who dominates practicing theism today."[68]

This justification was similar to the attempt of Richard Dawkins (quoted in Chapter 6) to justify his title, *The God Delusion.* After acknowledging that there were forms of religion centered around a non-supernatural, non-interventionist divine reality, Dawkins said that the "decent, revisionist religion is numerically negligible."

In response, I said, "regardless of how negligible may be the number of people who hold a non-fundamentalist version of theism, it was misleading of Dawkins to use objections to Gawd to criticize all belief in God." Likewise, no matter how dominant the Sistine God may be among practicing theists, it was misleading of Dworkin to call his position "religious atheism." As shown by various statements of his pantheism—that "inherent, objective value permeates everything," that "the universe and its creatures are awe-inspiring," that nature is "something of intrinsic wonder and beauty," that "some transcendental and objective value permeates the universe"—Dworkin could have been described with the term applied to Spinoza: "God-intoxicated."

QUESTIONS ABOUT DWORKIN'S PANTHEISM

Although Dworkin's *Religion without God* does not contradict the thesis of this chapter—that an adequate moral philosophy is impossible without the affirmation of a divine reality—there are questions to be asked about the adequacy of his pantheism. In particular, could he, unlike Larmore, provide answers to the Platonic and Benacerraf problems?

The Platonic Problem: Although Larmore built his moral argumentation primarily around an affirmation of Platonic realism, giving reasons why anti-Platonic naturalism is inadequate, his rejection of theism, as we saw, left his worldview with no place for Platonic values to exist. By the same token, Larmore could provide no answer to the Benacerraf problem of how Platonic values, even if they somehow existed, could exert any influence on our minds. Could Dworkin, by virtue of affirming pantheism rather than atheism, do better?

With regard to the Platonic problem, did Dworkin, insofar as he regarded the universe as a whole as God, provide a place for the Platonic forms to exist? According to Middle Platonism, as we have seen, the Platonic forms exist in God, understood as conscious. And Dworkin at places could be taken as regarding his pantheistic deity—that is, the universe—as conscious. For example, he said that "the universe as a whole . . . is itself sublime: something of intrinsic value."[69] And many philosophers hold that only entities with value for themselves, because they have experience, have "intrinsic value."

However, this seemed not to have been Dworkin's view: The attributes that he withheld from his pantheistic deity apparently included being personal, intelligent, and conscious.[70] It is unclear, accordingly, how the universe could have intrinsic value. It is equally unclear how the universe could include moral values—values that would make it true that, in Dworkin's words, "cruelty is really wrong," because this statement is "objectively true."[71]

In discussing "in what way is the universe that is composed of [the parts described by physics is] beautiful," Dworkin admitted that the answer is "obscure" and that the idea that the universe is beautiful rests "on faith." The same was evidently true of his idea that the universe contains values that "are as real as trees or pain."[72]

The Benacerraf Problem: Equally problematic would be the Benacerraf problem: how Platonic moral values, even if they somehow exist, could exert any influence on our minds, so that we would know of their existence. His pantheism certainly had more promise for answering this question than Larmore's atheism, given Dworkin's statements about "a 'force' in the universe, 'greater than we are,'" and his quotation of Shelley's "some unseen Power" that "floats though unseen among us."[73] But given his failure to explain how his pantheistic deity—the universe as divine—could contain Platonic values, it is unclear how the unseen power could impress such values on our minds.

Likewise, Dworkin provided no epistemological discussion of how, even if the unseen power is permeating the universe with moral values, our minds could perceive them. He knew that if we believe that cruelty is really wrong, then we must think we have a "way of being 'in touch with' moral truth."[74]

In raising a difficult question—"What reason do we have for supposing that we have the capacity for sound value judgment?"—Dworkin answered: "The only possible reason we could have—we reflect responsibly on our moral convictions and find them persuasive."[75]

In defending his answer, Dworkin spoke of an "innate capacity" for moral truth:

We know we have an innate capacity for logic and mathematical truth. But how do we know we have that capacity? Only because we form beliefs in these domains that we simply cannot, however we try, disown. So we must have such a capacity.[76]

The "innate capacity" to which Dworkin appealed is another term for the old idea of "moral sense," which was instilled in humans at creation, or at birth, by God.

But that idea presupposed a supernaturalistic, creationist context, which Dworkin certainly would not have endorsed. The question he needed to answer was how, within an evolutionary context, humans could have a capacity for moral, along with logical and mathematical, truths.

Therefore, Dworkin failed to answer the question of how we can "be in touch with" moral truth. We have an idea of how our physical senses put our minds in touch with trees and pains. But our physical senses do not help explain how we can be in touch with moral truth.

SUMMARY OF DWORKIN'S POSITION

Although Dworkin rightly held that the affirmation of moral realism does not require belief in Gawd, he could have developed a more adequate position by replacing his pantheism with the kind of panentheism suggested by Whitehead.

4. THEISM AND MORAL NORMS

The above writers together provide strong reason to believe that a world view that excludes nonsensory perception, along with any form of theism, cannot do justice to morality, just as it cannot do justice to mathematics. An affirmation of normative values is as indispensable as an affirmation of mathematical objects. Larmore rightly pointed out that we cannot self-consistently reject such values in the name of science, because to say that we should follow science is to say that there are values about "the way we ought to think."[77]

Likewise, Larmore pointed out, to reject objective cognitive values would mean that there is no reason that we should avoid self-contradiction. Given the agreement that we should avoid self-contradiction, moreover, we must affirm the reality of objective moral norms, because this reality is presupposed in our normal activities of living. We must "bow to those presumptions," in Whitehead's words, "which, in despite of criticism, we still employ for the regulation of our lives."[78]

THE NEED FOR AN EXPLANATION

If moral norms are inescapable, then any philosophical position is inadequate to the extent that it provides no explanation for them. Whitehead used the same explanation he used for our awareness of mathematical objects, saying that they reflected eternal objects in the primordial nature of God. In that explanation, however, Whitehead described the mathematical objects as "eternal objects of the objective species." Our awareness of moral norms, by contrast, reflect "eternal objects of the subjective species," which can inform not only the objects of perception but also the subjective forms of feelings.[79]

In referring to God as the source of moral experiences, Whitehead wrote:

> There are experiences of ideals—of ideals entertained, of ideals aimed at, of ideals achieved, of ideals defaced. This is the experience of the deity of the universe.[80]

In explaining how we know about these ideas, Whitehead was in effect referring to what is usually called "moral intuition" (just as Kurt Gödel used "mathematical intuition" to explain our awareness of mathematical objects).

As we saw earlier, Bernard Williams rejected this idea, saying that "the appeal to intuition as a faculty . . . seemed to say that these truths were known, but there was no way in which they were known." Similarly, John Mackie said: "'Moral sense' or 'intuition' is an initially more plausible description of what supplies many of our basic moral judgments than 'reason.'" He also admitted that people in making moral judgments implicitly claim, among other things, to be pointing to "something objectively prescriptive." But this claim must be false, Mackie argued, because to affirm moral realism would require an exception to the only way in which we know anything beyond our own minds: sensory perception.[81]

Indeed, if this were the case, then Whitehead in affirming moral intuition would have been rejecting scientific naturalism, according to which there can be no violation of the normal cause-effect relations. However, this is not the case. In rejecting sensate empiricism, Whitehead developed an epistemology in which sensory perception is derivative from a nonsensory mode of perception, which we share with all other living creatures.

In appealing to nonsensory perception to explain our awareness of moral norms, he was not providing an ad hoc explanation, because—as we saw in the previous chapter—nonsensory perception is needed to explain our awareness of causation, memory, the past, time, mathematics, and the existence of the external world (so no one in practice is afflicted with "solipsism of the present moment").

Accordingly, rather than being an exception to our normal experience, moral intuition is an example of the same mode of perception through which we intuit the reality of a wide range of indispensable beliefs.

MORALITY: THICK AND THIN

The idea that moral beliefs result from divine ideals as well as other factors, including cultural conditioning, can explain Michael Walzer's position in his book entitled *Thick and Thin: Moral Argument at Home and Abroad*.

Walzer had been widely regarded as a moral relativist, but while still emphasizing "difference," Walzer articulated "a certain sort of universalism."[82] Within every community's particularist moral tradition, which he called a "thick" morality, there are, he said, "the makings of a thin and universalist morality."[83]

Because there does seems to be a thin universalist morality—Gene Outka and John Reeder spoke, for example, of the emergence of a "remarkable kind of cross-cultural moral agreement about human rights"[84]—this would be hard to explain apart from a source of moral norms standing above and *embedded in* the various cultures and traditions.

Although many philosophers have noted this duality, Walzer said, they had usually described it "in terms of a (thin) set of universal principles adapted (thickly) to these or those historical circumstances," thereby wrongly suggesting that the thin, common morality is every culture's starting point. Instead, "Morality is thick from the beginning," and the thin element—which provides common principles with peoples of other cultures—is revealed "only on special occasions."[85]

Rather than being the starting point for more particular moralities, the universal, minimal morality results, Walzer said, from "mutual recognition among the protagonists of different fully developed moral cultures."

> [Minimal morality] consists in principles and rules that are reiterated in different times and places, and that are seen to be similar even though they are expressed in different idioms and reflect different histories and different versions of the world.[86]

Although Walzer declined to go into a discussion of "the reasons for the reiterations or for the differences," he did say that "a naturalist account seems best for the first, a cultural account for the second."[87] By "naturalist," Walzer was using the term with the meaning it has in international law, in which "naturalism" refers to laws or principles that exist in the nature of things.[88] The reiterated elements, therefore, would suggest a moral natural law.

This account, according to which the universal minimal morality reflects principles in the nature of things, fits with the position being developed in this chapter, according to which morality derives in part from intuitions of moral principles that are present in the primordial nature of God, hence in the fabric of the universe. The reason there is a universal minimal morality, Whitehead suggested, is because the universe contains a "character of permanent rightness."[89]

Given the ontological principle, of course, we can intuit the rightness in the universe only by means of nonsensory perceptions of God. "There is a unity in the universe," wrote Whitehead, "enjoying value and (by its immanence) sharing value."[90]

As indicated above, ethical intuitionism has in recent times been disparaged. But the major complaint has been that, as expressed by Mackie and Williams, any intuition of moral norms would be by means of a *special faculty*, hence by a way of knowing entirely different from our normal way of learning about things beyond our own minds.

But that complaint by Mackie and Williams was based on their sensate empiricism. Whitehead's position, by contrast, was that we learn about moral norms through the same mode of perception through which we learn about mathematical objects, logical principles, rational norms, the reality of causation, and the reality of an actual world.

There have indeed been problems with ethical intuitionism as it was commonly presented. One problem was that some advocates suggested that a moral code could be based on intuition alone, without support from cosmology. Referring to thinkers such as August Comte and Jeremy Bentham as two advocates of this view, Whitehead criticized their view for accepting moral norms as "ultimate moral intuitions, clear matter of fact, requiring no justification."[91]

Ethical intuition, in Whitehead's view, is merely one element, albeit an essential one, in a moral philosophy, just as moral minimalism is, in Walzer's view, merely an element, albeit an essential one, in a thick morality. Accordingly, Whitehead's philosophy can be used to flesh out Walzer's thick and thin morality. The nonsensory perceptions of moral principles inherent in God, as the "unity in the universe," account for the reiterations that constitute the makings of a natural moral law. Of course, people can be affected by the rightness in things without knowing that they are being affected by God. People can be highly moral without "believing in God." But the development of an adequate *moral philosophy* is another matter.

CONCLUSION

To have a self-consistent worldview, it appears, philosophers cannot explain our moral beliefs without reference to something beyond the totality of finite things, something from which we receive moral norms as well as mathematical truths.

This does not mean, to be sure, that our moral beliefs derive wholly from perceptions of the deity of the universe: In our moral convictions, moral norms are always intermixed with cultural conditioning, tradition, bias, and ignorance, so that the beliefs on which we form our ethical positions are often in tension with the underlying moral ideal. Accordingly, moral intuitions should be taken to establish only *prima facie*, not absolute, duties. In such situations—which are *most* situations—we can decide what should be done only through rational deliberation, taking into account all the relevant facts as well as all the relevant moral values.

A final comment: It is understandable that, given the long period during which philosophers assumed that all factual questions could in principle be answered without reference to a divine reality, there would be great resistance to the idea that moral norms could only be explained by referring to something divine.

Jeffrie Murphy, a highly respected professor of law and philosophy, has spoken to this issue. Having said that for him it was "very difficult—perhaps impossible—to embrace religious convictions," he wrote that "the idea that fundamental moral values may require [religious] convictions . . . appears to force choices that some of us would prefer not to make." However, he added, "it still might be true for all of that."[92]

ENDNOTES

1. Alfred North Whitehead, *Essays in Science and Philosophy* (Philosophical Library, 1947), 80.

2. Henry Sidgwick, ed. E. M. Sidgwick and A. Sidgwick, *The Methods of Ethics* (1874; seventh edition, 1907), Appendix I.

3. Whitehead, *Modes of Thought* (Free Press, 1968), 19.

4. John Passmore, *Philosophical Reasoning* (Basic Books, 1961), 60; Alfred North Whitehead, *Process and Reality: An Essay in Cosmology*, corrected edition, ed. David Ray Griffin and Donald W. Sherburne (1929; Free Press, 1978), 13.

5. John Mackie, *Ethics: Inventing Right and Wrong* (Penguin, 1977), 15.

6. Ibid., 17, 70–80.

7. Ibid., 24.

8. Ibid., 38, 40.

9. Ibid., 38–39.

10. Ibid., 48.

11. John Mackie, *The Miracle of Theism: Arguments for and against the Existence of God* (Clarendon, 1982), 1, 151.

12. Hilary Putnam, *Words and Life*, ed. James Conant (Harvard University Press, 1994), 170.

13. Gilbert Harman, *The Nature of Morality: An Introduction to Ethics* (Oxford University Press, 1977), 131–32.

14. Ibid., 11.

15. Ibid., 12-13.

16. Ibid., 131–32; emphasis added.

17. Gilbert Harman, "Is There a Single True Morality," in *Relativism: Interpretation and Confrontation*, ed. Michael Krausz (University of Notre Dame Press, 1989), 363–86, at 366; *The Nature of Morality*, 17.

18. Harman, "Is There a Single True Morality?" 365–66, 381.

19. Harman, *The Nature of Morality*, 8, 66.

20. Ibid., 9–10.

21. Ibid., 10.

22. Whitehead, *Modes of Thought*, 19.

23. Willard Van Quine, "Replies," Lewis Edwin Hahn and Paul Arthur Schilpp, eds., *The Philosophy of W. V. Quine,* Library of Living Philosophers, Vol. 18 (Open Court, 1986), 663–65.

24. Harman, "Is There a Single True Morality?" 366.

25. Bernard Williams, *Ethics and the Limits of Philosophy* (Harvard University Press, 1985), 22.

26. Ibid., 136, 149, 151–52.

27. Ibid., 94.

28. Bernard Williams, "Ethics and the Fabric of the World," in *Morality and Objectivity: A Tribute to J. L. Mackie*, ed. Ted Honderich (Routledge & Kegan Paul, 1985], 203–14, at 205; Williams, *Ethics and the Limits of Philosophy,* 53.

29. Martin Heidegger, "The Word of Nietzsche: 'God Is Dead,'" *The Question Concerning Technology: Heidegger's Critique of the Modern Age*, transl. William Lovett (Harper and Row, 1977), 61.

30. Richard Rorty, *Contingency, Irony, and Solidarity* (Cambridge

University Press, 1989), 20.

31. Ibid., 107–08.

32. Ibid., 15–17.

33. Ibid., 59.

34. Ibid., 3-5, 77.

35. Ibid., 44, 45.

36. Ibid., xv, 44-45, 53–54, 197.

37. Ibid., 191–92.

38. Ibid., 87.

39. Ibid., 68, 197, 87.

40. Charles Larmore, *The Morals of Modernity* (Cambridge University Press, 1966), 8, 86, 87, 89.

41. Ibid., 91–96.

42. Ibid., 86.

43. Ibid., 87, 99.

44. Ibid., 90.

45. Ibid., 100–02.

46. Ibid., 96-97, 62, 114, 8, 96.

47. Ibid., 115.

48. Ibid., 53, 51.

49. Ibid., 31–32, 40, 57, 62–63.

50. Ibid., 97, 215.

51. Ibid., 44.

52. Ibid., 92–93, 96–97.

53. Ibid., 96-98, 116.

54. Willard Van Quine, *From Stimulus to Science* (Harvard University Press, 1995), 14; *Theories and Things* (Harvard University Press, 1981), 14–15.

55. Ibid., 11–13.

56. Ibid., 22, 40.

57. Ibid., 40, 64.

58. Ronald Dworkin, *Religion without Theism* (Harvard University Press, 2013), 5.

59. Ibid., 1.

60. Ibid., 10.

61. Ibid., 12, 13.

62. Ibid., 22, 23.

63. Ibid., 9, 22, 27.

64. Ibid., 32.

65. Ibid., 31, 2, 3.

66. Ibid., 42.

67. Ibid., 42–43.

68. Ibid., 32.

69. Ibid., 10.

70. Ibid., 9, 30.

71. Ibid., 14.

72. Ibid., 49, 13.

73. Ibid., 2, 3.

74. Ibid., 14.

75. Ibid., 14–15.

76. Ibid., 17.

77. Larmore, *The Morals of Modernity*, 86.

78. Whitehead, *Process and Reality*, 151.

79. Ibid., 291.

80. Whitehead, *Modes of Thought*, 103.

81. Mackie, *Ethics*, 35, 38–39.

82. Michael Walzer, *Thick and Thin: Moral Argument at Home and Abroad* (University of Notre Dame Press, 1994), x.

83. Ibid., xi.

84. Gene Outka and John P. Reeder, Jr., eds., *Prospects for a Common*

Morality (Princeton University Press, 1992), 3.

85. Walzer, *Thick and Thin*, 4, 18.

86. Ibid., 17.

87. Ibid.

88. International lawyer Richard Falk, saying that naturalism holds that "the basis of human rights is prior to politics," calls naturalism "the essential ground for claiming that human rights are universally valid," *Human Rights and State Sovereignty* (Holmes and Meier, 1981), 43.

89. Alfred North Whitehead, *Religion in the Making* (1926; Fordham University Press, 1996), 61.

90. Whitehead, *Modes of Thought*, 119–20.

91. Alfred North Whitehead, *Adventures of Ideas* (Free Press, 1967), 37.

92. Jeffrie G. Murphy, "Afterword: Constitutionalism, Moral Skepticism, and Religious Belief," in *Constitutionalism: The Philosophical Dimension*, ed. Alan S. Rosenbaum (Greenwood, 1988), 239–49, at 248.

9

Logic and Rationality

Although logic and rationality are not the same, they are closely related, in that logic is basic to rationality and rationality would be impossible without logic. Indeed, Whitehead called logic "the general analysis of self-consistency."[1] In spite of this close relationship, self-consistency is one thing, the analysis of it is another thing. Also, there is more to rationality than self-consistency. So the two concepts can be discussed somewhat separately.

1. LOGIC

Just as mathematical objects and moral norms are indispensable for thought and yet pose problems, the same is true of logical truths. In fact, said Hilary Putnam, "the nature of mathematical truth" and "the nature of logical truth" are one and the same problem.[2] Accordingly, we have the same twofold problem: Where do logical truths exist, and how can they be effective in the world?[3]

WHAT IS LOGIC?

A prior question, of course, is: What is logic? This is a subject about which there have been great advances since the late 19th century, starting

204

especially with Gottlob Frege (1848–1925),[4] whose work then led to *Principia Mathematica* by Alfred North Whitehead and Bertrand Russell.[5] Frege reaffirmed the traditional idea that logic is, in Thomas Nagel's words, "the examination of mind-independent conceptions." In a fuller description, Nagel said that logic is "the system of concepts that makes thought possible and to which any language usable by thinking beings must conform."[6]

This point can be illustrated with the logical principle known as *modus ponens*, which says: "If p then q; p holds; therefore q is true." For example:

- If it is raining outside, my balcony is wet.

- It is raining outside.

- Therefore, my balcony is wet.

"No 'language' in which modus ponens was not a valid inference," wrote Nagel, "would be used to express thoughts at all."[7]

To say that logic consists of "mind-independent conceptions" is to say that logical truths are not dependent upon human thinking. Rather, a logical thought has a content, which is, in Nagel's words, "a logical proposition which would be true even if I were not in existence or were unable to think it. The thought is therefore something independent of my mind."[8]

Whitehead had earlier expressed this view. In discussing the need for a philosophical worldview to be logical, he added that "logical notions must themselves find their places in the scheme of philosophic notions."[9] In Whitehead's scheme of such notions, logical notions consist of "propositions," which are *potential matters of fact,* or "tales that might be told" about particular things.[10]

PROPOSITIONS AND VERBAL STATEMENTS

Rather than being a verbal statement, a proposition is a *meaning,* which could be expressed in a verbal statement. Because a proposition is distinct from a verbal statement, one and the same proposition can be expressed in various verbal statements. For example, these three sentences—"It is raining," "Es regnet," and "Il pleut"—all express the same proposition. The proposition is the *meaning* that is expressed in each of these sentences.[11]

A proposition must be either true or false.[12] Take, for example, the statement that "the first bound set of notes from Ludwig Wittgenstein's lectures was blue." This statement expresses a proposition, a meaning, that is either true or false. In this case, the proposition is true.

HOW CAN PROPOSITIONS BE GRASPED?

Because propositions, being meanings, are not linguistic entities, grasping propositions is distinct from learning a language. As meanings, propositions are not physical entities, so they cannot be seen, heard, touched, tasted, or smelt. How, then, can logical truths affect us? Colin McGinn raised this problem, asking "how a physical organism can be subject to the norms of rationality. How, for example, does *modus ponens* get its grip on the causal transitions between mental states?"[13] Being a materialist, who as such rejected the idea of propositions as non-physical entities, McGinn was expressing true puzzlement.

To explain Whitehead's answer to this question, it is necessary to introduce one of his technical terms: prehension. To prehend something is, as the term "prehensile" indicates, to grasp something. For Whitehead, it meant, more particularly, grasping something by taking it in, by incorporating it.

Prehensions are of various types, depending upon the objects being grasped. There are "physical prehensions," which refer not to what are normally called physical (material) things, but to prehensions of entities that are actual, rather than simply possible. The prehensions of merely possible entities, by contrast, are called "conceptual prehensions," which grasp possibilities such as numbers and colors. There are also "propositional prehensions," in which the non-actual entity prehended is a proposition. The various types of propositions include logical propositions.[14]

The Whiteheadian answer to McGinn's question is that we have nonsensory perceptions, one type of which is the prehension of logical propositions. Accordingly, logic, just like mathematical and moral objects, presupposes nonsensory perception.

LOGIC AND GOD

Moreover, by Whitehead's "ontological principle," just as mathematical objects and moral norms can exist and be effective only by virtue of something actual, the same is true of logical truths. Without reference to a cosmic actuality, the Platonic and Benacerraf problems would pose insuperable problems of understanding the status of logic as well as that of mathematics and morality.

Being a materialist, McGinn rejects the idea that a conceptual problem could be solved by reference to an omnipresent actuality, whether Gawd or God. But although traditional philosophical theology was wrong to say that logical truths point to the existence of Gawd (who allegedly created them),[15] the existence of logical truth does seem to point to the existence of a divine actuality, through which logical principles and truths can exist and be effective in the world.

LOGIC AND COMPUTER SCIENCE

An impressive new way in which logic has proved to be effective in the world is its use in computer science. Inspired by Wigner's essay, "The Unreasonable Effectiveness of Mathematics in the Natural Sciences," a group of computer scientists published a long paper in 2001 entitled "On the Unusual Effectiveness of Logic in Computer Science." Whereas logic has been very important for mathematics, the authors reported, "logic has turned out to be significantly more effective in computer science than it has been in mathematics." Indeed, they say, logic has been called "the calculus of computer science."[16]

An early discussion of this connection was a 1988 essay by Martin Davis entitled "Influences of Mathematical Logic on Computer Science," in which he said:

> When I was a student, even the topologists regarded mathematical logicians as living in outer space. Today the connections between logic and computers are a matter of engineering practice at every level of computer organization.

Davis then gave examples of how logical concepts have been crucial in computer science, such as the influence of logic on the design of programming languages, and the connections between digital circuits and Boolean logic.[17]

Then in 2000, Davis published a book called *The Universal Computer*, in which he traced the connection between logic and computation through the contributions of people from Leibniz to Boole, Frege, and Turing.[18]

In the essay "On the Unusual Effectiveness of Logic in Computer Science," the authors, after giving several examples, point out the difference between their argument and Wigner's: Whereas the phenomena of the natural sciences are not human creations, the phenomena of computer science are, which could explain "why the use of logic in computer science is both appropriate and successful." For this reason "the effectiveness of logic in computer science is perhaps not mysterious or unreasonable." Nevertheless, they add, this effectiveness is "still quite remarkable and unusual."[19]

In any case, the extraordinary effectiveness of logic in computer science provides visible evidence that logic, in spite of having ideal rather than physical existence, can be effective in "the real world."

2. HOW IS RATIONALITY POSSIBLE?

As stated earlier, logic makes rationality possible. To think rationally about any topic, be it physics, engineering, or theology, is to operate in terms of rules of rationality.

It has traditionally been thought that these rules are *a priori*, that is, prior to experience. However, in a famous essay entitled "Two Dogmas of Empiricism," Willard Quine rejected this idea, saying that the most fundamental laws of logic are in principle revisable. His Harvard colleague Putnam initially agreed, but later wrote an essay entitled "There Is At Least One A Priori Truth," in which he argued that the principle of noncontradiction is an absolutely unrevisable *a priori* truth.[20]

Charles Larmore has also made this point, emphasizing that the absence of objective rational rules "would mean that the idea that we *ought* to avoid self-contradiction is merely a preference, with no inherent authority." Saying that this Nietzschean outlook "boggles the mind," Larmore wrote:

> Imagine thinking that even so basic a rule of reasoning as the avoidance of contradiction has no more authority than what we choose to give it. Imagine thinking that we could just as well have willed the opposite, seeking out contradictions and believing each and every one. Has anyone the slightest idea of what it would be like really to believe this?[21]

However, although it is easy to declare (correctly) that rationality involves *a priori* principles, the question of how rationality is possible is more difficult.

MATERIALIST PHILOSOPHIES

Rationality is made impossible most obviously by materialist philosophies, which insist that all causation is *efficient* causation, meaning the influence of one thing or event on another. By contrast, the rational activity of a philosopher of science is action in terms of some norm, such as the norm of self-consistency. Rational activity is, in other words, an example of *formal* and *final* causation. Philosopher Jaegwon Kim made this point, saying that thinking of ourselves as capable of mental causation is closely related to thinking of ourselves "as reflective agents capable of deliberation and evaluation—that is, . . . as agents capable of acting in accordance with a norm."[22]

One problem with the materialist worldview is that it has no room for such activity, because the mind is equated with the brain and the brain's activities are said to be, like everything else, determined by the causal activities of the brain's elementary parts, which in turn are assumed to be fully determined by efficient causes.

McGinn acknowledged this problem in his question, "How, for example, does *modus ponens* get its grip on the causal transitions between mental states?"[23] The problem is that to operate in terms of *modus ponens* is to operate so as to avoid self-contradiction, which in no way can be understood mechanistically. By continuing to affirm materialism, McGinn illustrated Putnam's complaint that most science-based schools of thought have produced "philosophies which leave no room for the rational activity of philosophy," with the result that "these views are self-refuting."[24]

Such philosophies are self-refuting because they have such restricted understandings of what can be included in "naturalism." Norms in mathematics, science, and ethics point to the need for an "expansion of our conception of the natural order to include," Nagel said, "the source of our active capacity to think our way beyond those starting points."[25]

INFINITE THOUGHTS

However, Nagel added, understanding how rationality is possible within a naturalistic worldview is difficult, because reasoning involves infinite thoughts. The infinity of thought is easiest to see, he said, with regard to arithmetical reasoning. "Once we are able to count at all, we have the basis for realizing that every number has a successor, larger by one," so the number of arithmetical truths is infinite.[26]

To insert a personal note: When my brother and I were quite young, we decided to start writing down all the numbers, beginning with 1. After doing this for a day or so, we realized that we could continue doing this the rest of our lives without completing the task.

The same fact, Nagel pointed out, is true of logical truths. Expressing a resulting puzzle, Nagel said: "How is it possible for finite beings like us to think infinite thoughts." This question, Nagel believed, has "no imaginable answer."[27] To grasp how puzzling it is for "finite beings like us" to think infinite thoughts, be they arithmetical or logical, remember that we have evolved from bacteria. Imagining how people such as Frege, Whitehead, Russell, and Gödel evolved out of bacteria is not easy.

A RELIGIOUS ANSWER?

Nagel knows that some people give "the religious [answer]," but he rejected it, partly because he does not "understand the idea of God well enough to see such a theory as truly explanatory."[28] One could respond by pointing out that it makes no sense to speak of "the idea of God," because there are dozens of ideas of God.

But Nagel also admitted that he did not *want* the religious answer to be true, because he shared in the widespread "fear of religion." He wrote:

It isn't just that I don't believe in God and, naturally, hope that I'm right in my belief. It's that I hope there is no God! I don't want there to be a God; I don't want the universe to be like that.[29]

However, Nagel also pointed out that this reason for rejecting a religious answer was "somewhat ridiculous," for "it is just as irrational to be influenced in one's beliefs by the hope that God does not exist as by the hope that God does exist."[30]

Having said all of this, Nagel then observed that it would be difficult to avoid a position with no religious ring to it whatsoever. Noting that "the existence of mind is certainly a *datum* for the construction of a world picture," because the possibility of the existence of mind must be explained, he wrote:

I admit that this idea—that the capacity of the universe to generate organisms with minds capable of understanding the universe is itself somehow a fundamental feature of the universe—has a quasi-religious "ring" to it.[31]

However, he added, one could admit this "without going over to anything that should count literally as religious belief," since he was not implying "the existence of a divine person, or a world soul."[32]

It is true that his admission does not imply religion in either of these senses. But it is less clear that the question of how we can participate in logical truths and rationality more generally can be answered without positing a cosmic mind.

In evaluating Nagel's hope that "God does not exist," it is also relevant to know what he understands by "God." Having admitted in his 1997 book, *The Last Word,* that he did not "understand the idea of God well," he in his 2012 book, *Mind and Cosmos,* gave indications of what he meant by theism, saying:

- "[A] theistic explanation [of our capacities] poses the famous problem of evil."

- "If God exists, he is not part of the natural order but a free agent not governed by natural laws. . . . [W]hatever he does directly cannot be part of that order."

- "[Theism's] interventionist hypotheses amount to a denial that there is a comprehensive natural order."[33]

As these statements show, Nagel understood theism to be belief in Gawd.

A THIRD WAY

Besides indicating what he meant by a religious view of the universe, Nagel's *Mind and* Cosmos also gave good reasons for rejecting what he called "the materialist neo-Darwinian conception of nature." That type of naturalism, Nagel said, would:

- undermine our confidence in "our own cognitive capacities";

- weaken "the authority of reason";

- weaken "our confidence in the objective truth of our mathematical or scientific reasoning";

- weaken even more "our moral and normative capacities";

- "require us to give up moral realism—the natural conviction that our moral judgments are true or false independent of our beliefs";

- and mean "that we shouldn't take any of our convictions seriously, including the scientific world picture on which evolutionary naturalism itself depends."[34]

Accordingly, rightly finding both of the best-known worldviews—supernaturalism and neo-Darwinism—unsatisfactory, Nagel was confident that there must be a third view that avoids the problems of these positions—a third one that is "neither a [neo-Darwinian] naturalistic account nor a Cartesian theistic one."[35] His hope, Nagel said, is "the hope for an expanded but still naturalistic understanding that avoids psychophysical reductionism." Explaining more fully, he continued:

> The essential character of such an understanding would be to explain the appearance of life, consciousness, reason, and knowledge neither as accidental side effects of the physical laws of nature nor as the result of intentional intervention in nature from without but as an unsurprising if not inevitable consequence of the order that governs the natural world from within.[36]

A version of the third way for which Nagel hopes is presented in the present book. This third way does, to be sure, include a "world soul," which Nagel rejected. But in rejecting such a notion,[37] Nagel evidently was thinking of it as having the attributes of the traditional deity, so that the world soul would be a version of Gawd. The present book, by speaking of a world soul, describes a view of deity that is radically different from Gawd—a deity that is not an omnipotent, supernatural being, a deity that exerts influence by being part of (rather than intervening into) the normal cause-effect relations, and that, therefore, does not create a problem of evil.

ENDNOTES

1. Alfred North Whitehead, *Process and Reality: An Essay in Cosmology,* corrected edition, ed. David Ray Griffin and Donald W. Sherburne (1929; Free Press, 1978), 26, 192.

2. Hilary Putnam, *Words and Life*, ed. James Conant (Harvard University Press, 1994), 500.

3. Putnam himself would not have asked these questions, given his view that ethics should be discussed apart from ontology; see Hilary Putnam, *Ethics without Ontology* (Harvard University Press, 2005). But how can a realistic philosophy of morality be advocated apart from a philosophy of what exists?

4. See Edward N. Zalta, "Gottlob Frege," Stanford Encyclopedia of Philosophy, 25 July 2014.

5. Whitehead and Russell published *Principia Mathematica,* which contained three volumes, in 1910, 1912, and 1913. A second edition, with both of their names on it, was published in 1925 (Vol. 1) and 1927 (Vols. 2 & 3). However, pointed out Ray Monk in his biography of Russell, Whitehead had nothing to do with the second edition. Russell had wanted to produce a second edition that would "work out the technical consequences of the fundamental changes to the basic theory of logic in the book that would be required by an acceptance of [Ludwig] Wittgenstein's work." However, "Whitehead was deeply unsympathetic to Wittgenstein's work and thus to the general lines on which Russell sought to 'improve' their joint undertaking." This new edition, said Monk, "was unsatisfactory in almost every respect . . . and was disliked by both

Wittgenstein and Whitehead." Having been under the impression that "a general statement would appear in the new edition, making it clear that Russell alone was responsible for the new additions," Whitehead "wrote to *Mind* dissociating himself from the new material that Russell had added to it." (Russell had sent the new material to Whitehead but, after receiving no reply from him, went ahead and sent it, with Whitehead's name on it, to the publisher.) With respect to Russell's original hopes for mathematical logic, said Monk, "the second edition of *Principia Mathematica* represents a major step backwards." Ray Monk, *Bertrand Russell: 1921–1970, The Ghost of Madness* (Free Press, 2001), 44–48. (I am grateful to the late Tod Fletcher for discovering Monk's work.)

6. Thomas Nagel, *The Last Word* (Oxford University Press, 1997), 37–38.

7. Ibid., 39, 56.

8. Ibid., 66.

9. Whitehead, *Process and Reality*, 3.

10. Ibid., 256.

11. Ibid., 11–13.

12. Ibid., 256.

13. Colin McGinn, *The Problem of Consciousness: Essays Toward a Resolution* (Basil Blackwell, 1991), 23n.

14. Whitehead, *Process and Reality*, 164, 184, 185.

15. Just as William Lane Craig rejects the notion that numbers are eternal objects, because this idea would imply a restriction on Gawd's omnipotence, he for the same reason rejects the idea that logic is uncreated. See William Lane Craig (interviewed by Kevin Harris), "God, Abstract Objects, Platonism and Logic," Reasonable Faith, 2 August 2011.

16. Joseph Y. Halpern et al., "On the Unusual Effectiveness of Logic in Computer Science," *Bulletin of Symbolic Language*, 7/2 (January 2001).

17. Martin Davis, "Influences of Mathematical Logic on Computer Science," in Rolf Herken, ed., *The Universal Turing Machine: A Half-Century Survey* (Oxford University Press, 1988), 315–26.

18. Martin Davis, *The Universal Computer* (W. W. Norton, 2000).

19. Halpern et al., "On the Unusual Effectiveness of Logic in Computer Science."

20. W. V. Quine, *From A Logical Point of View* (Harvard University Press, 1953); Hilary Putnam, *Realism and Reason* (Cambridge University Press, 1985), 98–114.

21. Charles Larmore, *The Morals of Modernity* (Cambridge University Press, 1966), 86, 87, 99.

22. Jaegwon Kim, *Supervenience and Mind: Selected Philosophical Essays* (Cambridge: Cambridge University Press, 1993), 215.

23. McGinn, *The Problem of Consciousness*, 23n.

24. Hilary Putnam, *Realism and Reason* (Cambridge University Press, 1985), 191.

25. Thomas Nagel, *Mind and Cosmos: Why the Materialist Neo-Darwinian Conception of Nature Is Almost Certainly False* (Oxford University Press, 2012), 72.

26. Nagel, *The Last Word*, 70.

27. Ibid., 74.

28. Ibid., 75.

29. Ibid., 130.

30. Ibid., 131.

31. Ibid., 132.

32. Ibid.

33. Nagel, *Mind and Cosmos*, 25.

34. Ibid., 27–28.

35. Ibid., 31.

36. Ibid., 32.

37. Nagel, *The Last Word*, 132.

10

Truth

Although truth was central to the previous chapter, there the issue was truth as a norm—a norm to guide thought. As such, truth in that chapter was used, like the previous chapters in Part II, to argue for the reality of a cosmic actuality influencing the world. It hence dealt with what Whitehead called the "primordial nature of God." The present chapter is concerned with the existence of factual truth, including historical truth, as pointing to the influence of the world on the cosmic actuality, hence on what Whitehead called "the consequent nature of God."

The reality of factual truth is obvious—so obvious that most people would wonder why it needs to be stated. For example, if I go to get a blood test, I need to tell the nurse whether I had any food to eat that day. If people telephone my house asking for my wife, I need to let them know whether she is home. Or, if she is home, but does not want to talk to anyone, I need to decide how best to respond. Without the assumption that there is a truth about matters, all of our conversations would be meaningless.

The reality of truth is also presupposed in the discussions in the previous chapters. Is there a cosmic agent that can interrupt the normal cause-effect processes? Could this agent have prevented all the world's pain and suffering? Has human civilization arisen out of billions of years of evolution, or was it created only a few thousand years ago? Without the assumption that there is a truth about these issues, all such debates would be meaningless.

The same is the case with regard to controversies about fateful historical events: Is the standard account about the Pearl Harbor attack accurate? Was President Kennedy really killed by Lee Harvey Oswald? Were the 9/11 attacks engineered by Muslims? With all such questions, we presuppose that the answer is either true or false. Otherwise, there would be no debates about them.

1. COMPETING THEORIES OF TRUTH

If the reality of truth is presupposed, the next question is what we mean by "truth." There are, to be sure, many ways to use the term, such as speaking of a "true friend" or being "true to oneself." But with regard to factual matters, truth is the *correspondence of a proposition with the reality to which it refers*. For example, if witnesses at a criminal trial testify that they saw Joe Jones shoot Sam Smith, their testimony is true if and only if Jones really shot Smith and they actually witnessed this shooting. This should be too obvious to state—that an assertion is true if and only if it corresponds to what really happened.

EPISTEMIC THEORIES

However, during recent decades, many philosophers have rejected this conception of truth, offering alternative definitions. Most of these alternatives involve some version of an *epistemic* theory of truth. Whereas *truth as* correspondence says that facts are either true or false independently of what anyone thinks, the epistemic conception says that the truth of a proposition is dependent on human beliefs.

For example, assertions may be said to be true if they are rationally justifiable: Richard Rorty equated truth with "warranted assertability." More flippantly, Rorty said that truth is "what our peers will . . . let us get away with saying."[1] With regard to what provides a warrant for an assertion, philosophers who advocate an epistemic theory of truth commonly understood warrant in terms of the so-called coherence theory of truth, according to which a proposition is true if, and only if, it has a place in a coherent system. But all such definitions are problematic.

PROBLEMS WITH EPISTEMIC THEORIES

The primary problem with epistemic conceptions is that they lead to an unacceptable relativism. The assertion that the Earth is flat was at one time warranted. The idea that the Earth is the stationary center of the universe once fit within a coherent system of propositions. If you had lived in Europe five centuries ago, most of your peers would have let you get away with the claim that the Earth is only a few thousand years old. Surely we do not want to say that these ideas were true at one time. If we define truth in terms of justified human beliefs, this type of relativism to time and place is entailed.

Because of the problems created by epistemic theories of truth, some erstwhile advocates turned against it. At one time, Rorty had supported his position by appeal to Hilary Putnam's position. But Putnam later rejected epistemic theories of truth in favor of "common-sense realism." Rorty had attempted, Putnam said, "to show that the whole idea that our words and thoughts sometimes do and sometimes do not 'agree with' or 'correspond to' or 'represent' a reality outside themselves ought to be rejected as entirely empty." But Putnam later dissociated himself from that attempt.[2]

TRUTH AS CORRESPONDENCE

In a correspondence conception of truth, the truth of a proposition is independent of human beliefs; it depends entirely on the relation of the proposition to the state of affairs to which it refers. For example, take the proposition expressed by the sentence, "William James taught philosophy at Harvard." This proposition is true if and only if James taught philosophy at Harvard. Whereas "only if" means that James's having taught philosophy at Harvard is a necessary condition of the proposition's truth, "if" means that his having taught philosophy there is a sufficient condition. So James's having taught philosophy at Harvard is a necessary and sufficient condition for the truth of the proposition.

Nothing else is relevant. It matters not whether we have reached intersubjective agreement with our peers that James taught philosophy at Harvard. Many people today do not know that James taught philosophy at Harvard, so it might be impossible to reach agreement on this question. Some people, knowing his book *The Principles of Psychology*, may know that he taught psychology at Harvard but do not realize that he later changed to the philosophy department. That is entirely irrelevant to the truth of the assertion, which depends simply on the fact that James taught philosophy at Harvard.

TRUTH AS CORRESPONDENCE AS PRESUPPOSED

In a book entitled simply *Truth*, Paul Horwich said that the "common-sense notion [is] that truth is a kind of 'correspondence with the facts.'" The alternatives to correspondence theories have been problematic, he said, precisely because "they don't accommodate the 'correspondence' intuition."[3]

Although this point may seem too obvious to state, many modern philosophers have rejected it. Rorty, for example, rejected the claim that "some nonlinguistic state of the world . . . 'makes a belief true' by 'corresponding' to it." Rorty admitted, to be sure, that we have the "intuition that truth involves correspondence." However, he said, we should "do our best to *stop having* [this intuition]."[4] However, Rorty himself was not able to stop having it. For example:

- Having argued that truth is "made rather than found," Rorty spoke of "what was true in the Romantic idea that truth is made rather than found." Rorty thereby implied that it is true that some Romantics said that truth is made rather than found.

- Rorty said that this Romantic view expressed "the realization that a talent for speaking differently, rather than for arguing well, is the chief instrument of cultural change." Rorty thereby implied that this account corresponds to the facts about how cultural change occurs.

- Rorty told us that William James rejected the idea of truth as correspondence. In making this claim, Rorty implied that what he said about James corresponded to what James actually held[5] (which is, incidentally, not true[6]).

Rorty thereby illustrated the fact that it is impossible to deny, without falling into performative contradiction (as discussed above in the Introduction), the idea that the truth of an assertion consists in its correspondence to a reality beyond itself.

2. ARGUMENTS VS. TRUTH AS CORRESPONDENCE

However, some philosophers, perhaps concerned less with self-consistency than with other ideas to which they are committed, have argued that truth cannot be understood as the correspondence of a proposition to the facts, because this idea does not make sense. Here are four such arguments.

TRUTH AS VERIFICATION

One of the standard epistemic theories of truth held that the meaning of a proposition was its mode of verification. This idea was central to the movement known as "logical positivism." Although logical positivism is now generally rejected, its equation of meaning with verification has lingered.

This equation has led many philosophers to assume that to *define* truth as correspondence between proposition and reality is to prescribe a method of *verifying* that proposition. Then, arguing that we have no direct access to "reality in itself" apart from our ideas about it, they conclude that the notion of truth as correspondence must be rejected.

However, although the issue of direct access to reality is important, the question of what the truth *means* can be discussed independently. We can know what a proposition means, and what it would imply to consider it true, apart from there being a possible mode of verifying it.

For example, a recent president of the United States publicly expressed contrition for his wrongdoing and asked forgiveness. Some people believed the contrition to be genuine, whereas others suspected that it was feigned for political purposes. Most of us have no way of completely verifying whether the expressed contrition reflected sincerity or political expediency—or some combination thereof. But in spite of this lack of any means to verify the truth of the president's declarations of contrition, we know what they *mean*. Those who were uncertain as to whether he was genuinely contrite understand what they were in doubt about, which is whether the emotion that we call "contrition" was really experienced by the president or merely feigned.

Whitehead distinguished clearly between truth and verification. Important to this difference is the distinction between a proposition as such and a "propositional feeling," in which that proposition is prehended by someone. The proposition's truth or falsity depends on its relation to its *logical* subject (the thing or event to which it refers), not its relation to any *prehending* subjects.[7]

These prehending subjects may make a judgment about the proposition's truth, and may even set out to verify or falsify it. But these beliefs and operations will not affect the truth or falsity of the proposition, because this truth or falsity obtained prior to the proposition's being prehended by anyone.[8] In line with this point, Whitehead affirmed "a 'correspondence' theory of the truth and falsehood of propositions," while speaking of "coherence" and "pragmatic tests" in regard to attempts to *ascertain* the truth-value of particular propositions.[9]

Putnam was only one of a number of philosophers who, after having first affirmed an epistemic theory of truth, later changed their minds. For example, the University of California's Donald Davidson had long rejected correspondence theories on the basis of the "usual complaint" that "it makes no sense to suggest that it is somehow possible to compare one's words or beliefs with the world." With reference to the early Davidson, Rorty based much of his own case against correspondence on this complaint. But Davidson later said: "This complaint against correspondence theories is not sound [because] it depends on assuming that some form of epistemic theory is correct."[10]

CORRESPONDENCE AS IDENTITY

A second argument that correspondence is nonsensical is based on the assumption that to affirm *correspondence* between a proposition and its referent is to affirm their *identity*. To affirm that a proposition, such as "Caesar crossed the Rubicon," corresponds to the event itself is absurd, goes the argument, because it is ridiculous to hold that this proposition is identical with the event of Caesar's actually crossing the Rubicon.

However, to affirm a correspondence between a proposition and an event is not to affirm their identity. The false idea that correspondence means identity is derivative from the fact that a true proposition and the reality to which it refers contain the same elements: the same subject and the same predicate. For example, let's say that my wife believes that Bill Snyder became angry yesterday. If Bill did indeed become angry yesterday, then the proposition and the actual event contained the same subject, "Bill Snyder," and the same predicate, "became angry yesterday."

It could seem, therefore, that they are identical, which would imply that propositions would be able to exert agency. Accordingly, the ontological principle—that only actualities, not also propositions, can exert agency—would be contradicted.

However, Whitehead guarded against this interpretation. Although the proposition and the actual event contain the same elements, they contain these elements in different ways. The actuality contains those elements in "the mode of realization," whereas the proposition contains them only in "the mode of abstract possibility." Accordingly, Whitehead added, "[an actuality] and a proposition belong to different categories of being. Their identification is mere nonsense."[11]

PROPOSITIONS EQUATED WITH VERBAL STATEMENTS

Some claims that the correspondence notion of truth is nonsensical are based on the assumption that, when truth is defined as the correspondence of a proposition with the reality to which it refers, the word *proposition* means a *verbal statement*, a *sentence*.

One resulting problem is that it is often nonsensical to say that propositions (understood as verbal statements) are either true or false, because language can be very ambiguous. For example, it is meaningless to ask whether the statement "Caesar crossed the Rubicon" is true or false: It may be understood differently by the speaker and various hearers, depending upon (say) whether "Caesar" is understood to refer to an emperor, a puppy, or a movie star, and whether "the Rubicon" is understood to refer to a local stream, a river in Italy, or an irrevocable decision.

However, as clarified in the previous chapter, a proposition is not the same as a verbal statement. Rather, the proposition is the *meaning* that may be expressed and/or evoked by a verbal statement. The notion of correspondence applies only to a proposition. To call a verbal statement true is, therefore, really a short-hand way of speaking. It is a way of asserting, for example, that the proposition that a speaker *intended to express* corresponds with the facts in question. Or it may be a way of saying that the proposition that was *evoked in a hearer's mind* corresponds with reality—a proposition that might be quite different from the one intended by the speaker. The one may be true and the other false. This ambiguity does not mean, however, that the notion of truth as correspondence should be rejected, but only that we need to be alert to the distinction between verbal statements and propositions.

Whitehead gave great attention to this distinction. Warning against "trust in language as an adequate expression of propositions," he said: "It is merely credulous to accept verbal phrases as adequate statements of propositions." Although some thinkers "presuppose that language does enunciate well-defined propositions," Whitehead said, "This is quite untrue. Language is thoroughly indeterminate."[12]

However, once this distinction has been clearly made, it can be said that the practice of referring to verbal statements as either true or false is not wholly wrong, because such statements can be truth-bearers in a secondary, derivative sense. Although truth is a relation that *directly* applies to the relation between a proposition and that to which it refers, "There is," said Whitehead, "an indirect truth-relation of the sounds or of the visual marks on paper to the propositions conveyed." This is the case because, within any particular group of people, "There is a right and a wrong use of any particular language."[13]

Any human society, in order to communicate, must have widely shared understandings of the meanings of words and phrases, perhaps enshrined in dictionaries. Because of these shared understandings, linguistic statements have the capacity to evoke propositions in the conscious experience of readers and auditors that are identical with, or at least similar to, the propositions that the writer or speaker intended to convey.

The common practice is acceptable, therefore, if we keep in mind that verbal statements can be said to be true or false only in an indirect or derivative sense. In any case, the fact that language is indeterminate does not undermine the idea that truth means correspondence.

MATERIALISM VS. PROPOSITIONS

A fourth reason to reject the idea that truth means correspondence arises from the widespread acceptance of materialism, because it prevents a distinction between a proposition and a sentence. A sentence, whether spoken or written, is a material thing, but a proposition, as the *meaning* expressed or evoked by the sentence, is not.

According to a materialist ontology, the universe contains nothing but material entities, so propositions, understood as nonmaterial meanings, cannot exist.[14] This view provided Rorty's main argument against truth as correspondence. Truth must be a property of sentences, he said, not of propositions understood as meanings distinct from sentences. Although this may seem like a small distinction, the denial of the existence of propositions leads to drastic conclusions.

For example, the evolutionary sciences have taught us all sorts of things that were true before human beings arose—for example, that the universe had existed for billions of years or that chimpanzees evolved from bacteria. If truth is a property only of sentences, we cannot consider such facts to have been true prior to the human discovery of them, because, as Rorty put it, "where there are no sentences there is no truth." Accordingly, he said: "Truth cannot be out there—cannot exist independently of the human mind."[15]

On this point, Rorty at one time had the support of Putnam, who said: "It is statements (not abstract entities called 'propositions') that are true or false." This view led Putnam to make paradoxical assertions, such as: "While it is true that the stars would still have existed even if language users had not evolved, it is not the case that sentences would have existed. There would have still been a world, but there would not have been any truths."[16]

However, if it is now true that there would have been stars even if language users had never emerged, we cannot avoid saying that *it is true that* there were stars even before the rise of language users. And yet Putnam (at one time) and Rorty had to try to deny this, because of their materialistic rejection of propositions.

Given the fact that materialism leads to self-contradictory statements about truth, the need for self-consistency with regard to truth

provides one more reason, beyond those in previous chapters, for rejecting materialism.

In sum, there are no sound arguments against the idea that truth is
the correspondence of a proposition to its referent.

3. TRUTH AND GOD

Many philosophers and theologians have argued that truth, understood
as the correspondence of propositions with the realities to which they
refer, imply the existence of God. For many modern philosophers, one
of the attractions of epistemic theories of truth is that they undermine
that argument. But now that most philosophers have given up epistemic
theories, the question again arises whether factual truth implies theism,
in the sense of belief in an actuality with all-inclusive experience. This
question can be approached by considering whether truth could exist
if atheism were true.

ATHEIST THOUGHT EXPERIMENT

If the universe contained only a plurality of finite perspectives, there
would be no perspective that corresponds with the general nature of
reality, let alone one that correctly reflects the concrete events that have
occurred. Experience would consist of nothing but a vast plurality of
perspectives, with no impartial perspective that includes all of the partial
perspectives. These partial perspectives would often have radically different perspectives on the truth about this or that. There would, accordingly, be no place where truth as such—sometimes called *Truth with
a capital T*—could exist. But this would leave us with a paradox: The
ultimate truth about reality is that there is no ultimate truth.

A PLACE FOR TRUTH TO EXIST

This realization is one of the reasons why Whitehead, the erstwhile
agnostic or perhaps even atheist, came to affirm the reality of a divine
being who prehends the world in its entirety. He wrote:

> The truth itself is nothing else than how the composite
> natures of the organic actualities of the world obtain adequate

representation in the divine nature. Such representations com-
pose the 'consequent nature' of God, which evolves in its relationship to the evolving world.[17]

As to why the "truth itself" could not simply exist, even if there were
no God, Whitehead explained by employing the ontological principle,
saying:

> [T]here can be no determinate truth, correlating impartially
> the partial experiences of many actual entities, apart from one
> actual entity to which it can be referred.[18]

In other words, just as mathematical objects and moral norms could not
simply exist all by themselves—"in the void," as it were—the same is
the case with "truth itself." If, *per impossibile,* there were no God, there
would be no truth for scientists, philosophers, and theologians to be
seeking. We engage in this search without end because we presuppose
there is always a more complete truth to be reached.

GOD OR GAWD

Classical traditional theists, with their belief in Gawd, have generally said
that truth depends on theism. This point was especially emphasized by
St. Augustine.[19] But the deity in which he believed made the idea that
truth existed in God paradoxical. According to Augustine, the divine
reality is *immutable* in all respects, making it difficult to understand
how Gawd could embody the truth about history, with its ever-chang-
ing conditions. Augustine also held that the deity is entirely *impassible,*
which means that Gawd is not affected by what happens in the world.
Augustine also spoke of the divine being as *timelessly omnipotent,* so that
everything that happens in the world was ordained by Gawd from the
creation. So although the truth of the world is allegedly grounded in
Gawd, this truth is nothing but what deity had eternally ordained—a
paradoxical idea of truth at best.

By contrast, the idea that truth is in God, understood as temporal,
non-omnipotent, and receptive of the world, presents no paradoxes. In
Whitehead's terms, God has not only a primordial aspect but also a consequent aspect. Accordingly, we can understand—if only dimly—how

the "truth itself" could be the way in which the entities and events of the world receive "adequate representation in the divine nature," with these representations composing "the 'consequent nature' of God, which evolves in its relationship to the evolving world."[20]

To be sure, the non-classical version of traditional theism, according to which Gawd is *not* immutable, impassible, and timelessly omniscient, makes the idea that truth is in Gawd less self-paradoxical than it was for classical theism. But the idea of divine omnipotence by itself generates an insuperable problem of evil and the other problems discussed in Part I of this book, so there is more than sufficient reason for not thinking of the reality of factual truth as grounded in Gawd.

CONCLUSION

The argument of this chapter is that the existence of factual truth should be added to the list—along with the existence of mathematics, morality, logic, and rationality—of reasons for affirming the reality of God.

ENDNOTES

1. Richard Rorty, *Consequences of Pragmatism* (Minneapolis: University of Minneapolis Press, 1982), xxix–xxx; Rorty, *Philosophy and the Mirror of Nature* (Princeton University Press, 1979), 176.

2. Hilary Putnam, *Words and Life*, ed. James Conant (Harvard University Press, 1994), v, 297.

3. Paul Horwich, *Truth* (Basil Blackwell, 1990), 1.

4. Richard Rorty, *Contingency, Irony, and Solidarity* (Cambridge University Press, 1989), 5; Rorty, *Consequences of Pragmatism*, xxix–xxx.

5. Rorty, *Contingency, Irony, and Solidarity*, 7.

6. See Marcus Ford, *William James's Philosophy: A New Perspective* (University of Massachusetts Press, 1982), 59–74, or "William James," in David Ray Griffin et al., *Founders of Constructive Postmodern Philosophy: Peirce, James, Bergson, Whitehead, and Hartshorne* (State University of New York Press, 1993), 89–132, at 117–22.

7. Alfred North Whitehead, *Process and Reality: An Essay in Cosmology,*

corrected edition, ed. David Ray Griffin and Donald W. Sherburne (1929; Free Press, 1978), 258. "[T]he truth of a truth bearer consists," said William Alston, "in its relation to some 'transcendent' state of affairs, [not] in the epistemic virtues the former displays within our thought"; William P. Alston, *A Realist Conception of Truth* (Cornell University Press, 1996), 189.

8. The discussion here concerns propositions about the past, where the logical subject of the proposition is already fully determinate. The truth of propositions about the future can be affected by our actions, as in "self-fulfilling prophecies." William James's tendency to suggest a general "pragmatic" theory of truth on the basis of this characteristic of propositions about the future created much confusion, disguising the fact that James generally presupposed the notion of truth as correspondence, as Marcus Ford has shown; see note 5, above.

9. Whitehead, *Process and Reality*, 181, 191.

10. Donald Davidson, "The Structure and Content of Truth," *Journal of Philosophy* 87/6 (June 1990): 279–328, at 302.

11. Whitehead, *Adventures of Ideas*, 244–45.

12. Whitehead, *Process and Reality*, xiii, 11, 12.

13. Whitehead, *Adventures of Ideas*, 248–49.

14. It is widely agreed that the main reason for the denial of the reality of propositions is the nominalist rejection of "abstract entities" on the basis of a materialistic view of reality. See, for example, Alston, *A Realist Conception of Truth*, 9, 13; Paul Horwich, *Truth* (Oxford: Basil Blackwell, 1990), 92;, and Marian David, *Correspondence and Disquotation: An Essay on the Nature of Truth* (New York: Oxford University Press, 1994), 54–55.

15. Rorty, *Contingency*, 5.

16. Putnam, "Replies," *Philosophical Topics* 20/1 (Spring 1992): 347–408, at 368.

17. Whitehead, *Process and Reality*, 12.

18. Ibid., 13.

19. Ian Markham, *Truth and the Reality of God: An Essay in Natural Theology* (Bloomsbury T&T Clark, 2001).

20. Whitehead, *Process and Reality*, 12.

11

Religious Experience

Although traditional arguments for the existence of God did not generally have separate discussions of religious experience, this argument has been added to the list by some contemporary theists, most notably Oxford philosopher Richard Swinburne. Indeed, he has given this argument special status. Whereas the other arguments make theism "more probable than not," said Swinburne, adding the argument from religious experience makes theism "significantly more probable than not."[1]

If religious experience does indeed provide significant evidence for theism, the next question would be: What kind of theism? Much of the argumentation, assuming that religious experience would be supernatural, regards it as evidence for Gawd.

For example, in two books on the subject, Swinburne made clear that he was arguing for the existence of Gawd. In the smaller of his books—*Is There a God?*—Swinburne put the discussion of religious experience in a chapter dealing with miracles. And as we saw above in Chapter 5, Swinburne defined a miracle as "a violation or suspension of natural laws, brought about by [Gawd]."[2] In his larger book, *The Existence of God*, Swinburne said: "The argument from religious experience claims that . . . many have experienced [Gawd] (or some supernatural thing connected with [Gawd]) and hence know and can tell us of his existence."[3]

Swinburne thereby apparently assumed that any genuine religious experience would be miraculous. This assumption might seem to imply that supernatural miracles have occurred in the various religions of the world. However, Swinburne said, Christianity is the only religion with "good credentials" for having been founded on a miracle, namely, the resurrection of Jesus. Swinburne apparently used the supernatural origin of Christianity to treat Christianity as the One True Religion.[4]

However, in light of all the reasons for denying the reality of Gawd, we need not linger over this issue. More important is the question of whether religious experience provides evidence for God.

1. THE ACADEMIC STUDY OF RELIGION

Within the academy, the study of religion has been carried out largely in terms of a framework that gives a negative answer to that question. According to that framework, putative religious experience is not genuine, so that religion needs to be explained without referring to genuine religious experience. Putative religious experience could not, therefore, provide support for theism of any sort.

Referring to this approach as the "scientific study of religion," Robert Segal expounded it in his book *Explaining and Interpreting Religion*. He had also discussed this approach in his earlier book, *Religion and the Social Sciences*, which is subtitled, significantly, *Essays on the Confrontation*.[5]

Likewise, referring to the "naturalistic" approach to religion, Samuel Preus advocated it in a book entitled *Explaining Religion*.[6] The approaches of these two writers are essentially the same, as indicated by Segal's statement that Preus's book traced "the emergence of the social scientific, or naturalistic, explanation of religion." Indeed, "any naturalistic explanations," said Segal, "*are* social scientific ones."[7]

The main thing about religion that needs to be explained is the simple fact that religion exists. Every religion, said Segal, must have had "a naturalistic rather than divine origin." By this, he meant that there can be no explanation by means of an "experience of god," because this would be, asserted Segal, to posit a "supernatural origin" of religion. Indeed, Segal added, social scientists, being naturalists, hold that "believers never encounter God." Rather, said Preus, religion must be explained from "an altogether nonreligious point of view."[8]

Given these statements, the approach advocated by Preus and Segal could be called simply the "non-religious" or "atheistic" study of religion. Using these terms is better for this approach than "naturalistic," given the fact that there are types of naturalism that are religious and even theistic—using "theism" here to mean any view that affirms a divine being that influences the world.

In any case, behind this non-religious, atheistic approach there is a long history. According to Preus, Hume was the thinker who completed the paradigm shift in the study of religion to a thoroughgoing naturalism, so he called Hume "the founder of the scientific study of religion."[9] Preus then traced the development of this approach through August Comte, E. B. Tylor, Émile Durkheim, and Sigmund Freud. Segal used the same exemplars.

In addition, many other modern thinkers, having accepted the idea that all perception of things beyond our own mind are mediated by our sensory organs, have denied the possibility of genuine religious experience, in the sense of an experience of a divine reality. For example, J. J. C. Smart—the brother of the religion scholar Ninian Smart—said that mystical experiences are either "aberrations of feelings" or "miraculous," by which he meant impossible. To "get in touch" with things, said Smart, means receiving sensory stimuli from things, such as rabbits or electrons. Therefore, no naturalistic account could be given of getting in touch with something nonphysical, so all "mystical cognition of the supernatural," said Smart, is illusory.[10]

Accordingly, just as supernaturalists tend to hold that genuine religious experience is impossible *naturally*, atheists hold that it is impossible *altogether*. How, then, can they explain the fact that religion has been universal, in the sense that it has been in all human societies, as far back as we have records, and that it is still present in every society, even in those in which political authorities tried to stamp it out?

2. THE UNIVERSALITY AND VARIETY OF RELIGION

The universality of religion gives the advocates of the atheistic or non-religious approach a huge task. The central question for the academic study of religion, Preuss rightly said, is "if 'God is not given,' how is one to explain religions—that is, their universality, variety, and persistence until now?"[11]

NON-RELIGIOUS EXPLANATION

The position advocated by Preus and Segal can be considered a research hypothesis: On the assumption that there is no such thing as genuine religious experience, so that there is nothing about the fabric of the universe that tends to evoke experiences of the type that have been widely considered religious, how did religion get started and why has it persisted?

This question gave birth in the 19th century to various psychological and sociological theories of religion that tried to provide an answer. The primary problem for the scientific understanding of religion, said Émile Durkheim, is "explaining the sacred"—that is, explaining why religious people think in terms of the distinction between the "sacred" and the "profane," even though "nothing in sensible [sensory] experience seems able to suggest the idea of so radical a duality to them."[12]

The question of the origin of religion was answered by Durkheim and the other aforementioned thinkers—Comte, Tylor, Durkheim and Freud—but they all gave different answers. Preus, saying that Freud and Durkheim provided the most complete theories, suggested that a fully adequate theory of religion will need to combine their insights.[13] However, Preus's own account showed that neither Freud nor Durkheim came close to providing an adequate account of religion, and Preus gave no clue as to how Durkheim's sociological theory could be combined with Freud's psychological theory into an adequate psychosocial theory.

The problem is daunting because the task would not be simply to explain why something recognizable as religion has existed in every time and place. The task would be to provide a theory that would also explain the radical variety among religions. For example, Freud's theory, according to which religion expressed a desire for a powerful father-figure, was aimed at explaining biblical religion. Even if relevant for this goal, it had no relevance for Buddhism, Confucianism, Hinduism, Shinto, and Taoism.

The need to explain the universality as well as the variety of religion suggests that a non-religious theory of religion could never succeed.

RELIGIOUS EXPLANATION

If we do not insist that an academic explanation of religion must be non-religious, then formulating a theory to account for both the universality as well as the variety of religion might not be impossible. In broad strokes, such a theory, I suggest, can be modeled on the theory of morality, based on Walzer and Whitehead, sketched in Chapter 8.

The universality of religion—the fact that it has been a major feature of every human culture for which we have any evidence—can be explained by the fact that human beings prehend, along with everything else, the experiential unity of the universe, appropriately called "God."

Besides our constant prehension of God's primordial nature, which provides us with moral norms, mathematical objects, and the principles of logic and rationality, we also prehend God's "consequent nature," meaning God's response to the world. This response, the world's religions have testified, is characterized by love and compassion. Whitehead referred to the consequent nature as "the love in heaven," which "floods back again into the world."[14]

As to how this love is felt by us, every prehension includes an "objective datum," meaning the content of what is prehended, and also a "subjective form," meaning *the way* in which this content is felt. At the root of this subjective form is emotion. Whitehead wrote:

> The primitive form of physical experience is emotional—blind emotion—received as felt elsewhere in another [actuality] and conformally appropriated as a subjective passion. In the language appropriate to the higher stages of experience, the primitive element is *sympathy,* that is, feeling the feeling *in another* and feeling conformally *with* another.[15]

This idea is so central that Whitehead gave it a name: "the Doctrine of Conformation of Feeling."[16] According to this doctrine, when we experience God, we prehend God with a conformal subjective form. This idea provides the basis for an answer to Durkheim's question—why human beings have distinguished between the "sacred" and everything else.

THE HOLY OR SACRED

In at least most religious traditions, the divine reality is described as the "holy," or the "sacred." Rudolf Otto wrote a famous book about religious experience entitled *The Idea of the Holy;* Mircea Eliade wrote an equally famous book called *The Sacred and the Profane.* Unfortunately, neither Otto nor Eliade had a naturalistic explanation of such experiences.

Otto generally followed Kant, who affirmed that our theoretical (scientific) reason receives information only by means of our physical senses. Accordingly, to affirm a "feeling of the immediate presence of the Supreme Being," said Kant, would be a "fanatical religious illusion," because it would be to affirm "a receptivity for an intuition for which there is no sensory provision in man's nature."[17] However, convinced that religious experiences actually occur, Otto explained the idea of the holy as based on an *a priori* category of the mind.[18] Eliade, probably following Otto, said that "the 'sacred' is an element in the structure of consciousness."[19]

This answer understandably evoked sarcasm from Preus, who wrote:

> [I]n an academic setting where other scholars are struggling with the evolutionary emergence of our species, one legitimately wants to know how Eliade's remarkable 'element in the structure of consciousness' might have gotten there.[20]

However, given Whitehead's rejection of the view that all experience of things beyond our own minds is mediated by our sensory organs, he could give an explanation of religious experience that is not implicitly supernatural.

If, along with "love" and "compassion," the terms "holy" and "sacred" best characterize the nature of the experiential unity of the universe, we have a basis for understanding the origin and the persistence of religion. "[A]t the foundation of all religion," said Whitehead, is "the intuition of holiness, the intuition of the sacred."[21] That is, if the divine reality is characterized by the quality of *holiness* or *sacredness*, then by the conformation of feeling, this quality will also characterize the subjective form of our experience of God.

CONSCIOUS AND UNCONSCIOUS EXPERIENCE

Of course, the label "religious experience" is usually reserved for very exceptional experiences, in which people are consciously aware of holiness or sacredness. In general, being consciously aware of the things we experience is exceptional. In relation to our total experience, we become conscious of only a tiny portion, primarily objects of sensory perception.

For example, I am conscious of nearby mountains, which I see by means of a highly indirect process, involving trillions of photons and then billions of events in my eyes and my brain's optic system. But I am not conscious of my brain cells, which I prehend directly. As this example illustrates, consciousness primarily illuminates the products of sensory perception, tending to leave the objects of our more nonsensory perceptions in the dark, even though they are more fundamental.

Using "prehension in the mode of causal efficacy" for this nonsensory prehension and "prehension in the mode of presentational immediacy" for our perception by means of which we receive sensory data, Whitehead said:

> [C]onsciousness only dimly illuminates the prehensions in the mode of causal efficacy, because these prehensions are primitive elements in our experience. But prehensions in the mode of presentational immediacy are among those prehensions which we enjoy with the most vivid consciousness.[22]

Our prehensions of God, like our prehensions of our brain cells, are prehensions in the mode of causal efficacy, so they are ordinarily not illuminated by consciousness.

In certain extraordinary moments, however, our prehensions of God can rise to the level of consciousness. After such moments, we may say that we had a "religious" experience, an "experience of God," or an "experience of the holy"—the kinds of experiences described by William James in his *Varieties of Religious Experience*. What was extraordinary about those moments, however, was not that these people perceived God; by hypothesis, people are doing that all the time. What was extraordinary was only that this constant perception, with its subjective form of holiness, momentarily rose to the level of consciousness.

On this basis, religious experience can involve a direct experience of a Holy Actuality, in whom we live, move, and have our being. And on this basis, in turn, we can understand why human beings always and everywhere have been religious, orienting their lives around the idea of something holy or sacred. We can also understand why people have only occasionally reported having religious or mystical experiences, even though these experiences do not result from occasional divine interruptions of our normal perceptual processes.

BACKGROUND RELIGIOUS EXPERIENCE

Besides being essential for explaining the origin of religions without appeal to supernaturalism, the idea that everyone is experiencing a Holy Actuality all the time can explain why people in general, even if they have never had an extraordinary religious experience, understand the meaning of religious terms such as "God," "the holy," and "the sacred."

That is, in addition to the extraordinary kind of experience, to which the label "religious experience" is usually restricted, we can also speak of a general "background religious experience," through which all people are, more or less dimly, aware of the reality of something holy, so they are attracted to a religion. In this way, the extraordinary religious experiences of a few people can result in religions with large numbers of followers.

This background religious experience can also explain why all people, including ones who consider themselves nonreligious, consider some things, even apart from their own welfare, as especially important.

Whitehead considered the notion of *importance* so important that he had an entire chapter devoted to it. In spite of the positivistic effort to reduce everything to matter-of-fact, he said, "the notion of importance is like nature itself: Expel it with a pitchfork, and it ever returns." The "whole notion of importance," he said, is derived from "the unity of the Universe," which includes both "unity of purpose" (which is "the unity of ideal inherent in the universe") and "unity of enjoyment."[23]

As Whitehead saw it, the sense of importance arises from the immanence of the Universe as One, with its unity of ideal and purpose, in the universe as many—that is, from the "immanence of infinitude in the finite." Our sense of importance cannot be exorcised, because the universe's unity of purpose and enjoyment is immanent in our experience. That immanence in our experience, however, does not fully account for our sense of importance. "Does not 'importance for the finite,'" Whitehead asked rhetorically, "involve the notion of 'importance for the infinite'?"[24]

A discussion of importance by Bernard Williams can be used to illustrate the significance of this question. Besides having the merely *relative* idea of importance, according to which something is found important by someone, said Williams,

> we have another notion, of something's being, simply, important (important *überhaupt*, as others might put it, or important *period*). It is not at all clear what it is for something to be, simply, important. It does not mean that it is important for the universe: in that sense, nothing is important.

Accordingly, Williams said, "there is such a notion" as something being important *überhaupt*—important absolutely, not simply relatively—but we cannot understand why this is.[25] Whitehead would have agreed that, if the answer "important for the universe" is ruled out, no satisfactory notion of importance can be given.

The fact that we do have this notion of things being *important period*, accordingly, suggests that we have a sense for something behind the finite entities constituting the universe, to which things can be important. Whereas Williams held that nothing is important for the universe, panentheism holds that things in our lives *are* important for the universe.

3. COMBINING RELIGIOUS AND NON-RELIGIOUS EXPLANATIONS

A satisfactory treatment of religious experience, we have seen, requires a theory that can take account of both the universality and the variety of religious experience. But it should not be presupposed that either a religious or a non-religious (psychosocial) explanation could, by itself, be adequate. Perhaps an adequate theory requires a combination of both.

WILLIAM JAMES

William James wrote a classic book on this issue, *The Varieties of Religious Experience*. As his title emphasized, he discussed many varieties of religious experience. But he also discussed the nature of religion as such.[26] Indeed, without a description of religion meant to be universal, he could not have spoken of the varieties *of religious experience*.

Unlike Preus and Segal, James was able to see religious experience as providing knowledge about the universe. The difference is that James, rejecting the Humean, sensationist type of empiricism, affirmed a "thicker and more radical empiricism," which allows for nonsensory perception. This radical empiricism, he said, includes the examination of "the phenomena of psychic research so-called."[27] In fact, one of James's most famous statements, that it takes only one white crow to prove that not all crows are black, was aimed against the dogma quoted in Chapter 7—"that there can be nothing in any one's intellect that has not come in through ordinary experiences of sense."[28]

On the basis of this epistemology, James spoke of a "religious sense," through which we have an inkling of the existence of a religious reality. He said, for example, that religious experience might reveal to a man the existence of a "larger power which is friendly to him and to his ideals."[29] Indicating how important James considered the more radical empiricism for religion, he wrote:

> Let empiricism once become associated with religion, as hitherto, through some strange misunderstanding, it has been associated with irreligion, and I believe that a new era of religion as well as of philosophy will be ready to begin.[30]

The otherwise strange fact, that James was not even mentioned in Preus's historical survey of major modern thinkers engaged in the task of "explaining religion" scientifically, or in Segal's discussion of the academic study of religion, is probably explained by the fact that James affirmed genuine religious experience on the basis on nonsensory perception. Evidently James' rejection of Hume's sensationist empiricism meant for Preus and Segal that James' theory was not academic, not scientific.

Had Preus and Segal discussed James, their treatments would likely have been similar to that of Wayne Proudfoot. What James called a religious *sense*, said Proudfoot, is really a *thought*. In other words, what makes an experience a *religious* experience is simply the interpretive framework that the individual brings to the experience, not anything special about the experience itself. Proudfoot made this claim on the basis of his position—similar to that of Preus and Segal—that we need "a historical or cultural explanation of religious experience."[31]

COMBINING RELIGIOUS AND PSYCHOSOCIAL FACTORS

From an academic point of view, the main problem with the Preus-Segal-Proudfoot position is that it cannot provide a generic account of religion nor explain why religion is universal. Religion, according to Preus, is not even partly "a response to transcendence"—meaning something that transcends an individual's culture.[32] Rather, a *sufficient* explanation for religious experience, said Preus, is provided by "psychosocial causes."[33]

It is this idea—that psychosocial causes could and should provide a sufficient explanation[34]—is at the root of Segal's idea of a "confrontation" between religious and social-scientific explanations. He likewise assumes that, if a religious explanation were to be valid, it would need to provide a sufficient explanation of religious experience.

On the basis of these assumptions, Segal argues that non-religious explanations are superior. A non-religious, social-scientific account of religion, "however inadequate," said Segal, "is more adequate than a religious one." His argument here is that social scientists "provide a host of processes and entities like projection, wish fulfillment, complexes, collective representations, and symbols to account for how and why religion originates and functions," whereas religionists, such as Schleiermacher and Otto, "provide nothing"—except "the litany that religion originates as a response to the transcendent."[35]

However, there are two problems with this view. On the one hand, psychosocial explanations do not "account for how and why religion originates." They most certainly do not account for the universality of religion. On the other hand, religious explanations, speaking of experiences of "the holy" or "the transcendent," are intended only to explain why religion exists. They are not meant to be sufficient explanations, because they are not intended to provide explanations of the concrete details of all the various religions, or even one.

There needs to be, accordingly, a division of labor, with religious explanations accounting for the universality of religion and psychosocial explanations accounting for "the varieties of religious experience." This division of labor would be analogous to Michael Walzer's suggestion about morality—that the universal, minimal morality is based on factors existing in the nature of things, while the differences are to be explained in terms cultural factors.

CONCLUSION

Although some supernaturalists argue that religious experience provides evidence for the existence of Gawd, it provides much better evidence for God. Although religious experiences could be said to evidence for a supernatural deity,[36] this evidence is overwhelmed by the reasons to discount that evidence (as discussed in Part I of this book). But if we think in terms of a divine reality that is universal but not omnipotent in the traditional sense, the reality of religious experience simply adds one more reason to the list of reasons to believe in the existence of God.

Religious experience provides evidence for the existence of God in at least four ways.

- Religious experience in the usual sense, with its conscious experience of holiness or sacredness, can explain the origin and endurance of religions.

- Background religious experience gives people who have never had conscious religious experiences an inkling of its reality, thereby attracting them to religion.

- This background religious experience also accounts for the sense, even among non-religious people, that there are things that are important überhaupt—important without qualification.

- While explaining why religion has arisen and endured, genuine religious experience—the experience of a holy reality—can account for the universality of religion, while also allowing for its diversity.

ENDNOTES

1. Richard Swinburne, *Is There a God?* (Oxford University Press, 1996), 138–39.

2. Ibid., 101.

3. Richard Swinburne, *The Existence of God*, 2nd ed. (Oxford University Press, 2004), 293.

4. Swinburne, *Is There a God?* 110.

5. Robert A. Segal, *Explaining and Interpreting Religion: Essays on the Issue* (Peter Lang, 1992); *Religion and the Social Sciences: Essays on the Confrontation* (Scholars Press, 1989).

6. Samuel J. Preus, *Explaining Religion: Criticism and Theory from Bodin to Freud* (Yale University Press, 1987).

7. Segal, *Explaining and Interpreting Religion*, 123; *Religion and the Social Sciences*, 78.

8. Segal, *Explaining and Interpreting Religion*, 19, 71; *Religion and the Social Sciences*, 76–81; Preus, *Explaining Religion*, xi, xiii, xiv.

9. Preus, *Explaining Religion*, xi, 84n.

10. J. J. C. Smart, "Religion and Science," in Stephen H. Phillips, ed., *Philosophy of Religion: A Global Approach* (Fort Worth: Harcourt Brace, 1996), 217–24.

11. Preus, *Explaining Religion,* xv.

12. Émile Durkheim, *The Elementary Forms of the Religious Life,* trans. Joseph Ward Swain (Free Press, 1963), 57.

13. Preus, *Explaining Religion*, 158, 161–62, 196, 209.

14. Alfred North Whitehead, *Process and Reality: An Essay in Cosmology,* corrected edition, ed. David Ray Griffin and Donald W. Sherburne (1929; Free Press, 1978), 341.

15. Ibid., 162.

16. Ibid., 237–38; *Adventures of Ideas*, 183.

17. Immanuel Kant, *Religion within the Limits of Reason Alone,* trans. Theodore M. Greene and Hoyt H. Hudson (Harper & Row, 1960), 163.

18. Rudolf Otto, *The Idea of the Holy*, 2nd ed. (1923; Oxford University Press, 1950), 112–16.

19. Mircea Eliade, *History of Religious Ideas,* trans. W. R. Trask (University of Chicago Press, 1978), Vol. I: xiii.

20. Preus, *Explaining Religion,* xix.

21. Alfred North Whitehead, *Modes of Thought* (1938; Free Press, 1968), 120.

22. Whitehead, *Process and Reality*, 162.

23. Whitehead, *Modes of Thought,* 8, 28, 51.

24. Ibid., 20, 86–87.

25. Bernard Williams, *Ethics and the Limits of Philosophy* (Harvard University Press, 1985), 182.

26. William James, *The Varieties of Religious Experience: A Study in Human Nature* (Collier, 1961), 393–94.

27. William James, *Essays in Radical Empiricism* and *A Pluralistic Universe*, ed. Ralph Barton Perry (E. P. Dutton, 1971), 271.

28. James, *Essays in Psychical Research*, ed. Robert McDermott [Harvard University Press, 1986), 131.

29. James, *The Varieties of Religious Experience*, 407.

30. James, *Essays in Radical Empiricism*, 270.

31. Wayne Proudfoot, *Religious Experience* (University of California Press, 1985), 161, 223.

32. Preus, *Explaining Religion*, 204.

33. Ibid., 161, 197.

34. Segal, *Religion and the Social Sciences*, 82.

35. Segal, *Explaining and Interpreting Religion*, 70.

36. Unfortunately, in one place, William James said that he affirmed "piecemeal supernaturalism." This description of his position followed from two features of his position. On the one hand, he accepted the definition of "naturalism" as the doctrine that nature, understood as the world knowable through sensory perception, is all there is. Against

that view, James believed in "an altogether other dimension of existence," from which "our ideal impulses originate." James accordingly said that he had to be classified as a supernaturalist. On the other hand, James rejected absolute idealism, according to which "the world of the idea . . . relates only to the world as a whole." Rather, he said, he believed that the ideal world "interpolate[s] itself piecemeal between distinct portions of nature" (William James, *Varieties of Religious Experience* [Penguin Books, 1985], 510–12). Unfortunately, James's description of himself as a "piecemeal supernaturalist" was often misconstrued. For example, having defined miracles as "divine interventions which have disrupted the natural course of events," John Mackie took James's "piecemeal supernaturalism" to mean that he affirmed miraculous interruptions of the normal causal processes (John Mackie, *The Miracle of Theism: Arguments for and against the Existence of God* [Oxford: Clarendon, 1982], 13, 182).

12

Metaphysical Order

One of the traditional arguments for theism has been called the "cosmological argument." Beginning with the assessment of the world as contingent—that is, as not bearing the necessity for its existence within itself—this argument concludes that the world's existence can only be explained as the creation of a being that does exist necessarily. Declaring this "necessary being" to be divine, classical theists took the argument to point to a deity that is *in all respects* necessary and a world that is *in all respects* contingent.

The idea that God was necessary in all respects meant that the deity, as discussed above in the Introduction, was not affected by the world.[1] Although the deity was said to be loving, the deity was also impassible. Although the divine being was said to be omniscient and hence to know everything in the world, the divine being's knowledge could not be increased by occurrences and developments in the world. By virtue of its immutable omniscience, the divine being eternally knew, therefore, that a baby christened "John Fitzgerald Kennedy" would grow up to become the president of the United States and then be assassinated.

This idea of deity as immutably and impassibly omniscient, which was the idea of Gawd held by traditional theism in its classical form, was promulgated by Augustine and Aquinas. But arguments *against* the existence of this Gawd, said philosopher Charles Hartshorne, are "as conclusive as philosophical arguments could well be."[2]

In its non-classical form, as explained earlier, traditional theism does not hold that Gawd, as the necessarily existent being, is necessary in all respects. But it still holds the other half of the traditional view, according to which the world is contingent in all respects, because every detail was determined by the Omnipotent One.

In the present book, the divine reality, understood as God rather than Gawd, is not portrayed as either impassible or omnipotent. God is not portrayed, therefore, as a being that is necessary in all respects. The cosmological argument in its traditional form, therefore, is not applicable. But the basic idea still holds—that the world could not exist apart from a divine reality that exists necessarily. The very existence of the world, accordingly, is evidence for the existence of God.[3]

However, the fact that the world is contingent in some respects does not necessarily imply that it is contingent in *all* respects. Indeed, the idea that the present universe was created out of chaos, rather than out of absolutely nothing, implies that the existence of a universe—some universe or other—is necessary, because it has existed forever. That is, what we can call *the universe as such*, in the sense of a realm of finite beings, exists necessarily, whereas what we can call *our particular universe*, which came into being—according to the currently dominant view—about 14 billion years ago, is contingent. Therefore, the creation of our particular universe was "not the beginning of [finite] matter of fact, but the incoming of a certain type of order." The universe as such, accordingly, can have a sequence of particular universes, which Whitehead called "cosmic epochs."[4]

Given this distinction, the traditional cosmological argument must be divided into two parts: a *cosmological* argument, which deals with the order of our particular universe, and a *metaphysical* argument, which deals with the principles thought to obtain in the universe as such and hence in every cosmic epoch. The present chapter treats only the evidence for God provided by the metaphysical principles.

1. THE DIFFERENCE BETWEEN COSMOLOGICAL AND METAPHYSICAL ORDER

To refer to cosmological order is to refer to the fundamental laws or regularities of our particular cosmos, especially the laws of astronomy, physics, and chemistry. Examples are Kepler's laws of planetary motion, Newton's laws of motion, the conservation of mass-energy and momentum laws, the inverse-square law of gravitation, the electrostatic laws, the laws of thermodynamics, the laws of quantum mechanics, the invariance of the speed of light (as modified in relativity theory), and the most fundamental constituents of the world, such as quarks, electrons, protons, neutrons, neutrinos, and their combinations into atoms and molecules. These regularities, along with others, are usually called the "laws of nature."

However, these laws of our cosmos presuppose still more fundamental principles. For example, Hartshorne, focusing on aesthetic principles, said: "The most general principles of harmony and intensity are more ultimate than the laws of physics and are the reasons for there being natural laws." In saying that, Hartshorne was agreeing with Whitehead, who found "the foundations of the world in the aesthetic experience." Accordingly, he said, "All order is therefore aesthetic order."[5]

At least some of these more ultimate principles appear to be metaphysical, which means, in Whitehead's language, "characteristics so general that we cannot conceive any alternatives." If there really is no alternative to them, then they are *necessary* and hence would obtain in any possible universe (cosmic epoch).[6]

Some of these principles are non-controversial, at least largely, such as the principle of universal causation—that every event is causally influenced by previous events and then exerts influence on future events. But other putative metaphysical principles may be more controversial, because they are not endorsed by all metaphysical philosophies. For example:

- Chapter 4 gave reason to think that all actual things have experience or are composed of things with experience. The resulting metaphysical position has usually been called "panpsychism," although "panexperientialism" is better for Whitehead's position, which holds that the most ultimate things are momentary experiences, not enduring things such as bacteria and psyches.

- Panexperientialism is likely to affirm, as in Whitehead's view, that each experience has at least a tiny degree of spontaneity or self-determination, which in higher forms becomes freedom.

- In Whitehead's metaphysics, these two elements are also combined with the irreversibility of time, according to which time always moves from the past to the present and from the present to the future. Accordingly, the idea of particles going "backward in time," affirmed by some physicists, is ruled out.

- This point can also be discussed in terms of causation: Efficient causation—the causation of one event on another event—always goes from the past to the present, and from the present to the future. The idea of "retrocausation," affirmed by some physicists and parapsychologists, is ruled out.[7]

2. FORMATIVE ELEMENTS

The basic question of any metaphysical position is: What are the most fundamental ingredients in the universe as such, and hence in any cosmic epoch? In Aristotle's philosophy, the fundamental distinction was between "substances" and everything else. Substances were by definition the things that are real in the fullest sense, because they exert causation. These substances were composed of form and matter: The matter was the unformed stuff of which things are constituted, and the various substances resulted from being in-formed by various forms. However, Aristotle said, form and matter could result in substances only by virtue of a Prime Mover, understood to be divine.

Whitehead developed a somewhat similar position. In place of substances, he spoke of "actual entities," alternatively "actual occasions" or "occasions of experience." These actual entities exert both efficient causation, meaning the influence of one actual entity on others, and final causation, meaning each actual entity's self-causation. Final causation (self-determination) is exerted while the actual occasion is experiencing; efficient causation is exerted after the occasion has become fully determinate.

The formative elements of actual entities include "creativity" (as discussed in earlier chapters) and forms, which Whitehead called "eternal objects." Replacing Aristotle's "matter," creativity is the power of every actuality to exert self-causation and then to exert efficient causation on subsequent actualities.

At this point, Whitehead said, "an analogous metaphysical problem arises which can be solved only in an analogous fashion." That is, just as "Aristotle found it necessary to complete his metaphysics by the introduction of a Prime Mover—God," Whitehead was led to affirm "an entity at the base of all actual things," thereby affirming God as a third formative element in all actual occasions.[8] According to Whitehead's analysis, "the universe exhibits a creativity with infinite freedom, and a realm of forms with infinite possibilities." By themselves, however, "this creativity and these forms are together impotent to achieve actuality."[9]

Whitehead's explanation for the joint impotence of creativity and the eternal forms is that, for an occasion of experience to come into existence, a task must be performed that cannot be assigned to either creativity or forms, or to both of them together. The reason for holding this is the ontological principle, which says that only *actual* entities can act. Creativity is not an actual entity,[10] and the ideal forms are, by definition, ideal rather than actual.

The act that needs to be performed involves the fact that every actual entity—that is, every actual occasion, or occasion of experience— is a process of self-causation, which achieves a unity of experience. This is a teleological process, in which the occasion of experience receives influences from the past universe, most fully from the immediately previous occasions.

Given the infinity of possibilities, the occasion can only get started if it is given an initial direction. Because only actual entities can act, this initial direction could be supplied only by something actual. Because actualities-in-the-making always and everywhere need initial directions, this actuality must be everlasting and omnipresent. It was this train of thought that first led Whitehead to affirm the existence of a divine actuality.

3. METAPHYSICS AND THE EXISTENCE OF GOD

Whereas the logic of the above reasoning can be difficult to grasp, there is another version of the ontological principle that is much simpler. According to this version, "Everything must be somewhere; and here 'somewhere' means 'some actual entity.'" The "everything" here, which applies to Platonic forms, also applies to metaphysical principles. Because these principles must be in some actuality, Whitehead said, there must be some necessarily existent actuality in which they reside.

Whitehead also discussed the ontological principle in terms of *reasons,* saying that "the reasons for things are always to be found in the composite nature of definite actual entities." Reasons referring to "a particular environment" are found in "the nature of definite temporal actual entities," whereas "reasons of the highest absoluteness" are found "in the nature of God." Whitehead then added, "The ontological principle can be summarized as: no actual entity, then no reason."[11]

The "reasons of the highest absoluteness," of course, are the metaphysical principles. The existence and universality of these principles, Whitehead said, imply that "a primordial actual entity constitutes the metaphysical stability whereby the actual process exemplifies general principles of metaphysics."[12]

Most people, of course, do not think in terms of metaphysical principles, and most of the people who do think in terms of them seem to assume that their existence requires no explanation. But these principles could not, any more than mathematical objects or logical principles, simply exist in the void: "It is a contradiction in terms," said Whitehead, "to assume that some explanatory fact can float into the actual world out of nonentity."[13]

The metaphysical principles also could not be located in the world of finite occasions: Although some such world exists necessarily and therefore always, there is no finite enduring individual that has always existed. Any finite being, furthermore, could not explain the universality of the metaphysical principles. What could explain their existence and universality, Whitehead suggested, is that "the primordial Being shares his nature with the world," thereby being "a component in the natures of all [finite things]."[14]

The notion that the metaphysical principles exist in God reflects one of the respects in which the God-world relation differs from the Gawd-world relation. According to traditional theism, Gawd as the creator is completely different in kind from the world as a creature. Insofar as the world could be said to be based on metaphysical principles, therefore, those principles were imposed on the world by the creator, who did not need to operate in terms of these principles.

Whitehead, by contrast, said that "God is not to be treated as an exception to all metaphysical principles," but instead as "their chief exemplification."[15] So the metaphysical principles exist, in the first place, because they are embodied in God, as the primordial being. But because all finite things prehend God, the nature of God, with its metaphysical principles, is shared with them.

However, the fact that God is the "chief exemplification" of the metaphysical principles does not mean that these principles are less necessarily embodied in the world than in God. Metaphysics should, said Whitehead, exhibit "the World as requiring its union with God, and God as requiring his union with the World."[16] By capitalizing "World," Whitehead indicated that he was speaking of the world as such, not merely our particular cosmic epoch: God does not require our particular world, only the universe as such (which is always embodied in *some* particular world).

This way of understanding the God-world relation provides further clarification of the idea, discussed in Chapter 2, that it is impossible for God to interrupt the normal cause-effect relations. Those relations reflect metaphysical principles, which belong to the nature or essence of God.

Because the way in which God and the world interact belongs to the very nature of God, the idea that God could occasionally act in another way, as supernaturalists such as Millard Erickson and Alvin Plantinga suggest, would be as self-contradictory as suggesting that God could create a round square, change the past, or become forgetful.

"[Metaphysics] requires," wrote Whitehead, "that the relationships of God to the World should lie beyond the accidents of will."[17]

Accordingly, he said, "the ultimate creativity of the universe is [not] to be ascribed to God's volition."[18] We finite actualities do not have our creativity—our power to exert self-causation and other-causation—because God granted it to us (in which case God could cancel it). Rather, creativity belongs to the world as eternally as it belongs to God. Put otherwise, there is worldly creativity (meaning creativity as embodied in the world) as well as divine creativity (creativity as embodied in God).

CONCLUSION

The fact that the "actual process exemplifies general principles of metaphysics" can be understood only by positing the existence of a necessarily existent, omnipresent, everlasting being who, as the chief exemplification of the metaphysical principles, shares these principles throughout the universe by being prehended by all finite actualities. The existence of metaphysical principles, thereby, provides a distinct argument for the reality of God.

ENDNOTES

1. The eleventh-century Islamic philosopher Avicenna, who heavily influenced St. Thomas Aquinas, defined God primarily as "the necessary being." He commonly referred to God as being "necessary in all respects" and, said Rahim Acar in his essay on the two thinkers, Avicenna's "conception of God as necessary being equals Aquinas' conception of God as immutable" (*Talking about God and Talking about Creation: Avicenna's and Thomas Aquinas' Positions* [E. J. Brill Academic, 2005], 86–89). In a commentary on Aquinas' *Summa Theologica*, Reginald Garrigou-Lagrange wrote: "From the very fact that God is the self-subsisting Being, it likewise follows that He is absolutely immutable" ("The One God: A Commentary on the First Part of St Thomas' Theological Summa," The Summa and Other Matters).

2. Charles Hartshorne, *Man's Vision of God and the Logic of Theism* (Harper & Row, 1941), 58.

3. The argument that the existence of the world implies the existence of a necessary being has recently been formulated rigorously by Lorenz B. Puntel in *Being and God: A Systematic Approach in Confrontation with Martin Heidegger, Emmanuel Levinas, and Jean-Luc Marion* (Northwestern University Press, 2012).

4. Alfred North Whitehead, *Process and Reality: An Essay in Cosmology*, corrected edition, ed. David Ray Griffin and Donald W. Sherburne (1929; Free Press, 1978), 96.

5. Charles Hartshorne, "A Reply to My Critics," in *The Philosophy of Charles Hartshorne*, Library of Living Philosophers Vol. 20, ed. Lewis Edwin Hahn (Open Court, 1991), 569–731, at 590; Whitehead, *Religion in the Making* (1926; Fordham University Press, 1966), 101.

6. Whitehead, *Process and Reality*, 3, 4, 288.

7. Although this principle arguably should be non-controversial, there are some philosophies that allow for backward causation, according to which events in the future exert efficient causation on the present—an idea that implies that future events are already settled.

8. Alfred North Whitehead, *Science and the Modern World* (1925; Free Press, 1967), 173–74; Whitehead, *Religion in the Making*, 90.

9. *Religion in the Making*, 119-20.

10. Whitehead, *Process and Reality*, 222.

11. Ibid., 19.

12. Ibid., 40.

13. Ibid., 46.

14. Alfred North Whitehead, *Adventures of Ideas* (Free Press, 1967), 130.

15. Whitehead, *Process and Reality*, 343.

16. Whitehead, *Adventures of Ideas*, 168.

17. Ibid., 168.

18. *Process and Reality*, 225.

13

Cosmological Order

Whereas metaphysics is the attempt to discern the necessary principles of this and every possible universe, cosmology is the attempt to go beyond metaphysics by adding an account of the contingent laws of our particular universe. Cosmology, Whitehead said, is "the effort to frame a scheme of the general character of the present stage of the universe."[1] The fundamental problem set by these contingent laws is how we can explain their existence and universality.

Just as the previous chapter developed Whitehead's explanation of the existence of metaphysical principles by reference to the reality and efficacy of a Primordial Being, the present chapter follows Whitehead's treatment of the most fundamental of the contingent features of our universe, along with the ways in which their existence points to the reality of such a Primordial Being.

Cosmology was, in fact, Whitehead's central concern: Although he discussed metaphysics, his major work, *Process and Reality*, was subtitled *An Essay in Cosmology*. He made clear, moreover, that God was central to his cosmology, saying: "'God' is that actuality in the world, in virtue of which there is physical 'law.'"[2]

1. THE COSMOLOGICAL ARGUMENT: FOR GAWD OR GOD?

Although Whitehead developed a cosmological argument for the existence of God, this argument is very different from the traditional argument of that name. This difference results primarily from the fact that the traditional argument was meant to prove the existence of Gawd.

WHITEHEAD VS. NEWTON

This difference is shown in Whitehead's endorsement of Hume's reason for rejecting the cosmological argument as articulated by Newton. Pointing out that Newton's version of the argument involved a "supernatural origin" of the world, Whitehead said that this argument is "now generally abandoned as invalid; because our notion of causation concerns the relations of states of things within the actual world, and can only be illegitimately extended to a transcendent derivation."[3]

In other words, the traditional cosmological argument employed the human use of matter to make things, such as the use of wood to make a table, as an analogy for a supernatural being making a world out of nothing. This is illegitimate, Hume and Whitehead pointed out, because there is no analogy between creating a table out of wood and the alleged creation of the world out of nothing. The latter kind of "causation" is different in kind from our experience of causation, so the terms "causation" and "creation" are used equivocally, making the argument invalid.

In introducing his own version of the cosmological argument, Whitehead called it "an attempt to add another speaker" to Hume's *Dialogues*. These dialogues involved a discussion of Philo, representing Hume, with Demea, representing an orthodox theist, and Cleanthes, a deist who, like Demea, believed the world to have been created out of nothing. Whitehead meant, therefore, adding a speaker who, besides rejecting Humean skepticism, also did not define God as a supernatural being who could create a world *ex nihilo*.

The correctness of this interpretation is shown by the fact that Whitehead's statement about adding another speaker was immediately followed by his dictum, "God is not to be treated as an exception to all metaphysical principles."[4]

The implication of Whitehead's discussion is that his cosmological argument for the existence of God is not refuted by Hume's criticism of the cosmological argument for Gawd.

WHITEHEAD VS. KANT

Whitehead's cosmological argument for the existence of God is also not touched by Kant's reason for rejecting the traditional cosmological argument. In Kant's critique of the argument, which he called the "physico-theological proof," he said that the argument shows "the contingency of the [world's] form merely, but not of [its] matter." Accordingly, Kant said, the cosmological argument can at most "demonstrate the existence of an *architect of the world*, whose efforts are limited by the capabilities of the material with which he works."

Spelling out his critique, Kant said that the cosmological argument does not demonstrate the existence "of a *creator of the world*, to whom all things are subject."[5] In other words, the argument does not point to the existence of a being who created the world out of nothing.

It has widely been said that Hume and Kant destroyed the cosmological argument. For example, in a book subtitled *In Defense of Atheism*, Kai Nielsen reported with approval the "very considerable consensus among contemporary philosophers and theologians that arguments like those developed by Hume and Kant show that no proof (*a priori* or empirical) of God's existence is possible."[6]

But Kant's critique, like Hume's, only points out that the argument does not prove the existence of Gawd. If we do not insist that the term "creation" can refer only to *creation ex nihilo*, Kant suggested that the argument does point to a creator, in the sense of a being responsible for the world's order. And this was precisely Whitehead's position, endorsing Plato's view that "the creation of the world is not the beginning of [finite] matter of fact, but the incoming of a certain type of social order."[7]

2. THE LAWS OF NATURE: IMPOSED OR IMMANENT?

The contrast between Whitehead's concept of deity and that of Newton is illustrated by their respective explanations of the relationship of the divine being to the "laws of nature." Newton thought of these laws as wholly imposed by a "transcendent imposing Deity": An atom behaves as it does because Gawd imposed certain laws on it. By virtue of being imposed, Whitehead wrote, "the Laws of Nature will be exactly obeyed."[8]

For Whitehead himself, by contrast, actualities exert causation on other actualities by entering into them—in other words, by being prehended by them. As a result, held Whitehead, law is immanent in nature, rather than being imposed upon it from without.

> [T]he order of nature expresses the characters of the real things which jointly compose the existences to be found in nature. . . . [A]ccording as there are common elements in their various characters, there will necessarily be corresponding identities in their mutual relations. In other words, some partial identity of pattern in the various characters of natural things issues in some partial identity of pattern in the mutual relations of those things. These identities of pattern in the mutual relations are the laws of Nature.

Given the view of the laws of nature as immanent, Whitehead explained, "the exact conformation of nature to any law is not to be expected." Indeed, the hypothesis that the laws would be "exactly obeyed" has not been supported by modern science. Rather, "most of the laws of physics," physicists now hold, "have a statistical character."[9]

However, a doctrine of law as immanent based solely on the internal relations of finite things with each other, added Whitehead, would not be adequate. Such a doctrine would never have inspired science, because it would not have provided the faith in definite laws underlying the apparent capriciousness of nature. Also, "apart from some notion of imposed Law, the doctrine of immanence provides absolutely no reason why the universe should not be steadily relapsing into lawless chaos."[10]

What is needed, in Whitehead's view, is a doctrine that could be called *quasi-imposition*, resulting from the immanence of a supreme being in all other beings. In a statement partially quoted earlier, Whitehead wrote:

> [T]he primordial Being, who is the source of the inevitable recurrence of the world towards order, shares his nature with the world. In some sense he is a component in the natures of

all [finite things]. Thus, an understanding of the nature of temporal things involves a comprehension of the immanence of the Eternal Being. This doctrine effects an important reconciliation between the doctrines of Imposed Law and Immanent Law. For, with this doctrine, the necessity of the trend towards order does not arise from the imposed will of a transcendent God. It arises from the fact, that the existents in nature are sharing in the nature of the immanent God.[11]

My term "quasi-imposition" can be used for this doctrine because, although it is really a doctrine of immanence, the immanence of a primordial, omnipresent being in all finite things produces regularities similar to laws that would result from divine imposition. Of course, the effect is only similar, not identical, because the laws of nature are only statistical. But it had seemed like true imposition, before scientists had become able to discern the microcosmic constituents of nature, because only at this level is the statistical nature of laws apparent.

In any case, an adequate doctrine of law as immanent, Whitehead held, must include "a stable actuality whose mutual implication with the remainder of things secures an inevitable trend towards order. The Platonic 'persuasion' is required."[12]

With regard to the idea of "Platonic persuasion," Whitehead said that Plato's final conviction—"that the divine element in the world is to be conceived as a persuasive agency and not as a coercive agency"—was "one of the greatest intellectual discoveries in the history of religion."[13]

Unfortunately, Christian thinkers for almost twenty centuries ignored this discovery, instead teaching people that the divine element in the world is Gawd—an omnipotent deity, belief in which resulted in an insuperable problem of evil, a conflict with scientific naturalism, and the other problems discussed in the first part of this book.

3. EVOLUTION AND TELEOLOGY

In his book *Mind and Cosmos*, Thomas Nagel said, as quoted in Chapter 4, that he "reject[ed] both supernaturalism and neo-Darwinism's explanation of the sources of evolutionary change." An adequate worldview, he said, would need to include "a naturalistic teleology."[14]

Whitehead provided this kind of worldview, except that Nagel expressed hope for a teleology that would be "naturalistic" in the sense of requiring no reference to a deity—a goal that Whitehead considered impossible. But Whitehead's view is naturalistic in the more fundamental sense, explaining evolution without any supernatural assistance.

His view can also be called deep evolution, encompassing the entire history of the universe.

DEEP EVOLUTION

Some treatments of evolution deal only with biological evolution, ignoring the issue of prebiotic terrestrial evolution—the roughly half-billion years of evolution on our planet prior to the emergence of life. In addition to discussing this prebiotic evolution, a still deeper view would include the fact that our universe had been evolving for billions of years before the formation of our planet. With regard to the earliest stages of our particular universe, Whitehead said that "there must have been some epoch in which the dominant trend was the formation of protons, electrons, molecules, the stars."[15]

Whitehead's perspective on evolution was based on the view that our universe was created out of chaos, rather than out of nothing. As stated earlier, Whitehead agreed with Plato's Timaeus, for which "the creation of the world is not the beginning of [finite] matter of fact, but the incoming of a certain type of order." Thinking in terms of a series of cosmic epochs, Whitehead held that the present cosmic epoch would have emerged out of "a state of chaotic disorder." In speaking of the emergence of very elementary forms of order, Whitehead referred to "electronic and protonic actual entities" and the "yet more ultimate actual entities which can be dimly discerned in the quanta of energy."[16]

Whitehead wrote that back in 1929. In the intervening period, there has been much development in the thinking about the earliest phases of evolution. The currently dominant view is the so-called Big Bang cosmology, according to which our universe began about 13.8 billion years ago. In the view of many scientists, this beginning involved the creation of the world out of nothing (although, some thinkers hold, without a Gawd to do the creating). This Big Bang event involved not only the creation of our world's basic entities—such as electrons, protons, neutrons, and neutrinos—but also time itself, so that it would be meaningless to ask what happened *before* the Big Bang.

But that is only one view of Big Bang cosmology. For example, Professor Sean Carroll of the California Institute of Technology wrote:

> The issue of whether or not there actually is a beginning to time remains open. Even though classical general relativity predicts a singularity at the Big Bang, it's completely possible that a fully operational theory of quantum gravity will replace the singularity by a transitional stage in an eternal universe.[17]

The idea of a singularity, which posits a beginning of time, is rejected in "bouncing" and "cyclic" cosmologies, which are more similar to Whitehead's idea of "cosmic epochs." According to these cosmologies, one *can* ask what happened before the Big Bang, which most fundamentally means only—according to Paul Steinhardt, the director of the Princeton Center for Theoretical Science—"that the universe was once hot and dense and has been expanding and cooling."

However, Steinhardt continued, there is little if any evidence for "the big bang beginning, the idea that the universe, at one time didn't exist and suddenly sprang from nothingness into somethingness." If you ask physicists whether they are confident in this idea, said Steinhardt, "the answer is no." Steinhardt considers it much more likely that rather than a "big bang," understood as "the beginning of space and time," what we call a bang "is really a bounce: a transition from a preexisting phase—let's say of contraction—[followed by] a bounce into expansion." In other words, rather than thinking of a single Big Bang, there is a series of big bangs. With this theory, said Steinhardt, "suddenly there's a whole new domain of time."[18]

It was an idea of this type, according to which there was a "domain of time" prior to the beginning of our cosmic epoch, that Whitehead had accepted for both philosophical and scientific reasons. He believed, accordingly, that a complete theory of evolution needed to include speculation about processes that occurred before the beginning of our particular universe.

THE ULTIMATE REALITY OF TIME

The idea that time had no beginning was expressed in a 2015 book by philosopher Roberto Mangabeira Unger and physicist Lee Smolin.

Most physicists, following Einstein, have held that time for physics is symmetrical and reversible, providing no basis for distinguishing between past, present, and future, hence no basis for speaking of "now." This idea makes time in physics completely different from time as known in human experience—an idea that has led many to the conclusion that time is illusory: that past, present, and future all co-exist simultaneously. The idea that time is illusory easily leads to the conclusion that moral effort, such as the effort to prevent destructive climate change, is unimportant.

Einstein himself was troubled by "the problem of the Now," as he called it. Whereas for us "the experience of the Now means something . . . essentially different from the past and the future," this difference, said Einstein, "cannot occur within physics." This conclusion, reported Rudolf Carnap, "seemed to [Einstein] a matter of painful but inevitable resignation."[19]

Whitehead held that Einstein's painful resignation was based on an error, which Whitehead called the "fallacy of misplaced concreteness"— equating scientific abstractions with concrete entities, such as those we call photons, electrons, and protons. Holding that these enduring entities consist of rapidly repeating events, each of which inherits from previous events and then influences subsequent events, Whitehead said that the distinction between past, present, and future is real for these entities. Time, accordingly, is ultimately real—being as real for photons and electrons as it is for bacteria and human beings.

As indicated by the title of their book, *The Singular Universe and the Reality of Time*,[20] Unger and Smolin affirm the ultimate reality of time, saying that "time goes all the way down."[21] Identifying with the tradition pioneered by Heraclitus, Hegel, Bergson, and Whitehead, Unger and Smolin call their position "temporal naturalism." Besides affirming "the radical and inclusive reality of time," they call time "the most real feature of the world."[22]

This thesis is revolutionary, point out Unger and Smolin, because it reverses the view that time, if real in any sense, is at best an emergent reality.[23] Instead, Unger and Smolin call time "the only feature of nature that enjoys absolutely the attribute of non-emergence."[24] Being non-emergent, time did not begin in a Big Bang. Rather, Unger and Smolin, like Whitehead, say that our universe was formed after a previous universe had come to an end, with no interruption in the reality of time.[25] They have thereby provided a naturalistic cosmology that, in their words, "does not reduce human experience and aspirations to illusion."[26]

Although their position has weaknesses, primarily because of their insistence that *everything* is temporal (so there are no eternal objects and no divine reality), their work is a big step forward in the development of physics, including astrophysics, based on the fundamental reality of process.

PREBIOTIC EVOLUTION

Darwin assumed that life had been supernaturally created out of the organic molecules created by the deity, so that he could focus on how higher forms of life evolved. But Whitehead, like contemporary evolutionists, had to deal with the billions of years of evolution that occurred before the emergence of life, and even before the evolutionary formation of the inorganic entities that provided the preconditions for the emergence of life. He needed, therefore, a theory of evolution that dealt with the billions of years of prebiotic evolution in our cosmic epoch.

In reflecting on the phase "in which the dominant trend was the formation of protons, electrons, molecules, the stars," Whitehead suggested that the "material universe has contained . . . some mysterious impulse for its energy to run upwards."[27] This trend is continuous with the "upward trend" in biological evolution.

BIOLOGICAL EVOLUTION

This trend raises a big question, namely, "Why has the trend of evolution been upwards?" This question is, Whitehead pointed out, "not in the least explained by the doctrine of the survival of the fittest." That doctrine explains why some kinds of organisms, having emerged, manage to survive. But if survival were the only goal, then the very emergence of living things would be inexplicable, because "life itself is comparatively deficient in survival value. The art of persistence is to be dead." In fact,

"The problem set by the doctrine of evolution is to explain how complex organisms with such deficient survival power ever evolved."[28]

Neo-Darwinists avoid this question—of why the evolutionary trend has been upwards—by denying the very idea of "higher" organisms. For example, Stephen Jay Gould said: "[I]f an amoeba is as well adapted to its environment as we are to ours, who is to say that we are higher creatures?" Evolution brings about "improved fitness," to be sure, but this means, Gould insisted, only "better designed for an immediate, local environment," not improvement in any "cosmic sense."[29] In other words, survival is the only criterion of success.

For Darwin himself, by contrast, the idea of progress was central. According to historian Dov Ospovat, "Darwin never seriously doubted that progress has been the general rule in the history of life." Robert Richards agreed, saying that "Darwin crafted natural selection as an instrument to manufacture biological progress."[30]

The difference between Darwin and the neo-Darwinists on this point was based on the fact that the latter are atheists (at least methodologically), while Darwin was an "evolutionary deist," as John Greene called him, and this conception of the universe, Ospovat pointed out, lay behind Darwin's belief in progress.[31]

Richards agreed, saying that Darwin's belief in evolutionary progress was "a direct consequence of Darwin's . . . regarding natural selection to be a secondary cause responsive to the primary cause of divine wisdom." According to Darwin himself, "from the war of nature from famine and death," he said in the final paragraph of *The Origin of Species*, "the most exalted object which we are capable of conceiving, namely, the production of the higher animals, directly follows."[32]

But neo-Darwinists, having rejected the idea of any purpose behind the universe, have no criterion for success other than adaptability for survival. William Provine brought out this point in an essay entitled "Progress in Evolution and Meaning in Life." While denying the idea of a cosmic purpose, he wrote, "Some neo-Darwinists have tried to hold on to an idea of progress." But this attempt, he pointed out, was self-contradictory, because without a cosmic purpose, there can be no cosmic progress: "The problem is that there is no ultimate basis in the evolutionary process from which to judge true progress."[33]

Another reason for the neo-Darwinists' denial of the possibility of progress is that their materialism directs their attention to the external characteristics of things, as known through sensory perception. From that external perspective, the survival of organisms is all there is, and survival is survival—hence there is no basis for regarding elephants and gibbons as in any way superior to amoebae and fleas. Indeed, the amoebae and fleas will survive longer.

Whitehead, by contrast, had a twofold basis for talking about "higher organisms": Like Darwin, he regarded the universe as the creation of a purposive deity; and he focused less on the external features of organisms than on their inner experiences. On these bases, Whitehead rejected the belief that "fitness for survival is identical with the best exemplification of the Art of Life." Rather than evolutionary success being mere survival, progress involves "increase in satisfaction," meaning increase in the realization of intrinsic value. The cosmic aim, he said, encourages "a three-fold urge: (i) to live, (ii) to live well, (iii) to live better"—with the latter meaning "to acquire an increase in satisfaction."[34]

Just as Hartshorne (in a statement quoted above) said that the laws of physics are less ultimate than aesthetic principles, Whitehead held that the laws of physics reflect an aim towards value. His philosophy, he said, "finds the foundations of the world in the aesthetic experience," after which he said:

> The laws of physics reflect the fact that the endurance of individuals such as electrons, atoms, and molecules involves the repetition and intensification of a certain kind of value.[35]

Stating that the best word for the "intrinsic reality of an event"—meaning what an event is for itself—is *value*, Whitehead wrote: "The endurance of things has its significance in the self-retention of that which imposes itself as a definite attainment for its own sake."[36] In other words, the simplest kinds of enduring entities already reflect the cosmic aim at value.

With regard to this cosmic aim, which is reflected at every level of the evolutionary process, Whitehead declared: "What is inexorable in God, is valuation as an aim towards 'order,'" with "order" understood as structure allowing for actualities with greater intrinsic value.

Although all actual entities have *some* intrinsic value, they "differ in importance of actuality." This difference provides the reason for the continual creation involved in evolutionary advance: "[T]he purpose of God in the attainment of value," wrote Whitehead, "is in a sense a creative purpose."[37]

The idea of divine perfection is understood by Whitehead in terms of acting to achieve this purpose. Offering "an alternative rendering of Descartes' notion of perfection," Whitehead described perfection as "the notion of that power in history which implants into the form of process, belonging to each historic epoch, the character of a drive toward some ideal, to be realized within that period."

Accordingly, whereas believers in Gawd think of divine perfection as divine omnipotence, Whitehead defined divine perfection in terms of persuasion. Moreover, although Whitehead saw the basic divine aim as remaining the same throughout the evolutionary process, he portrayed the various epochs as receiving new goals, saying that "as the present becomes self-destructive of its inherited modes of importance, then the deistic influence implants in the historical process new aims at other ideals."[38]

4. COMPOUND INDIVIDUALS

The unchanging divine purpose, with its ever-new goals, lies behind the direction of evolution towards more complex organisms:

> The problem of evolution is the development of enduring harmonies of enduring shapes of value, which merge into higher attainments of things beyond themselves.[39]

For example, electrons, protons, and neutrons can merge to combine into atoms; atoms can be combined into molecules; simple molecules can combine to form organic molecules (macromolecules), including lipids, carbohydrates, proteins, and nucleic acids (DNA and RNA); with these four organic molecules, plus some other ingredients, they can be combined into organelles, which in turn can be combined into prokaryotic cells, such as bacteria. And, as we saw in Chapter 4, prokaryotic cells can be compounded into eukaryotic cells, from which plants and animals are formed.

Although this is the (now) standard account of the evolution of these structures, the Whiteheadian treatment of this evolution adds that each step involves the emergence of a higher type of experience and therefore of "compound individuals," a concept that was introduced in Chapter 4 (where Lynn Margulis was described as having a similar view). The emergence of higher-level compound individuals brings richer experience, hence greater intrinsic value.

For example, when electrons, protons, and neutrons form the compound individuals that we call atoms, the electronic, protonic, and neutronic occasions of experience give birth to atomic occasions of experience,[40] which in turn can give birth to molecular and then macromolecular occasions of experience, which can in turn give birth to higher-level experiences enjoyed by organelles and prokaryotic cells, which can in turn be combined to give birth to eukaryotic cellular occasions of experience. And then, the most complex compound individuals, at least on this planet, are humans and other animals, the central experiences of which we call *minds, psyches*, or *souls*.

ORGANIZATIONAL DUALITY

Not all combinations of things are compound individuals. Besides being combined into macromolecules, simple molecules can also form what we call "matter," which can be solid, liquid, gas, or plasma (the latter being the dominant naturally-occurring state of matter). In the resulting aggregations of things large enough to see, such as sticks, stones, telephones, houses, mountains, and human corpses, there is no unified experience. Such things are non-individualized aggregations of matter. To refer to Whitehead's worldview as "panexperientialism" does not mean, therefore, that literally *all things* have experience. Rather, the "pan" refers to *all genuine individuals*—which can be either simple or compound individuals.

The failure to recognize the distinction between compound individuals and non-individualized aggregations has been the major reason that philosophers and others have dismissed panexperientialism (or panpsychism) as obviously false. Some forms of panpsychism have, to be sure, regarded literally all things as having experiences,[41] but that is not true of the panexperientialism of Whitehead and Hartshorne: Rocks and telephones do not have central experiences, do not have psyches. There is an organizational duality between visible things that have central experiences and those that do not. In making this distinction, said Hartshorne,

> Leibniz took the single greatest step in the second millennium of philosophy (in East and West) toward a rational analysis of the concept of physical reality.[42]

I have suggested, accordingly, that rather than referring to Whitehead's position as simply "panexperientialism," we should call it "panexperientialism with organizational duality."[43] The organizational duality takes care of the obvious difference between things with and without central experiences, while avoiding Descartes' disastrous ontological dualism, according to which there are two kinds of actual entities.

However, the idea of "organizational duality" is evidently too simple. Regarding humans and other animals as "monarchical societies," Whitehead described plants as "democracies," which makes them structurally similar to sticks and stones. However, evidence has been gathering that plants are aware and even have intelligence. It would seem, therefore, that plants exemplify a third type of organization, as do bee and ant colonies.[44] For the sake of simplicity, however, we can limit the discussion here to organizational duality.

COMPOUND INDIVIDUALS AND FREEDOM

The notion of organizational duality is crucial for the discussion of freedom. Whereas nineteenth-century physics had encouraged the idea of a deterministic universe, quantum physics showed that processes in nature's most elementary constituents are not completely deterministic. This development provided a basis for seeing how human beings can have a degree of freedom.

Being able to affirm human freedom is a necessary condition of a self-consistent worldview, because freedom is one of those things that we inevitably presuppose in practice. "This element in experience," observed Whitehead, "is too large to be put aside merely as misconception. It governs the whole tone of human life."[45]

Some other philosophers agree, even if they personally feel compelled to affirm determinism. One example is University of California philosopher John Searle. On the one hand, Searle said that the scientific worldview entails determinism. On the other hand, he stated that no matter how many arguments against freedom may be marshaled by philosophers, including himself, it is "impossible for us to abandon the belief in the freedom of the will."[46] Nevertheless, Searle said, we must conclude that the feeling of freedom is an illusion: "Science allows no place for freedom of the will." Part of Searle's basis for this conclusion is his view that science tells us that the world "consists entirely of mindless, meaningless, physical particles." But another part of his argument is that quantum indeterminacy is irrelevant, because in entities composed of large numbers of particles, whatever freedom characterizes individual particles is canceled out in entities with large numbers of particles. Accordingly, said Searle, "the statistical indeterminacy at the level of particles does not show any indeterminacy at the level of the objects that matter to us—human bodies, for example."[47]

As these statements show, Searle's argument was based on the assumption that the organization of rocks and bowling balls is not different in kind from that of dogs and humans. So the actions of human beings involve no more self-determination than a bowling ball headed for either a strike or a gutter. Specifically ruling out the idea that human brains are organized to give birth to a mind as a higher-level actuality, Searle said of the human head, "the brain is the only thing in there."[48]

That assumption, pointed out Whitehead, leads to the conclusion that the activity of shipbuilders is "analogous to the rolling of the shingle on the beach"—an idea, he said, that is "ridiculous."[49] The doctrine of "panexperientialism with organizational duality" allows us to avoid that this ridiculous idea must be accepted.

According to this panexperientialist worldview, the evolutionary process gives birth to higher-level compound individuals, which as part of their greater experience have more capacity for self-determination and hence freedom. Rather than suggesting that human freedom is either illusory or a miraculous exception to the rest of nature, we can say that, in the line of genuine individuals, a degree of freedom goes all the way down, to the most elementary individuals.

Just as a naturalistic view of evolution must, as discussed in Chapter 4, hold that experience goes all the way down, a naturalistic view must say the same thing about freedom. Just as *pour soi* (experiencing things) could not have emerged out of *en soi* (non-experiencing things), so beings with freedom could not have emerged out of things totally devoid of any capacity for self-determination.

This point was made by Princeton mathematicians John Conway and Simon Kochen, who said that, "if indeed we humans have free will," as presupposed by every scientist setting up an experiment, "then elementary particles already have their own small share of this valuable commodity."[50] At that level, to be sure, it would be better to speak of "proto-freedom," or "incipient freedom," saving the term "freedom" for living beings.

In any case, Conway and Kochen reject the assumption, held by Searle and many others, that freedom (even proto-freedom) is canceled out in all visible things. With regard to their conviction that "fundamental particles are continually making their own decisions," Conway and Kochen say:

> Most of their decisions, of course, will not greatly affect things
> —we can describe them as mere ineffectual flutterings, which on
> a large scale almost cancel each other out, and so can be ignored.

However, they believe, "there is a way our brains prevent some of this cancellation, so allowing us to integrate what remains and producing our own free will."[51]

Accordingly, although they do not use the language of compound individuals, Conway and Kochen suggest the position held by Whitehead and Hartshorne: that thanks to the organization of the central nervous system, especially the brain, it evokes the self-determining experiences of what we call mind or psyche.

NAGEL ON WHITEHEAD, HARTSHORNE, AND FREEDOM

This view of the emergence of human freedom out of self-determining events at the most elementary level of nature is needed to fulfill

Thomas Nagel's desire for a naturalistic view of evolution that is fully self-consistent.

In his 1986 book, *The View from Nowhere,* Nagel said that he changed his mind about free will every time he thought about it. On the one hand, he said, he had found no way to give a coherent account of freedom. On the other hand, he added, "I can no more help holding myself and others responsible in ordinary life than I can help feeling that my actions originate with me."[52]

However, while expressing the same contradiction expressed by Searle, Nagel may have implicitly indicated how to resolve this contradiction in his 2012 book, in which he, as pointed out in Chapter 4, spoke of both Whitehead and Hartshorne. Having referred in a footnote to Galen Strawson's *Consciousness and Its Place in Nature,* Nagel described Hartshorne's essay, "Physics and Psychics: The Place of Mind in Nature," as an "acute and historically informed discussion." With regard to Whitehead, Nagel wrote:

> Whitehead argued that to identify the abstractions of physics with the whole of reality was to commit the fallacy of misplaced concreteness, and that concrete entities, all the way down to the level of electrons, should all be understood as somehow embodying a standpoint on the world.[53]

Like Whitehead, Hartshorne, and Strawson, Nagel sees that a fully naturalistic worldview requires some version of panexperientialism or panpsychism, according to which "organisms with mental life are not miraculous anomalies but an integral part of nature."[54] To complete this naturalistic worldview, one needs only to add that, along with experience, Whitehead's "concrete entities" include self-determination, which at the highest level of nature becomes the kind of freedom we recognize in ourselves.

One serious problem in Strawson's version of panexperientialism, incidentally, is that he retains the view, entailed by materialism, that freedom is impossible. His argument is that, although everything has a mental aspect, this mental aspect does not prevent anything from being completely determined by antecedent causes, because "[n]othing can be *causa sui*" (cause of itself) in a way that would allow for freedom.[55]

According to Whitehead's version of panexperientialism, by contrast, to say that every individual has a mental pole is to say that every individual is partly *causa sui*. That is, every individual is "physical" to the extent that it is determined by antecedent causes, whereas every individual is "mental" to the extent that it is self-determining. In his technical language: "To be *causa sui* means that the process of concrescence is . . . finally responsible for the decision by which any lure for feeling is admitted to efficiency. The freedom inherent in the universe is constituted by this element of self-causation."[56] Of course, the mental poles of low-grade actual occasions, such as those of electrons and atoms, are extremely limited, so there is no real freedom, merely an element of spontaneity. But the evolutionary development of compound individuals has produced higher-grade occasions, especially human occasions of experience, in which mentality, hence self-determination, plays a much bigger role.[57]

This self-determining freedom also, of course, is necessary for the capacity for logic and rationality discussed in Chapter 9.

5. NOVELTY

Given the fact that Whitehead presented God as the ground of our world's metaphysical and cosmological order, one would not be surprised that Whitehead typically referred to God as the *ground of order*. But he also referred to God as the *ground of novelty*.[58] The primordial nature of God, said Whitehead, answers the question, "where does novelty come from?"[59]

This question is crucial, because evolution presupposes the emergence of novel forms. The argument to God from novelty is based on the fact that novel eternal objects—meaning possibilities previously unrealized in our cosmic epoch—do get realized. This fact implies that these possibilities, before they got realized, were somehow *relevant* to the actual entities that realized them.

How could this relevance be understood? Whitehead's answer is contained in a passage about the ontological principle that was only partially quoted earlier:

> Everything must be somewhere; and here "somewhere" means "some actual entity." Accordingly the general potentiality of

the universe must be somewhere; since it retains its proximate relevance to actual entities for which it is unrealized. . . . This "somewhere" is the non-temporal actual entity. Thus "proximate relevance" means "relevance as in the primordial mind of God."[60]

In a parallel passage, Whitehead made the point in a way that more clearly brought out the argument from novelty:

In what sense can unrealized abstract form be relevant? What is its basis of relevance? "Relevance" must express some real fact of togetherness among forms. The ontological principle can be expressed as: All real togetherness is togetherness in the formal constitution of an actuality. So if there be a relevance of what in the temporal world is unrealized, the relevance must express a fact of togetherness in the formal constitution of a non-temporal actuality.[61]

This argument from novelty is presupposed in the notion of God as the ground of the upward trend of the evolutionary process, because every stage of this upward trend involves the realization of novel forms.

Like order, novelty is not good in itself, but only as it serves the divine aim: "'Order' and 'novelty' are but the instruments of [God's] subjective aim," which is the growth of intrinsically valuable experiences.[62]

SUMMARY

In a statement summarizing his arguments from metaphysical order, cosmological order, progress, and novelty, Whitehead wrote that, apart from God, "there could be nothing new in the world, and no order in the world." The novel forms derived from God, therefore, "are the foundations of progress."[63]

ENDNOTES

1. Alfred North Whitehead, *The Function of Reason* (1929; Beacon Press, 1968), 76.

2. Alfred North Whitehead, *Process and Reality: An Essay in Cosmology,* corrected edition, ed. David Ray Griffin and Donald W. Sherburne

(1929; Free Press, 1978), 283.

3, Ibid., 93.

4, Ibid., 343.

5. Immanuel Kant, *Critique of Pure Reason*, trans. N. Kemp Smith (St. Martin's Press, 1929), A627/B655.

6. Kai Nielsen, *Philosophy and Atheism: In Defense of Atheism* (Prometheus Books, 1985), 18.

7. Whitehead, *Process and Reality*, 96.

8. Alfred North Whitehead, *Adventures of Ideas* (Free Press, 1967), 113–14.

9. Ibid., 111–12.

10. Ibid., 114–15.

11. Ibid., 130.

12. Ibid., 115.

13. Ibid., 166.

14. Thomas Nagel, *Mind and Cosmos: Why the Materialist Neo-Darwinian Conception of Nature Is Almost Certainly False* (Oxford University Press, 2012), 7, 92, 93.

15. Whitehead, *The Function of Reason*, 24.

16. Whitehead, *Process and Reality*, 96, 92, 91.

17. Sean Carroll, "Does the Universe Need God?" *The Blackwell Companion to Science and Christianity,* ed. James B. Stump and Alan G. Padgett (Oxford: Wiley-Blackwell, 2012).

18. Maggie McKee, "Ingenious: Paul J. Steinhardt," Nautilus, 25 September 2014.

19. Rudolf Carnap, "Intellectual Autobiography," in *The Philosophy of Rudolf Carnap*, ed. P. A. Schilpp (Open Court, 1963), 37.

20. Roberto Mangabeira Unger and Lee Smolin, *The Singular Universe and the Reality of Time* (Cambridge University Press, 2015).

21. Ibid., 11.

22. Ibid., xiii, 357, 167, 164.

23. Ibid., 7, 162.

24. Ibid., xi, 37.

25. Ibid., 42–43, 112, 145, 186.

26. Ibid., 357.

27. Whitehead, *The Function of Reason*, 24.

28. Ibid., 4, 5.

29. Stephen Jay Gould, *Ever Since Darwin* (W. W. Norton, 1977), 36, 45.

30. Dov Ospovat, *The Development of Darwin's Theory: Natural History, Natural Theology & Natural Selection 1838–1859* (Cambridge University Press, 1981), 212; Robert J. Richards, "Moral Foundations of the Idea of Evolutionary Progress," in Matthew Nitecki, ed., *Evolutionary Progress* (University of Chicago Press, 1988), 129–48, at 131.

31. Ospovat, *The Development of Darwin's Theory*, 72.

32. Richards, "Moral Foundations," 142.

33. William Provine, "Progress in Evolution and Meaning in Life," in Nitecki, ed., *Evolutionary Progress*, 49–74, at 63.

34. Whitehead, *The Function of Reason*, 4, 8.

35. Whitehead, *Religion in the Making*, 101.

36. Whitehead, *Science and the Modern World*, 94.

37. Whitehead, *Process and Reality*, 244; *Religion in the Making*, 100.

38. Whitehead, *Modes of Thought* (1938; Free Press, 1968), 120, 103.

39. Whitehead, *Science and the Modern World*, 94.

40. Whitehead said that "our cosmic epoch is to be conceived primarily as a society of electromagnetic occasions, including electronic and protonic occasions"; *Process and Reality*, 92. Today this statement would need to be modified to mention more primitive occasions, not simply electronic and protonic ones.

41. See, for example, Bernard Rensch, "Arguments for Panpsychistic Identism," in John B. Cobb, Jr., and David Ray Griffin, eds., *Mind in Nature: Essays on the Interface of Science and Philosophy* (University Press of America, 1977), 70–78.

42. Charles Hartshorne, "Physics and Psychics: The Place of Mind in Nature," in Cobb and Griffin, eds., *Mind in Nature*, 89–96, at 95.

43. Griffin, *Reenchantment without Supernaturalism: A Process Philosophy of Religion* (Cornell University Press, 2001), Introduction.

44. See, for example, Daniel Chamovitz, *What a Plant Knows: A Field Guide to the Senses* (Scientific American/Farrar, Straus and Giroux, 2013), and Stefano Mancuso and Alessandra Viola, *Brilliant Green: The Surprising History and Science of Plant Intelligence* (Island Press, 2015). A much earlier book was Peter Tompkins and Christopher Bird, *The Secret Life of Plants: A Fascinating Account of the Physical, Emotional, and Spiritual Relations Between Plants and Man* (Harper & Row, 1973).

45. Whitehead, *Process and Reality*, 47.

46. John R. Searle, *Minds, Brains, and Science: The 1984 Reith Lectures* (British Broadcasting Corporation, 1984), 94.

47. Ibid., 92, 13, 87.

48. Ibid., 248.

49. Whitehead, *The Function of Reason* (1929; Beacon Press, 1968), 14.

50. John H. Conway and Simon Kochen, "The Free Will Theorem," *Foundations of Physics* 38/10 (2006), 1.

51. Ibid., 26–27.

52. Thomas Nagel, *The View from Nowhere* (Oxford University Press, 1986), 110–17, 123.

53. Nagel, *Mind and Cosmos*, 33, 57-58 n. 16; referring to Hartshorne, "Physics and Psychics: The Place of Mind in Nature."

54. Ibid., 34.

55. Galen Strawson, "The Impossibility of Ultimate Moral Responsibility," Chapter 13 of Strawson's *Real Materialism and Other Essays* (Oxford University Press, 2008), 319–36.

56. Whitehead, *Process and Reality*, 88.

57. I developed this argument in Griffin, *Unsnarling the World-Knot: Consciousness, Freedom, and the Mind-Body Problem* (University of California Press, 1998).

58. Whitehead, *Process and Reality*, 67, 88, 108, 164, 247, 349.

59. William E. Hocking, "Whitehead as I Knew Him," in *Alfred North Whitehead: Essays on His Philosophy*, ed. George L. Kline (Prentice-Hall, 1963), 7–17.

60. Whitehead, *Process and Reality*, 46. As Charles Hartshorne pointed out, it was a mistake, or at least confusing, for Whitehead to refer to God as a "non-temporal actual entity," as if there were no process in God. Given the fact that Whitehead regarded God as having both a primordial and a consequent nature, with the consequent nature being in process with the temporal process of the world, it is best to understand "non-temporal actuality" to mean: an enduring actuality with a non-temporal aspect." For an extensive discussion, see Chapter 4 of David Ray Griffin, *Reenchantment without Supernaturalism: A Process Philosophy of Religion* (Cornell University Press, 2001).

61. Ibid., 32. On the reference to God as "non-temporal actuality," see the previous note.

62. Ibid., 88.

63. Ibid., 247.

14

Teleological Order

According to the cosmological order of the universe, as developed in the previous chapter, this order includes a divinely inspired drive toward evolutionary progress. This way of looking at the universe is a type of teleology. The teleological order of the universe is part of its cosmological order.

Customarily, however, the teleological argument for a divine reality has been treated separately. In addition to custom, moreover, it makes sense to devote a separate chapter to the universe's teleological order, because of the complexity of the issue and hence the number of pages needed to discuss it. This discussion builds on the teleological naturalism introduced in the previous chapter.

Thomas Nagel, as we have seen, believes that an adequate world-view requires a naturalistic teleology. The present chapter shows that Whitehead's teleological view of the universe can be deepened on the basis of recent developments in cosmology.

1. TELEOLOGY AS FINE-TUNING

Nowadays, the description of the universe as teleological is usually discussed in terms of the idea that the universe has been "fine-tuned" to enable the possibility of life.

276

THE BEGINNING OF FINE-TUNING ARGUMENTS

One of the first arguments for this conclusion was by a biochemist at Harvard University named Lawrence Joseph Henderson, who in 1913 wrote a book entitled *The Fitness of the Environment: An Inquiry into the Biological Significance of the Properties of Matter*.

As a biochemist, Henderson focused especially on the properties of water, along with its prevalence on the Earth. Saying that the properties of matter can now be said to be "intimately related to the structure of the living being," Henderson suggested that "the whole evolutionary process, both cosmic and organic, is one," and that the universe in its very essence is "biocentric." In a 1917 book entitled *The Order of Nature*, Henderson, speaking of the properties that served as the precondition for life, said: "The chance that this unique ensemble of properties should occur by 'accident' is almost infinitely small."[1]

THE ANTHROPIC PRINCIPLE

In the 1970s, physicists started engaging in that type of argumentation. In 1974, Brandon Carter published an essay entitled "Large Number of Coincidences and the Anthropic Principle in Cosmology."[2] But the subsequent discussion of the so-called anthropic principle, also called "anthropic reasoning," has been confused and confusing. University of Toronto computer scientist Radford Neal said: "There is a large literature on the Anthropic Principle, much of it too confused to address." And Canadian philosopher John Leslie has said: "The ways in which 'anthropic' reasoning can be misunderstood form a long and dreary list."[3]

This confusion would not have resulted if other scientists had simply stuck with Brandon Carter's definition, according to which the anthropic principle is a tautology—a logically necessary truth. One can ask, "Why do we observe a universe having conditions making the emergence of intelligent life possible?" The simplest answer is that, by definition, only a universe allowing for intelligent beings could be observed by such beings. Carter did distinguish between a "weak" and a "strong" anthropic principle, but the difference was not great. They both, in Leslie's words, "describe logically necessary links between observations and observation-permitting conditions."[4]

However, the fact that the anthropic principle is tautologous does not mean that it cannot teach us anything. For example, Leslie, paraphrasing Carter, pointed out that the principle says that "our universe must now be *old enough* for heavy elements—needed to build our bodies—to have been formed inside stars and then scattered by stellar explosions."[5]

ANTHROPIC PHILOSOPHIES

However, many writers have redefined the anthropic principle so that it is no longer a tautology but instead provides the basis for an "anthropic philosophy." There are, moreover, two types of anthropic philosophies: one reductive, the other expansive.

An *expansive* anthropic philosophy was developed in a 1986 book by John D. Barrow and Frank J. Tipler entitled *The Anthropic Cosmological Principle*.[6] This book was valuable in going beyond Carter by including the constants of physics in describing the fine-tuning of the universe. But as University of Sydney physicist Luke Barnes has explained, Barrow and Tipler changed the very meaning of the anthropic principle.[7]

Whereas Carter had distinguished between a Weak Anthropic Principle (WAP) and a Strong Anthropic Principle (SAP), as mentioned, Barrow and Tipler defined them very differently. They also added John Wheeler's Participatory Anthropic Principle (PAP),[8] based on his version of quantum mechanics, according to which "observers are necessary to bring the Universe into being."[9] Barrow and Tipler then added the Final Anthropic Principle (FAP). Inspired by Teilhard de Chardin's Omega Point, FAP says that, once intelligent information-processing comes into existence, it will never die out. Barrow and Tipler concluded the description of FAP with these words:

> At the instant the Omega Point is reached, life will have gained control of *all* matter and forces not only in a single universe, but in all universes whose existence is logically possible; life will have spread into *all* spatial regions in all universes which could logically exist, and will have stored an infinite amount of information, including *all* bits of knowledge which it is logically possible to know.[10]

Martin Gardner justly dubbed this the Completely Ridiculous Anthropic Principle (CRAP).[11]

In 1989, John Gribbin and Martin Rees wrote a much more sober book entitled *Cosmic Coincidences: Dark Matter, Mankind, and Anthropic Cosmology,* which argued that a large number of apparently independent physical constants were all necessary for the evolution of carbon-based life. Although they spoke positively of "anthropic cosmology," Gribbin and Rees rejected what they called Barrow and Tipler's "baroque elaboration." Rather, they advocated only

> the mildest form of what is now known as anthropic reasoning, or anthropic cosmology. Given the brute fact that we are a carbon-based form of life, which evolved slowly on a planet orbiting around a star like our Sun . . . , there are some features of the Universe, some constraints on the possible values of physical constants which can be inferred quite straightforwardly. . . . Simply from the fact that we are a carbon-based life form we can deduce that the Universe must be a certain size and a certain age.[12]

However, having advocated only the "mildest form" of anthropic reasoning, Gribbin and Rees then used anthropic reasoning to argue that that the universe was "tailor-made for man"[13]—which is far from being a logical truism.

Moreover, if one were to go beyond the anthropic principle to argue that the universe is tailor-made for anything, it would be better to speak of the physical universe as "tailor-made for life," while adding that the possibility of human-like intelligence was made possible by the non-physical factors of the universe discussed above in Chapters 7, 8, 9, and 10—namely, the principles of mathematics, morality, logic, rationality, and truth. Unless these principles belong to the fabric of the universe, human-like beings could never have emerged.

In the *reductive* anthropic philosophy, the anthropic principle is used to argue not only that we should not be surprised that we observe a life-supporting universe, but also that we should not be surprised that there *is* a life-supporting universe. This type of anthropic philosophy implies that our existence as observers can serve as an explanation of our universe, so that no further explanation is needed. John Leslie explained why this is not true with a firing-squad parable, which he made famous.

According to this parable: You are dragged before a firing squad of 100 expert marksmen, all of whom have their rifles aimed at your heart. After you hear the order to fire, you observe that you are still alive. An acquaintance says that you should not be surprised, because you could not possibly have observed anything else; you could not have observed that you were dead. However, you point out, the fact that you are still alive is indeed surprising, because it is most unlikely that all 100 marksmen would have missed.

By analogy, although it is not surprising that the universe we observe is life-permitting, it *is* surprising that that there is a life-permitting universe, which is partly surprising because of the fineness of the fine-tuning.

2. THE FINENESS OF THE FINE-TUNING

At some point, some physicists began to speak about the universe as having been "fine-tuned for life." The fineness of the tuning was expressed by Paul Davies—an English physicist now at Arizona State University—who said: "Had this exceedingly delicate tuning of values been even slightly upset, the subsequent structure of the universe would have been totally different."[14]

However, calling such features "fine-tuned" does not merely mean that they were all necessary if life was to develop. As Luke Barnes says, "Fine-tuning involves a comparison between the life-permitting range of the fundamental parameters with their possible range."[15] Put otherwise, calling features "finely-tuned for life" does not imply only that they allow for life. It implies that they are *surprising*. As Christian philosopher Peter S. Williams said, we should "be surprised at observing features of the universe" that, besides being "necessary for our existence," are also "highly improbable."[16]

These fine-tuned characteristics are generally discussed in terms of laws of nature and initial conditions as well as the constants of physics.[17] But scientists usually focus primarily on the constants. A discussion of these constants can begin with the four forces of physics—gravity, the strong force, the weak force, and electromagnetism.

THE FOUR FORCES OF PHYSICS

Gravity is a long-range attractive force. Without it, there could be no stars and no planets.

- Gravity is extremely weak, but if it had been still weaker, the stars would have been red dwarfs. While lasting for a very long time, they would not have burned hot enough to support planets on which life could develop.

- But if gravity had been a bit stronger, all stars would have been blue giants, which would have been so hot that they could not have lasted the billions of years it takes life to develop.[18]

The Strong Force is a very powerful but short-range force, exerting influence only within the atom's nucleus, where it binds protons and neutrons together. This strong force determines the amount of energy released when simple atoms undergo nuclear fusion. When hydrogen in a star turns into helium, the helium atom is slightly lighter than the two protons and two neutrons that went into making it. So 0.007 of the hydrogen's mass is converted into energy.

If this figure were 0.006 instead 0.007, protons and neutrons would not bond together, so helium could not be formed. The result would be an all-hydrogen universe. But if this figure were instead 0.008, then protons would bond together without the aid of neutrons, so that no hydrogen would remain. "[W]hat is remarkable," said Martin Rees—who is Great Britain's astronomer royal—"is that no carbon-based biosphere could exist if this number had been 0.006 or 0.008 rather than 0.007."[19]

The Weak Force also exerts influence only within the nucleus, where it is responsible for converting neutrons into protons (by radioactive decay, in which a neutron is changed into a proton and an electron). The weakness of this force allowed the sun to "burn its hydrogen gently for billions of years," thereby allowing the universe to have time to bring about life.[20]

- If this force had been much weaker, there would have been no excess protons to make hydrogen, leading to all-helium stars, which would not provide the basis for the emergence of life.[21]
- But if this force had been much stronger, then "the Big Bang's nuclear burning would have proceeded past helium and all the way to iron," making fusion-powered stars impossible.[22]

In other words, if the weak force had been significantly weaker or stronger, there would have been no hydrogen and hence no life as we know it.

Electromagnetism is essential for the formation of atoms, because it holds electrons, which are negatively charged, in orbit around the nucleus, which is positively charged. But electromagnetism, which exerts repulsive as well as attractive force, had to have about the same strength it actually does have if the universe were to make the creation of life possible (see below).

OTHER CONSTANTS OF PHYSICS

In addition, there are many constants of physics involving ratios that need to be approximately what they are if life was to develop:

The Ratio of Gravity to Electromagnetism: Whereas gravity attracts and compresses, electromagnetism repulses in some situations. Electromagnetism is much stronger than gravity—about a trillion, trillion, trillion times stronger. In spite of the enormity of this ratio, scientists say, it could not have been much different if life were to be possible.

- If gravitational attraction were much stronger, stars would be smaller and would burn so hot that their life spans would be too short for life to develop.
- But if gravitation were much weaker, electromagnetism would become competitive with it for small objects, so planet masses would be much smaller, and a miniaturized sun would burn much more quickly, lasting perhaps only 10 thousand rather than the 10 billion years needed for the creation of the heavier elements—including carbon and oxygen—and the evolution of life.

The Strong Force-Electromagnetism Ratio: If the strong force were much stronger, the electromagnetic force would not have been strong enough to prevent protons from sticking together, so there would be no free protons to form hydrogen. But if the strong force had been much weaker, then complex atomic nuclei, upon which life depends, would be unable to form. Looked at from the other side: Stephen Hawking says that "if the electric charge of the electron had been only slightly different, stars either would have been unable to burn hydrogen and helium, or else they would not have exploded."[23] According to astrophysicists John Barrow and Joseph Silk, "small changes in the electric charge of the electron would block any kind of chemistry."[24] Indeed, such changes would make the electron's orbit unstable, preventing the existence of atoms.

The Ratio of Gravity to the Strong Force: Gravity is 10,000 billion billion billion billion times weaker than the strong nuclear force. If gravity were, say, only 10,000 billion billion billion times weaker than the strong force, stars would not to exist for more than a billion years—not nearly long enough for life to develop.[25]

The Mass Difference of Protons and Neutrons: Neutrons are heavier than protons, but only *very* slightly—the ratio of their masses is 939.56563 to 938.27231. If the mass of neutrons were increased a tiny bit more—by one part in seven hundred—hydrogen could not be turned into helium, so stars could not be formed. But if neutrons were slightly lighter, an all-helium universe would have resulted.[26]

These are only a few of the many fundamental constants that had to be fine-tuned for life in our universe to have developed—by one count, 26 such constants.[27]

3. EXPLAINING FINE-TUNING

According to physicist Paul Davies, "There is now broad agreement among physicists and cosmologists that the Universe is in several respects 'fine-tuned' for life."[28] This agreement is shared by traditional theists and deists, which is not surprising, but also by atheists, such as Stephen Hawking.[29] For example, Hawking wrote:

The laws of science, as we know them at present, contain many
fundamental numbers, like the size of the electric charge of the
electron and the ratio of the masses of the proton and the electron. . . . The remarkable fact is that the values of these numbers
seem to have been very finely adjusted to make possible the
development of life.[30]

The fact that our universe appears to be fine-tuned for life, it is
generally agreed, cannot be simply explained as a lucky accident—at
least in the normal sense, as when a poker player gets a straight flush and
then, with no cheating, in the very next game is dealt four aces. Rather,
it is generally accepted that some explanation is needed. Competing
explanations have been offered.

4. AN INTELLIGENT COSMIC AGENT

The simplest explanation is that the fine-tuning was the work of an
intelligent cosmic agent. As Paul Davies put it: "It seems as though
someone has fine tuned nature's numbers to make the universe. . . . The
impression of design is overwhelming."[31] According to John Lennox in
God's Undertaker, "the more we get to know about our universe, the more
the hypothesis that there is a Creator . . . gains in credibility as the best
explanation of why we are here."[32]

The most outspoken advocates of this interpretation are traditional
theists and deists. For example, philosopher Robin Collins of Messiah
College, advocating the "theistic hypothesis," said:

According to this hypothesis, there exists an omnipotent, omniscient, everlasting or eternal, perfectly free creator of the universe whose existence does not depend on anything outside
itself.[33]

Writing from a deistic perspective, author Michael Corey argued that
"the theological doctrine of omnipotence can be *justified purely from a
scientific point of view,*" partly because "the universe's many constituent
parameters were perfectly fine-tuned to bring about life *from the very
beginning.*"[34]

Also, people who had not believed in any cosmic intelligence can be converted by the evidence for fine-tuning. An example is provided by famous astronomer Fred Hoyle, who had long been so opposed to theism that he rejected the Big Bang—the name of which he had sarcastically coined—in favor of the steady-state view of the universe, because it seemed less suggestive of theism.

But his atheism was "shaken," said Hoyle, by a discovery he made about the carbon nucleus.[35] This nucleus, which involves six protons and six neutrons, is formed by combining three helium nuclei. However, explained Martin Rees,

> There is negligible chance of all three coming together simultaneously, and so the process happens via an intermediate stage where two helium nuclei combined into beryllium (four protons and four neutrons) before combining with anther helium nucleus to form carbon.

But unfortunately, "the beryllium nucleus is unstable: it would decay so quickly that there seemed little chance of a third helium nucleus coming along and sticking to it before it decays." Fortunately, however, the carbon nucleus has a "resonance" with a very particular energy that "enhances the chance that beryllium will grab another helium nucleus in the brief interval before it decays."[36]

Hoyle had predicted this particular resonant energy, which is just higher than the combined energies of beryllium and helium. Some experimental physicists then demonstrated this prediction to be correct.[37] "Some supercalculating intellect," the erstwhile atheist Hoyle declared, "must have designed the properties of the carbon atom," after which he added: "The numbers one calculates from the facts seem to me so overwhelming as to put this conclusion almost beyond question."[38] (Hoyle would later argue that the universe as a whole is intelligent, evolving itself in accordance with a great plan, becoming more complex.[39])

Another example of a thinker converted from atheism by fine-tuning was philosopher Antony Flew, who had been one of the world's best-known atheists. (Some of Flew's argumentation against the existence of Gawd was discussed in Chapter 1.) After becoming aware of the evidence for fine-tuning, Flew concluded that "the only viable explanation [for] the origin of the laws of nature" is "the divine Mind."[40] Flew made clear, however, that he did not accept traditional theism. Calling himself a deist, he described his deity as "the first initiating and sustaining cause of the universe."[41]

A pantheistic example of explaining fine-tuning by affirming a cosmic intelligence has been provided by John Leslie.[42] Given the common understanding of pantheism, according to which "God" is simply the world as a whole but not a conscious being, fine-tuning could not be explained in terms of an intelligent cosmic agent. According to Leslie's version of pantheism, however, God is a unified consciousness, and all the "intricately structured things of our universe exist merely because [the divine mind] thinks of this universe in all of its details."[43] From this point of view, Leslie said:

> The fine-tuning, together with the life-permitting nature of the basic laws of physics, probably cannot be understood without something with some right to be called *belief in God*. However, perhaps only pantheism can make such belief at all plausible.[44]

If theists, deists, and pantheists all explain the fine-tuning of the universe as the effect of an intelligent agent, how could atheists explain it?

5. ADDING A MULTIVERSE TO THE ANTHROPIC PRINCIPLE

Some thinkers have suggested that the idea of intelligence behind fine-turning can be avoided by the anthropic principle in the context of a "multiverse." According to the multiverse idea, what we have considered "the universe" is, rather than being the totality of everything that exists, simply a tiny piece of a much larger whole.

As discussed above, the anthropic principle is based on the fact that our universe is well-suited for the existence for beings who can observe it. Far from being a surprise, this principle is a tautology: The universe we observe is necessarily fit for observers.

Brandon Carter later regretted that he had described this principle as "anthropic," because it does not refer to human observers in particular, but simply any observers.[45] It would seem, therefore, that his principle should be renamed the "observer principle." This principle does not either support or undermine belief in an intelligent creator, because it is a tautology. But the anthropic (observer) principle in conjunction with the multiverse hypothesis can be used to call the idea of an intelligent creator unnecessary.

To explain: Given the realization that our universe was able to support life depended on an enormous amount of fine-tuning, it would be surprising if (a) our universe had come about by chance, without a purposeful creator, and if (b) it were the only universe. The possibility that our universe came by chance would be so improbable as to be virtually impossible. This degree of impossibility would virtually entail that our universe was purposively created. This line of thought led scientists opposed to the idea of a divine creator to promote the multiverse idea.

A MULTIVERSE AS ALTERNATIVE TO DIVINE CREATION

Although there are many versions of the multiverse hypothesis, it is basically the idea that our universe is only one of a large number, perhaps an infinite number, of parallel universes, each of which has its own laws. This hypothesis provides a basis for thinking of our universe, in spite of its fine-tuning, as an "accidental universe."[46] The idea is that, given every possible type of universe, one of them was bound by chance to be a universe that promotes life and, by the anthropic principle, we necessarily observe such a universe.

Scientists on both sides of the issue agree that the multiverse idea has been motivated by the desire to avoid a divine creator:

- Arno Penzias, who won the Nobel Prize as co-discoverer of the cosmic microwave background, said: "Some people are uncomfortable with the purposefully created world. To come up with things that contradict purpose, they tend to speculate about things they haven't seen."[47]

- "The many improbable occurrences that conspired to enable our existence," wrote Stephen Hawking, would seem to be a miracle created by a benevolent God, "if ours were the only solar system in the universe." However, if there are many parallel universes, each with different laws, then the "apparent miracle" that our universe is ideally fit for life disappears: "the multiverse concept can explain the fine-tuning of physical law without the need for a benevolent creator who made the universe for our benefit."[48]

- "If one does not believe in providential design, but still thinks the fine-tuning needs some explanation," said Martin Rees, the multiverse hypothesis provides an option.[49]

- Cal Tech's Sean Carroll, saying that most scientists "would prefer a theory that was completely free of appeals to supernatural agents," wrote: "Given the number of potential universes, it wouldn't be surprising that one (or an infinite number) were compatible with the existence of intelligent life. Once this background is in place, the 'anthropic principle' is simply the statement that our observable universe has no reason to be representative of the larger whole: we will inevitably find ourselves in a region that allows for us to exist."[50]

CRITIQUES OF THE MULTIVERSE HYPOTHESIS

The multiverse hypothesis has developed quite a following. In addition to Hawking, Rees, and Carroll, many other physicists have written positively about the multiverse hypothesis, including Columbia University's Brian Greene, who has advocated it in two best-selling books.[51] But many physicists have written about it negatively, criticizing it on several grounds:

Violation of Occam's Razor: One of the most common objections to the multiverse idea is that it dramatically violates Occam's razor, according to which, all other things being equal, the simplest hypothesis should be chosen. For example, Paul Davies said that "the multiverse represents an inconceivably flagrant violation of Occam's razor—postulating an enormous ensemble of essentially unobservable universes, just to explain our own."[52] To postulate billions or trillions—perhaps an infinite number—of universes, rather than a single deity, does seem to violate Occam's principle.

It can be argued, to be sure, that the multiverse idea does not necessarily violate Occam's principle, because the meaning of "simplest" is debatable. For example, Max Tegmark said:

As a theoretical physicist, I judge the elegance and simplicity of a theory not by its ontology, but by the elegance and simplicity of its mathematical equations—and it's quite striking to me that the mathematically simplest theories tend to give us multiverses.[53]

Nevertheless, no such refinement of the meaning of "simplest theory" can support a plausible claim that the simplest explanation of the apparent fine-tuning of the universe is the existence of billions of universes. This explanation is indeed, as Davies said, a "flagrant violation of Occam's razor."

Not Really Scientific: According to Luke Barnes, the multiverse idea "will surely forever hold the title of the most extreme extrapolation in all of science, if indeed it can be counted as part of science."[54] Several physicists, moreover, have argued that it indeed *cannot* be regarded as a scientific hypothesis.

- Princeton University's Paul Steinhardt, after having helped create the multiverse idea, rejected it. "It's not even a scientific theory," said Steinhardt, because "it allows every conceivable possibility."[55]

- In an article entitled "You Think There's a Multiverse? Get Real," Perimeter Institute's Lee Smolin said that "the multiverse theory has difficulty making any firm predictions and threatens to take us out of the realm of science."[56]

- English physicist and theologian John Polkinghorne wrote: "Let us recognize these speculations for what they are. They are not physics, but in the strictest sense, metaphysics. There is no purely scientific reason to believe in an ensemble of universes."[57]

- Similarly, according to South African applied mathematician George Ellis, "the case for the multiverse is inconclusive. The basic reason is the extreme flexibility of the proposal: it is more a concept than well-defined theory." Ellis added: "Nothing is wrong with scientifically based philosophical speculation. . . . But we should name [the multiverse proposal] for what it is."[58]

Science Stopper: A third objection to the multiverse theory is that it is unscientific in a different sense—that it could be used as an excuse to accept a premature answer. Even Brian Greene has admitted that it could be a "science stopper," saying:

> If true, the idea of a multiverse would be . . . a rich and astounding upheaval, but one with potentially hazardous consequences. Beyond the inherent difficulty in assessing its validity, when should we allow the multiverse framework to be invoked in lieu of a more traditional scientific explanation? Had this idea surfaced a hundred years ago, might researchers have chalked up various mysteries to how things just happen to be in our corner of the multiverse and not pressed on to discover all the wondrous science of the last century? . . . When faced with seemingly inexplicable observations, researchers may invoke the framework of the multiverse prematurely—proclaiming some phenomenon or other to merely reflect conditions in our own bubble universe and thereby failing to discover the deeper understanding that awaits us.[59]

Well-known physicist Heinz Pagels was even more negative, saying that those physicists and cosmologists who took this approach were "gratuitously abandoning the successful program of conventional physical science of understanding the quantitative properties of our universe on the basis of physical laws."[60]

Unnecessary: A fourth reason for rejecting the multiverse view is that it is not needed to solve the scientific problems for which it was created. To understand this objection, it is necessary to know that the multiverse idea arose out of the idea of cosmic "inflation," according to which the expansion of the universe began with a very brief inflationary phase, during which the size of the universe accelerated very rapidly, doubling and redoubling many times in a very small period to time.

The hypothesis of this inflation was regarded as necessary to overcome some problems with the original Big Bang theory, such as the so-called horizon problem.[61] According to Steinhardt, these problems can all be avoided by replacing the idea of a "big bang" with that of a "big bounce"—that is, an infinite cyclical universe (which is a version of the same basic idea accepted by Whitehead).[62]

Does Not Eliminate Fine-Tuning: A fifth problem with the multiverse theory is that, although it was motivated by the desire to eliminate fine-tuning and thereby a divine creator, it does not really do this.

- According to Paul Davies, "the scientific multiple worlds hypothesis merely shifts the problem up a level from universe to multiverse." Explaining why, Davies said: "The multiverse comes with a lot of baggage, such as an overarching space and time to host all those bangs, a universe-generating mechanism to trigger them, physical fields to populate the universes with material stuff, and a selection of forces to make things happen. Cosmologists embrace these features by envisaging sweeping 'meta-laws' that pervade the multiverse and spawn specific bylaws on a universe-by-universe basis. The meta-laws themselves remain unexplained—eternal, immutable transcendent entities that just happen to exist and must simply be accepted as given. In that respect the meta-laws have a similar status to an unexplained transcendent god."[63]

- Paul Steinhardt agreed, saying: "From the very beginning, even as I was writing my first paper on inflation in 1982, I was concerned that the inflationary picture only works if you finely tune the constants that control the inflationary period. . . . The whole point of inflation was to get rid of fine-tuning—to explain features of the original big bang model that must be fine-tuned to match observations. The fact that we had to introduce one fine-tuning to remove another was worrisome." Continuing, Steinhardt said: "I did not take the multiverse problem seriously at first even though I had been involved in uncovering it. I thought someone would figure out a resolution once the problem was revealed. . . . Unfortunately, what has happened since is that all attempts to resolve the multiverse problem have failed."[64]

In sum: There are many good reasons for rejecting the multiverse hypothesis.

6. FINE-TUNING: EVIDENCE FOR GAWD OR GOD?

As we have seen, it is widely agreed that our universe seems to be fine-tuned for life and, in addition, that the recognition of this fact is widely thought to have forced people to choose between a multiverse and a divine creator. Indeed, as we have seen, the main motivation for pursuing the multiverse idea has been the desire to avoid affirming a divine creator.

However, pointed out deity-averse Thomas Nagel, "it is just as irrational to be influenced in one's beliefs by the hope that God does not exist as by the hope that God does exist."[65] Accordingly, scientists and others should do their best to avoid being unduly influenced by their hopes, looking as dispassionately as possible at which alternative has the best evidence.

As to why many science-based thinkers have wanted to explain away fine-tuning in order to remove its support for a divine creator, they have usually done so on the assumption that such a creator would necessarily be a supernatural being, which could interrupt the normal cause-effect relations. For example, in explaining why he has rejected the idea of a divine creator, Stephen Hawking said: "Religion believes in miracles," which "aren't compatible with science."[66] However, a divine creator responsible for fine-tuning would not necessarily be a supernatural, omnipotent being.

It is true that most of the thinkers who believe that the universe has been finely tuned while rejecting the multiverse idea—such as Peter Williams, Robin Collins, and Michael Corey—argue that it points to the existence of an omnipotent deity. The list of such thinkers also includes George Ellis, who proposed a Christian Anthropic Principle, combining design with divine omnipotence.[67]

Still another example is Richard Swinburne, who has argued that the existence of a benevolent and omnipotent creator would make a universe fine-tuned for human life much more probable than would otherwise be the case. Accordingly, Swinburne argued, fine-tuning provides evidence for Gawd.[68]

However, Quentin Smith has argued that, given the fact that our universe has "a large amount of gratuitous natural evil," it is reasonable to conclude that "[Gawd] does not exist, since [Gawd] is omnipotent, omniscient and perfectly good and thereby would not permit any gratuitous natural evil." Moreover, said Smith, "gratuitous natural evils are precisely what we would expect if a malevolent spirit created the universe." The fine-tuning of the universe, accordingly, leads to this conclusion: "If any spirit created the universe, it is malevolent, not benevolent."[69]

Although Swinburne would reject Smith's claim that *prima facie* gratuitous evil points to a malevolent creator, he would say that at least Smith recognized that the fine-tuning of the laws to allow for life supports the existence of an omnipotent creator!

However, that claim can be challenged. One could reject Smith's claim by arguing that the creation of our world, with its fine-tuning for life, does not require divine omnipotence.

NO EVIDENCE FOR GAWD: WHITEHEAD

Alfred North Whitehead, who endorsed Lawrence Joseph Henderson's argument that our universe is biocentric and that this fact is not accidental, did not accept the idea that the creation of a universe suited for life required a supernatural, omnipotent deity.

Although Whitehead only occasionally cited recent books in his writings, in *Process and Reality* he called the books by Henderson "fundamental for any discussion of [the order of nature]."[70] Whitehead made abundantly clear in *Process and Reality* and other books that he rejected the notion of a supernatural, omnipotent deity. As quoted in Chapter 1, Whitehead rejected belief in "one supreme reality, omnipotently disposing a wholly derivative world," in favor of the view "that the divine element in the world is to be conceived as a persuasive agency and not as a coercive agency."[71] Consistently with that view of divine power, as stated in the previous chapter, Whitehead held that "the creation of [our] world is not the beginning of [finite] matter of fact, but the incoming of a certain type of social order."[72]

Whitehead must, accordingly, have considered Henderson's conclusion—that the universe is non-accidentally biocentric—consistent with his non-omnipotent deity. Indeed, Henderson's thinking may have played a role in the development of Whitehead's position, according to which the distinctively cosmological features of our world—all the general features beyond the metaphysical principles—are rooted in a primordial decision (with "primordial" meaning not *eternal* but *at the outset of this cosmic epoch*).[73]

Like Darwin, Whitehead did not believe that absolutely everything about our world came about through evolution. Rather, both men believed, the basic framework within which evolution could occur was established by a divine creator. But Darwin considered the deity omnipotent, whereas Whitehead did not. The question is: How could a non-omnipotent deity have fine-tuned our universe? Whitehead did not discuss this matter, at least in print. But there is a possible way to understand it.

Like C. S. Peirce and William James, who regarded the laws of nature as habits,[74] Whitehead considered the regularities discovered by science as simply the most widespread, long-standing "habits of nature," its "communal customs."[75] The reason why the God of process theism cannot usually bring about effects unilaterally, or even virtually so, one can say, is that the divine influence always faces enormous competition from the past world. This past world largely involves well-entrenched habits, which are involved in long-lasting enduring individuals such as protons, molecules, bacteria, eukaryotic cells, and animals of all types.

However, prior to the beginning of our particular cosmic epoch, the realm of finite actualities was (by hypothesis) in a state of chaos, in the sense that there were no enduring individuals, not even extremely simple ones, such as photons, electrons, and quarks. So, although our universe was not created out of absolutely nothing, in the sense of a complete absence of finite actualities, it *was* created out of a state of no-thing, in the sense of a state of affairs in which there were no "things" in the ordinary sense of the term, namely, *enduring* things. Instead, there *was,* by hypothesis, a multiplicity of finite actual occasions, which were extremely brief events—enduring less than a billionth or even a trillionth of a second[76]—happening at random. Because there were no enduring individuals, these fleeting events embodied no habits, no principles other than the purely metaphysical principles.

The present cosmic epoch began (by hypothesis) with the creation of extremely small enduring individuals—such as quarks, photons, neutrinos, and electrons—with each such individual being a serial-ly-ordered society of actual occasions (such as electronic occasions). In such serially-ordered societies, each occasion embodies not only the metaphysical principles but also the more-or-less complex contingent form embodied in its predecessors in that society. Each such enduring individual, in other words, embodies a habitual way of being, which through its long-standing repetition of a contingent form gives this form considerable power to implant itself in future events.

But prior to the emergence of any such habits, the divine influence, in seeking to implant a set of contingent principles in the universe, would have had no competition from any contingent principles. In that situation, divine persuasion could produce quasi-coercive effects—that is, effects that could appear to result from Gawd, although really from God.

From then on, however, the divine persuasive activity would always face competition from the power embodied in the habits reflecting these contingent principles, so that divine persuasion would never again, as long as this cosmic epoch exists, be able to guarantee quasi-coercive results. In this way, one can understand how the fine-tuning of our universe does not imply the existence of Gawd, but rather a non-omnipotent deity whose goodness is not contradicted by the evils of the universe.

According to this account, the behaviors of things reflect influences from four sources: (1) God; (2) the metaphysical principles; (3) the cosmological laws (about which Whitehead said: "'God' is that actuality in the world, in virtue of which there is physical 'law'"[77]); and (4) the habits that have developed. Of course, the metaphysical principles and cosmological principles are effective by virtue of being embodied in God; but God is also directly effective, providing possible novelty.

This way of explaining our universe, by employing the idea of God, is not "scientific" in the sense that, given these four sources, one should be able to predict the nature of the next cosmic epoch. But this way of explaining the universe is scientific in the sense of not being *anti*-scientific.

AVOIDING AD HOC EXPLANATIONS

It is generally agreed that one way to be anti-scientific is to employ *ad hoc* explanations. An *ad hoc* explanation is one that exists for no other reason than saving a favored hypothesis. That is, it is ad hoc because it does not help explain any other data. The multiverse idea, developed to explain away the apparent fine-tuning of the universe in order to save the hypothesis that the universe has no divine creator, can be considered the ultimate ad hoc hypothesis.

It might seem, therefore, that the multiverse and the idea of a divine creator would be in the same boat, because both would be ad hoc hypotheses. That would certainly be true of the hypothesis that the reason for the fine-turning is that the universe was created by Gawd. This fact becomes obvious when one sees the many reasons, discussed in Part I, for rejecting the existence of Gawd.

However, the idea that the universe was fine-tuned by a non-omnipotent universal mind is not an *ad hoc* hypothesis: As shown in the second part of this book, such a cosmic mind is needed to explain a wide range of features of our universe. So to explain fine-tuning by reference to God (thus understood) is simply to add one more reason for affirming the existence of God.

To be sure, even with this kind of theism, many scientists and philosophers will, in spite of all the problems with the multiverse hypothesis, prefer it to a theistic explanation of fine-tuning. This preference would follow from the widespread assumption that only the multiverse explanation could count as scientific. This assumption was reflected, for example, in the title of an article in *Discover* magazine, "Science's Alternative to an Intelligent Creator: the Multiverse Theory."[78] That title assumes that the multiverse hypothesis is scientific by virtue of not being theistic.

Scientists and philosophers might be able to overcome this bias if, rather than using the term "God," proponents simply spoke of a cosmic mind, or the mind of the cosmos. A scientific theory about anything can be called a satisfactory theory if it, besides being coherent, is also adequate to all of the relevant facts. With regard to a theory of the universe, *all* of the facts are relevant. If one philosopher concluded that there are various phenomena that are explainable only by positing a cosmic mind, while another philosopher concludes that these phenomena must be ignored, should the second philosopher's theory be considered more scientific than the first one, simply because it does not offer an explanation in order to avoid positing a cosmic mind? Surely not.

7. FINE-TUNING WITHOUT EITHER A CREATOR OR A MULTIVERSE?

In spite of the widespread belief that fine-tuning can be explained only by either affirming a multiverse or a divine creator, Roberto Unger and Lee Smolin have suggested a third option in their book, *The Singular Universe and the Reality of Time*. The second part of that title was discussed in the previous chapter; the present discussion deals with the first part.

In speaking of the "singular universe," Unger and Smolin mean that there is only *one universe at a time*. Like Whitehead, they believe that there have been *successive* universes. Unlike Whitehead, however, they employ the notion of successive universes to explain the fine-tuning of the present universe.

The discovery that the universe appears to be fine-tuned for life, they say, has created what they call cosmology's "greatest crisis of its short history." This discovery caused a crisis, in their view, because there has been no acceptable explanation for the fine-tuning.[79] On the one hand, the multiverse idea is both unscientific (because it is untestable) and absurd, being an "ontological fantasy."[80] On the other hand, Unger and Smolin also evidently believe—they do not explicitly discuss this issue—that any appeal to a divine creator would be unacceptable.

According to their alternative explanation, there is a causal connection from one universe to the next, so many features of our universe could have been inherited from the previous one. In particular, the universe's constants could be explained historically.[81] "Their seemingly arbitrary values may be the result of an earlier universe," being "vestigial forms of a suppressed and forgotten history: testimonials to a vanished world—the one real world earlier on."[82]

By itself, however, Unger and Smolin's solution is inadequate. Insisting that *everything* is temporal, they reject the reality of anything eternal, which leaves them with an inability to be adequate to mathematics, which deals with eternal objects.[83] Unger and Smolin also reject an even partially unchanging divine reality.[84] As a result, their historical explanation of the constants suffers from an infinite regress. That is, the seemingly arbitrary constants of our universals were inherited from the previous universe, which were inherited from an earlier universe, which were inherited from a still earlier universe, and so on back. An infinite regress provides no answer to their question, "Where do these regularities come from."[85]

Moreover, there is a further problem with Unger and Smolin's explanation. They say that our early universe, after the end of the previous universe, had no recurrent phenomena, and hence no laws, for millions of years.[86] Insofar as we accept Whitehead's ontological principle, according to which anything non-actual can exist only in something actual, there would have been nothing in which the constants of the previous universe could have subsisted.

Accordingly, it seems that Unger and Smolin's book, in spite of its admirable focus on the reality of time and the rejection of the multiverse idea, provides no way to avoid the conclusion that the fine-tuning of the universe points to the reality of some form of theism.

CONCLUSION

The scientific community rightly rejects supernatural theism, with its omnipotent deity that can interrupt the world's normal cause-effect relations. But Whitehead, who in *Process and Reality* endorsed a very early version of fine-tuning, provided a basis for explaining the contingent laws of nature in terms of a *naturalistic* theism. So there is no good reason why scientists could not entertain this explanation.

ENDNOTES

1. Lawrence Joseph Henderson, *The Fitness of the Environment: An Inquiry into the Biological Significance of the Properties of Matter* (Macmillan, 1913), 312; *The Order of Nature* (Harvard University Press, 1917), 191.

2. Brandon Carter, "Large Number of Coincidences and the Anthropic Principle in Cosmology," in M.S. Longair, ed., *Confrontation of Cosmological Theories with Observation* (Reidel, 1974).

3. Radford M. Neal, "Puzzles of Anthropic Reasoning Resolved Using Full Non-indexical Conditioning," University of Toronto, 23 August 2006; John Leslie, *Universes* (1989; Routledge, 1996), 136; both quoted in Luke Barnes, "The Traps of WAP and SAP" (Letters to Nature [blog], 4 August 2012).

4. Leslie, *Universes*, 132.

5. Ibid., 128.

6. John D. Barrow and Frank J. Tipler, *The Anthropic Cosmological Principle* (Oxford University Press, 1986).

7. Luke Barnes, in "The Traps of WAP and SAP," showed that "the formulation of WAP and SAP in Barrow and Tipler's [book] is different to Carter's."

8. "The Anthropic Universe," *Science Show*, 18 February 2006.

9. Barrow and Tipler, *The Anthropic Cosmological Principle*, 22.

10. Ibid., 677.

11. Martin Gardner, "WAP, SAP, PAP, and FAP," *New York Review of Books* 23/8 (8 May 1986): 22–25.

12. John Gribbin and Martin Rees, *Cosmic Coincidences: Dark Matter, Mankind, and Anthropic Cosmology* (1989; CreateSpace Independent Publishing Platform, 2015), 8.

13. Ibid., 241, 261, 279.

14. Paul C. W. Davies, *The Accidental Universe* (Cambridge University Press, 1981), 90.

15. Luke A. Barnes, "The Fine-Tuning of the Universe for Intelligent Life," *Publications of the Astronomical Society of Australia*, 29/4 (2012): 529–64.

16. Peter S. Williams, "The Anthropic Design Argument" (extract from *A Sceptic's Guide to Atheism* [Paternoster, 2009], 191–97).

17. More complete discussions speak also of the "initial conditions" of our universe. See, for example, Robin Collins, "The Evidence for Fine-Tuning," in Neil A. Manson, ed., *God and Design: The Teleological Argument and Modern Science* (Routledge, 2003), 178–99.

18. See Barrow and Tipler, *The Anthropic Cosmological Principle*, 336.

19. Martin Rees, *Just Six Numbers: The Deep Forces that Shape the Universe* (Basic Books, 2000), 54–57.

20. Leslie, *Universes,* 34 (quoting Freeman Dyson, "Energy in the Universe," *Scientific American*, September 1971: 51–59).

21. Paul Davies, *Cosmic Jackpot: Why Our Universe is Just Right for Life* (Houghton-Mifflin Co., 2007), 143.

22. Leslie, *Universes*, 34.

23. Stephen Hawking, *A Brief History of Time* (Bantam, 1998), 129.

24. John D. Barrow and Joseph Silk, "The Structure of the Early Universe," *Scientific American*, April 1980.

25. For discussion, see (in addition to Gribbin and Rees) Robin Collins, "The Teleological Argument: An Exploration of the Fine-Tuning of the Cosmos," in *The Blackwell Companion to Natural Theology*, ed. William Lane Craig and J. P. Moreland (Oxford: Wiley Blackwell, 2009); Michael A. Corey, *The God Hypothesis: Discovering Design in Our 'Just Right' Goldilocks Universe* (Rowman & Littlefield, 2001).

26. Oliver Sacks, "My Periodic Table," *New York Times*, 24 July 2015; Paul Davies, *The Goldilocks Enigma: Why Is the Universe Just Right for Life?* (Mariner Books, 2006), 141-43.

27. Ethan Siegel, "It Takes 26 Fundamental Constants to Give Us Our Universe, But They Still Don't Give Everything," *Forbes*, 22 August 2015.

28. Paul Davies, "How Bio-Friendly is the Universe?" *International Journal of Astrobiology,* 2 (2003). The idea that the universe is in any sense fine-tuned for life was rejected in a 2011 book by Victor J. Stenger, *The Fallacy of Fine-Tuning: Why the Universe is Not Designed for Us* (Prometheus Books, 2011). But Luke A. Barnes, in his aforementioned essay "The Fine-Tuning of the Universe for Intelligent Life," argued that Stenger's argument "is so deeply flawed that its results are meaningless." Although Stenger wrote a response called "Defending *The Fallacy of Fine-Tuning,*" Barnes provided an effective counter-response, "In Defence of the Fine-Tuning of the Universe for Intelligent Life," Letters to Nature (blog), 2 May 2012.

29. Many people assumed that Hawking was not an atheist because he had spoken about the possibility of knowing "the mind of God." However, in 2014, he said: "Before we understand science, it is natural to believe that God created the universe. But now science offers a more convincing explanation. What I meant by 'we would know the mind of God' is, we would know everything that God would know, if there were

a God, which there isn't. I'm an atheist"; Alan Boyle, "'I'm an Atheist': Stephen Hawking on God and Space Travel," NBC, 23 September 2014.

30. Stephen Hawking, *A Brief History of Time* (Bantam Books, 1988), 125.

31. Paul Davies, *The Cosmic Blueprint* (Simon & Schuster, 1988), 203.

32. John C. Lennox, *God's Undertaker: Has Science Buried God?* (Lion Hudson, 2007), 68.

33. Collins, "The Teleological Argument: An Exploration of the Fine-Tuning of the Cosmos."

34. Michael A. Corey, *The God Hypothesis: Discovering Design in our 'Just Right' Goldilocks Universe* (Rowman and Littlefield, 2001), 244.

35. Robin Collins, "The Evidence for Fine-Tuning," 184.

36. Martin Rees, *Just Six Numbers*, 50.

37. D. N. F. Dunbar, et al., "The 7.68 MeV State in C12," *Physical Review* 29/3 (1 November 1953).

38. Sir Fred Hoyle, "The Universe: Past and Present Reflections," *Engineering and Science*, November 1981.

39. Fred Hoyle, *Intelligent Universe* (Holt, Rinehart, and Winston, 1983). Incidentally, the fact that Hoyle gave up his atheism does not mean that he adopted the Big Bang cosmology. Rather, continuing to criticize this framework, he argued for an updated, quasi-steady-state model; see Fred Hoyle et al., *A Different Approach to Cosmology: From a Static Universe Through the Big Bang Towards Reality* (Cambridge University Press, 2000).

40. Antony Flew with Roy Varghese, *There is a God: How The World's Most Notorious Atheist Changed His Mind* (Harper Collins, 2007), 121.

41. William Grimes, "Antony Flew, Philosopher and Ex-Atheist, Dies at 87," *New York Times*, 17 April 2010.

42. John Leslie, who explained his pantheism in the first chapter of his *Immortality Defended* (Blackwell, 2007), gave an extensive defense of fine-tuning in "The Prerequisites of Life in Our Universe," *Newton and the New Direction in Science*, ed. G. V. Coyne et al. (Specola Vaticana, 1988).

43. Leslie, *Immortality Defended*, 3.

44. Ibid., 83.

45. Brandon Carter, "Anthropic Interpretation of Quantum Theory," *International Journal of Theoretical Physics*, 43/3 (March 2004).

46. See Davies, *The Accidental Universe.*

47. Denis Brian, *Genius Talk: Conversations with Nobel Scientists and Other Luminaries* (Plenum Press, 1995), 164.

48. Stephen Hawking and Leonard Mlodinow, *The Grand Design* (Bantam, 2012), 153, 165. For an insightful critique of *The Grand Design,* see Wolfgang Smith, "Response to Stephen Hawking's Physics-as-Philosophy," *Sophia: The Journal of Traditional Studies,* 16/2 (2011), 5–48.

49. Martin Rees, *Our Cosmic Habitat* (Phoenix, 2003), 164.

50. Sean Carroll, "Does the Universe Need God?" *The Blackwell Companion to Science and Christianity,* ed. James B. Stump and Alan G. Padgett (Wiley-Blackwell, 2012).

51. Brian Greene, *The Elegant Universe: Superstrings, Hidden Dimensions, and the Quest for the Ultimate Theory* (Norton, 2010) and *The Hidden Reality: Parallel Universes and the Deep Laws of the Cosmos* (Vintage, 2011).

52. Davies, *Cosmic Jackpot*, 179–85.

53. Alexander Vilenkin and Max Tegmark, "The Case for Parallel Universes," *Scientific American*, 19 July 2011.

54. Barnes, "The Fine-Tuning of the Universe for Intelligent Life."

55. Maggie McKee, "Ingenious: Paul J. Steinhardt," *Nautilus*, 25 September 2014.

56. Lee Smolin, "You Think There's a Multiverse? Get Real," *New Scientist*, 20 January 2015.

57. John Polkinghorne, *One World* (London, SPCK, 1986), 80.

58. George Ellis, "Does the Multiverse Really Exist?" *Scientific American,* August 2011.

59. Brian Greene, "The Multiverse," in John Brockman, ed., *What Is Your Dangerous Idea? Today's Leading Thinkers on the Unthinkable* (Harper Perennial, 2007), 120–21.

60. Heinz Pagels, *Perfect Symmetry* (Simon & Schuster 1985), 359.

61. The "horizon problem," also called the "uniformity problem," is how the universe could be so uniform. Uniformity usually comes about by the exchange of information. For example, when a door is opened between a warm room and a cold room in a building, the rooms will begin equilibrating toward a common temperature. Analogously, different regions of the universe should, according to the original Big Bang cosmology, begin with different temperatures, because of the random nature of the initial conditions. But through mutual exchanges of information, these different regions would have equilibrated. However, because of the expansion of space, some of the regions would be so distant from each other that they are beyond each other's "horizon"—meaning that they cannot share information, because it cannot be transmitted faster than the speed of light. Accordingly, there could be no equilibrating between these regions. In fact, however, evidence indicates that all regions of the universe have the same temperature. How can this be explained?

The dominant solution is inflationary cosmology, which says that, in the first split-second after the Big Bang, the universe expanded exponentially, faster than the speed of light, after which the expansion slowed down. Before the brief period of exponential inflation, the whole universe was in causal contact, so that it could equilibrate to a common temperature.

62. Paul J. Steinhardt, "The Cyclic Theory of the Universe," Department of Physics, Princeton University; John Horgan, "Physicist Paul Steinhardt Slams Inflation, Cosmic Theory He Helped Conceive," *Scientific American,* 1 December 2014.

63. Davies, *The Goldilocks Enigma,* 204; Davies, "Stephen Hawking's Big Bang Gaps," *Guardian,* 4 September 2010.

64. Horgan, "Physicist Paul Steinhardt Slams Inflation."

65. Thomas Nagel, *Mind and Cosmos: Why the Materialist Neo-Darwinian Conception of Nature Is Almost Certainly False* (Oxford University Press, 2012), 131.

66. Carroll, "Does the Universe Need God?"; Hawking and Mlodinow, *The Grand Design,* 34; Stephen Hawking, interviewed by Pablo Jáuregui, "No hay ningún dios. Soy ateo," *El Mundo,* 26 October 2014.

67. George F. R. Ellis, "The Theology of the Anthropic Principle," in Robert J. Russell et al., eds., *Quantum Cosmology and the Laws of Nature: Scientific Perspectives on Divine Action* (Vatican Observatory Publications & The Center for Theology and the Natural Sciences, 1993), 363–99.

68. Richard Swinburne, *The Existence of God* (Oxford University Press, 2004), 97, 189. See also Swinburne, "The Argument to God from Fine-Tuning Reassessed," in Manson, ed., *God and Design*, 80–105.

69. Quentin Smith, "The Anthropic Coincidences, Evil and the Disconfirmation of Theism," *Religious Studies*, 1992.

70. Alfred North Whitehead, *Process and Reality*, corrected edition, ed. David Ray Griffin and Donald W. Sherburne (Free Press, 1978), 89 n2.

71. Alfred North Whitehead, *Adventures of Ideas* (1933; Free Press, 1967), 166.

72. Whitehead, *Process and Reality*, 96.

73. Whitehead spoke of God as the "Primordial Being" and also of the "primordial nature of God." God's "primordial nature" is distinct from God's "consequent nature," whereas God as a whole is the Primordial Being, being the one and only actual being who has existed forever. The metaphysical principles are rooted in God as primordial in the sense of "eternal," whereas the cosmological laws are rooted in a divine decision that was primordial in the sense of occurring at the outset of the present cosmic epoch. Although Whitehead sometimes wrote as if the primordial nature involved a "primordial decision," I explained elsewhere why that would be incoherent (*Reenchantment without Supernaturalism*, Chapter 4).

74. William James, *The Principles of Psychology* (1890; Dover, 1950), Vol. 1: 104; Charles Peirce, "A Guess at a Riddle," in *Collected Papers of Charles Sanders Peirce*, ed. Charles Hartshorne and Paul Weiss (Harvard University Press, 1931-58), Vol. 1: 385-94; Peirce, "A Survey of Pragmaticisms," ibid., Vol. 5: 480.

75. Alfred North Whitehead, *Adventures of Ideas* (Free Press, 1967), 41; Whitehead, *Modes of Thought* (Free Press), 154.

76. "Ultra-Short X-ray Pulses Could Shed New Light on the Fastest Events in Physics," University of Oxford, 16 November 2015.

77. Whitehead, *Process and Reality*, 283.

78. "Science's Alternative to an Intelligent Creator: The Multiverse Theory," *Discover*, December 2008.

79. Roberto Mangabeira Unger and Lee Smolin, *The Singular Universe and the Reality of Time* (Cambridge University Press, 2015), 353–54, 360.

80. Ibid., 117–19, 160.

81. Ibid., 11, 155, 173.

82. Ibid., 10.

83. Ibid., 302–47.

84. Ibid., 37, 132.

85. Ibid., 10. Indeed, Unger and Smolin speak of the "conundrum of the meta-laws," ibid., 9, 524–25.

86. Ibid., 35, 101, 172, 173, 513.

Postscript

Why Belief in God,
Not Gawd, Is Important

The second part of this book provides a cumulative argument for the existence of God as understood in panentheism. In our time, however, such an argument can be convincing to well-informed and morally sensitive people only if it is made clear that Gawd—often mistakenly equated with God—does *not* exist. Accordingly, this book began by arguing, in agreement with atheists, that our world was not created by an omnipotent being. The second part of the book argues that, nevertheless, God does exist.

This book closes here with a discussion of why belief in God—rather than either atheism or belief in Gawd—is important with regard to the overriding issue of our time: whether civilization will be destroyed by global warming and the climate change it causes.

Even if people agree that, although Gawd does not exist, God does, they might still ask: So what? Although it is obvious that it is good to believe in the non-existence of Gawd, why is it important to believe in the existence of God—at least the panentheistic deity advocated in this book?

At this point in our history, the most important reason for belief in God, rather than either Gawd or atheism, involves the overriding threat of global warming and the climate change it causes: If the global

307

warming continues, it threatens to destroy civilization and perhaps even to extinguish humanity, along with most of the other forms of life on our planet. I have argued this case in a 2015 book, *Unprecedented: Can Civilization Survive the CO_2 Crisis?*[1] The remainder of this chapter compares belief in Gawd, atheism, and God in relation to this issue.

I. WHY BELIEF IN GAWD IS HARMFUL

There are at least four reasons why belief in Gawd is harmful with regard to the need to stop further global warming.

DIVINE OMNIPOTENCE AND CLIMATE COMPLACENCY

In the United States, belief in Gawd has been very destructive to the effort to stop global warming, because this belief has resulted in climate complacency. According to the title of a *Washington Post* article in 2013, "Americans Are Less Worried about Climate Change than Almost Anyone Else." According to a Pew poll of the same year, only 33% of the American public considered global warming a "very serious" problem, and only 28% thought it should be a "top priority" for the politicians in Washington. Of 21 priority issues, moreover, global warming was at the bottom of the list.[2]

American complacency about climate change is no coincidence: According to a 2015 poll, 35 percent of Americans identify as Evangelical Christians, and Evangelicals are, as polls have consistently shown, less likely than Americans in general to be very concerned about global warming.[3]

This climate complacency is especially problematic when it is embodied in national political leaders. A prime example is Republican Senator James Inhofe of Oklahoma. In 2012, he published a book in which he called claims about the dangers of climate change *The Greatest Hoax*. In response to people he called climate "alarmists," Inhofe said: "[Gawd] is still up there, and He promised to maintain the seasons."[4] It is arrogant, said Inhofe, to "think that we, human beings, would be able to change what He is doing in the climate."[5] These beliefs became especially dangerous in 2015, when Inhofe became the chairman of the Senate's Committee on Environment and Public Works.

As Inhofe's statements show, his climate complacency is based upon his belief in Gawd's omnipotence. Another example is provided by Republican Congressman John Shimkus of Illinois. Saying that he believes the Bible to be "the infallible word of [Gawd]," he quoted a biblical passage to conclude, "The Earth will end only when [Gawd] declares it's time to be over."[6]

National political life has also been influenced by talk-show host Rush Limbaugh, who said: "If you believe in [Gawd], then intellectually you cannot believe in manmade global warming." We are not so "omnipotent," said Limbaugh, that we could "destroy the climate."[7]

Likewise David Crowe, the executive director of an Evangelical organization called Restore America, said that human-caused global warming is not responsible for devastating hurricanes: "[M]an is not in control. God is! Everything in the sky, the sea and on earth is subject to His control."[8]

The issue of divine responsibility for evil was thrust into the national debate by a headline on the cover of the *New York Daily News* proclaiming, "GOD ISN'T FIXING THIS." The paper was talking about the mass shootings in San Bernardino on December 2, 2015. In response to tweets from Republican presidential candidates sending their thoughts and prayers, Democratic Senator Chris Murphy sent a tweet saying: "Your 'thoughts' should be about steps to take to stop this carnage. Your 'prayers' should be for forgiveness if you do nothing—again."[9]

Murphy's tweet and the *New York Daily News* headline both went viral and evoked many responses. Many of the responses were by Christians expressing outrage, charging the *Daily News* with mocking God. In an article entitled (without irony) "God Responds to the New York Daily News," the *Federalist* charged that the newspaper had "mock[ed] God for failing to 'fix' the problem of sinful mankind."[10] The *Christian Post* asked why the *Daily News* was "pointing blame at God?"[11] Another writer, calling the headline "arrogant," said that it was "not just an attack on Republican presidential hopefuls, but on all Christians and God Himself."[12]

The headline was indeed an attack on Republican presidential candidates, as indicated by the sub-headline: "As latest batch of innocent

Americans are left lying in pools of blood, cowards who could truly end gun scourge continue to hide behind meaningless platitudes." But the charge that the *Daily News* had criticized God was misplaced. It simply stated the fact that God has *not* stopped gun violence in the country. That seems obvious enough. However, people who assume traditional theism naturally read the headline as a criticism of God, because divine omnipotence implies that the deity *could* have presented the shootings. At most, therefore, the headline could be considered an attack on Gawd.

As this debate about the San Bernardino massacre shows, any public discussion about deity and evil revolves, more or less explicitly, around the question of divine omnipotence. In this case, those who assume divine omnipotence felt a need to explain *why* the shootings were not prevented. Some writers defended the free-will theodicy.[13] Others argued that the problem has already been "fixed" (through the death and resurrection of Jesus), or at least soon will be.[14]

By contrast, those who do not think in terms of divine omnipotence tend to agree with the charge by the *Daily News*. For example, the president of Auburn Theological Seminary wrote:

> Prayer alone cannot fix these troubled and dangerous times. Nor can prayer be used by politicians—or any of us—to excuse inaction or to demonstrate one's compassion, while continuing to support gun policies that will only allow more shootings.[15]

Jesuit priest James Martin wrote:

> How does God most often act? *Through* us. The disgust and anger and sadness that we feel over these kinds of violent acts are precisely *God's* disgust and anger and sadness. This is God inspiring us, urging us, begging us to act. How else would God act in our world other than through us? This is God's voice in us, also called our conscience. It's up to us, however, to decide to act. Or not. In other words, it's up to us to listen to that voice. So don't blame God for not acting. Blame us.[16]

The relevance of this discussion about gun violence is obviously that the *Daily* News headline—"God Isn't Fixing It"—could have equally been about global warming. Just as some politicians and others use their belief in divine omnipotence to say that we do not need to reduce the availability of guns, others use their belief in Gawd to say that we do not need to reduce the use of fossil fuels.

GAWD AND ANTI-EVOLUTIONISM

In addition to belief in the omnipotence of Gawd, American climate complacency is also based upon the astoundingly high percentage of the country's citizens who reject evolution. According to a 2012 Gallup poll, 46% of Americans say that Gawd created our world within the past 10,000 years.[17]

Evolution has, of course, long been rejected in America by fundamentalist Christians, now generally called "Evangelicals" (although not all Evangelicals should be considered fundamentalists). In recent years, the rejection of both evolution and climate change has virtually become a plank in the national platform of the Republican Party. The recognition of this double rejection was acknowledged in 2012, when the National Center for Science Education expanded its mission: Having been founded in 1981 to defend the teaching of evolution, the NCSE expanded its mission to "defending the teaching of evolution and climate science."[18]

The rejection of evolution and climate change by almost half of Americans means that they and other Americans live in essentially two worlds with regard to these issues.

According to those who accept science with respect to both evolution and climate change, humans and other mammals developed only after billions of years of biological evolution, built upon billions of years of cosmic and then geological evolution. Having long oscillated between ice ages and warming periods, our planet's most recent warming resulted about 10,000 years ago in the Holocene era, with a climate warm enough, but not too warm, for civilization to arise. But if the climate were to become either much warmer or much cooler, civilization would be brought to an end. Global warming is, therefore, an existential threat.

But for people who reject evolution on the basis of biblical faith in Gawd, the 10,000-year period during which our civilization developed constitutes the entire history of the universe. There was no need for billions of years of evolution before humans, along with other mammals, could emerge, and there was no need for many million more years to occur until our planet would have a climate that would allow the emergence of civilization. Instead, Gawd simply created the universe, our planet, and human beings virtually all at once, along with the climate that the Earth had at the beginning of the 20th century.

Given how easy it was for Gawd to create human civilization, the destruction of it would be no great tragedy. Gawd could simply create a "new heaven and earth" in a "twinkling of an eye."[19]

GAWD AND END-TIMES BELIEF

Complacency about climate change is also supported by the traditional Christian belief in "the Second Coming of Jesus Christ," according to which Jesus will return to bring the world to an end. According to a 2013 article published in the *Political Research Quarterly*, "believers in Christian end-times theology are less likely to support policies designed to curb global warming than are other Americans." Whereas it makes sense that most other Americans "would support preserving the Earth for future generations," the "end-times believers would rationally perceive such efforts to be ultimately futile, and hence ill-advised."[20]

GAWD AND EVIL

Belief in Gawd's omnipotence is usually combined with belief in divine goodness, with this combination resulting in climate complacency. But the acceptance of divine omnipotence can also, as discussed in Chapter 1, lead to the belief that the world has been created by an indifferent or even evil power. Given the tendency of human beings to want to be in harmony with the ultimate power of the universe, the belief that we have been created by a power that is indifferent to us or even evil, at least partly, could reinforce the human tendency to behave accordingly. This negative view of the universe can led people to believe that life on or planet is not worth saving.

2. WHY ATHEISM CAN BE HARMFUL

People who reject Gawd are often led to atheism. Some of them are led to this position simply because they do not realize that the rejection of Gawd-belief does not necessarily imply the rejection of belief in God.

Some of them are led to atheism out of the belief that science and philosophy have shown the truth of complete materialism. Some are led to atheism for other reasons.

But whatever be the reason, atheism is the rejection of not merely some particular view of deity, such as Gawd, but of any divine reality whatsoever.[21] There are at least three reasons why atheism in this sense is harmful to the effort to stop global warming before it destroys civilization.

NO MORAL NORMS

To affirm atheism is to hold the view of John Mackie, Gilbert Harman, Bernard Williams, and Richard Rorty, as described in Chapter 8, according to which moral norms do not belong to the fabric of the universe. According to this view, morality is simply a social convention, which human societies have invented. As Mackie said, it is generally thought that "if someone is writhing in agony before your eyes," you should "do something about it if you can." However, said Mackie, this is not an objective requirement "in the nature of things."[22]

This is the complete opposite of the moral attitude that is needed. To stop increasing global warming, civilization must reduce the burning of fossil fuels to virtually zero over the next two to three decades. To do so will require many changes, from diet to industrial production to transportation to home heating and cooling. Whether these changes will be made quickly will depend upon moral motivation—by individuals, communities, corporations, and entire societies—to do so.

"The basic matter," said leading climate scientist James Hansen, "is a matter of morality—a matter of intergenerational justice." That is, climate morality is policies and practices aimed at acting justly with regard to future generations. Central to such justice is preventing global warming from changing the climate so much that future generations will suffer from more heat waves, drought, sea-level rise, and violent storms.

Although native Americans taught their children to take account of the needs of the next seven generations, atheism implies that we have no obligation even to the next generation. If no moral norms exist in the fabric of the universe, we are doing nothing wrong if we use up all the remaining fossil fuels, even if this brings about the end of civilization.[23]

NO ULTIMATE MEANING OR IMPORTANCE

Atheism also entails the doctrine of nihilism, according to which the universe and hence our lives have no ultimate meaning. The absence of ultimate meaning implies that nothing is really important. One of the most explicit statements of this idea was provided by Cambridge University philosopher Bernard Williams. To repeat his statement quoted in Chapter 11: In discussing the idea of "importance," Williams said that we have a *relative* idea of importance, according to which something is found important by someone. However, he said,

> we [also] have another notion, of something's being, simply, important (important *überhaupt*, as others might put it, or important *period*). It is not at all clear what it is for something to be, simply, important. It does not mean that it is important for the universe: in that sense, nothing is important.[24]

As to why we nevertheless have this notion of something "important *überhaupt*," he said that there is no explanation. Williams' judgment on this point presupposed his endorsement of atheism and thereby his rejection of a teleological worldview.[25]

The survival of civilization will require a worldwide mobilization to eliminate the use of fossil fuels quickly. This mobilization will need the leadership of many types of people—including national political leaders, CEOs of energy corporations, and heads of the major media. But belief that life has no ultimate meaning, so that nothing is of ultimate importance—nothing important enough to forgo immediate comforts and riches for the sake of allowing future generations to have a livable world—will cut against the likelihood that such people will provide the needed leadership.

NO BASIS FOR HOPE

For individuals and societies to achieve anything difficult, it usually requires sacrifice, hard work, and persistence. The task of stopping further global warming quickly enough to save civilization is arguably the most difficult task ever undertaken. According to climate activist Bill McKibben, it is "the greatest challenge humans have ever faced."[26] To take on the sacrifice and hard work, and to persist in it for the coming decades, we need to believe that there is at least hope for success.

Atheism implies, however, that this hope cannot be based on anything beyond ourselves, and a critical examination of the human race can easily lead to the conclusion that hope for success would be foolish. A combination of ignorance, greed, cowardice, and selfishness has prevented any significant reduction in the use of fossil fuels since society became aware three decades ago of the threat to civilization posed by these fuels. One could easily conclude cynically that there is no basis for hoping that anything will overcome these human failures in the coming decades.

In sum: Although atheism does not have all the negative consequences of belief in Gawd, it provides no assistance to the motivation needed to overcome global warming before it leads to climate change too drastic to permit survival.

3. WHY BELIEF IN GOD CAN BE HELPFUL

In contrast to both atheism and belief in Gawd, belief in God can add motivation for engaging in the needed work and sacrifice. "Belief in God" here means, of course, belief in the panentheistic conception of deity portrayed in this book.

GOD'S POWER IS PERSUASIVE, NOT CONTROLLING

The central difference between God and Gawd is that God is not in complete control. We humans exist only because God persuaded the evolutionary process to bring forth higher forms of life, but to believe in God as our creator is not to believe that our planet's climate is controlled by God. It is also not to believe that—now that we have thus far failed to respond to the divine persuasion—the increasingly ferocious heat, drought, deluges, hurricanes, and tornadoes will be miraculously prevented from destroying us. Belief in God does not encourage climate complacency.

DIVINE POWER DOES NOT CONTRADICT DIVINE GOODNESS

As discussed in Chapter 1, the omnipotence of Gawd undermined the conviction that our universe was brought about by a wholly good creator. If our creator is in complete control of the universe, this creator would seem to be evil or at best indifferent (as is the case when neo-Darwinian evolution is considered our creator). But belief in God, with power that is persuasive rather than coercive and controlling, is fully consistent with the idea that our universe has been brought about by a divine power that is wholly good—an idea that implies that our world is basically good.

Leibniz's conviction that ours is "the best of all possible" worlds was rendered implausible by his doctrine that Gawd is responsible for every detail of our world. However, by combining the view of divine power as persuasive with what science has taught us about the only ways in which cosmic, geological, and biological evolution could have proceeded, we can hold that ours is likely *one of the best* of all possible worlds. This realization can help inspire us to do everything possible to save this precious planet's life.

LIFE WAS INTENDED

Whereas divine power is not capable of controlling events in the world (because the world is comprised of entities with some degree of self-determining power), it appears that the creator of our universe was able to fine-tune its laws so as to make the emergence of life possible, albeit only after many billions of years. The fact that our universe appears to be biocentric suggests that life on our planet illustrates what the universe is all about. Rather than being an accident, the existence of life appears to be of great importance from a cosmic point of view. Moreover, the fabric of the universe, by virtue of containing the forms for morality, mathematics, logic, and rationality, suggests that human-like creatures were not simply a cosmic accident.

SOMETHING OF ULTIMATE IMPORTANCE

Atheism suggests that nothing is ultimately important because, as Bernard Williams put it, nothing is "important for the universe." From the perspective of panentheism, by contrast, life is important to God, understood as the mind or soul of the universe. The idea that divine persuasion could bring about life only when certain conditions were present, and that higher forms of life could emerge only after many billions of years more, suggests that the preservation of higher forms of life for as long as possible is of ultimate importance. The premature extinction of higher forms of life on our planet, therefore, would be an enormous tragedy.

MORAL NORMS

One of the worst consequences of atheism is that it implies that there are no moral norms in the fabric of the universe. Aside from social conventions, according to this view, we have no moral obligation to preserve the conditions for civilization for future generations. According to panentheism, by contrast, moral norms belong to the fabric of our universe as fully as do physical, chemical, biological, mathematical, and logical principles. As intelligent creatures, we can feel, and even become consciously aware of, moral norms.

Because of this awareness, we know basic moral principles, such as the "silver rule"—that we should not do to others what we would not want done to us.[27] We know, therefore, that we should not destroy the conditions for the existence of future generations. Although atheists, of course, also feel these moral norms, their atheism leads them to dismiss them as non-cognitive, that is, as not providing any knowledge about the world. Belief in panentheism, by contrast, encourages us to take our moral intuitions seriously.

BASIS FOR HOPE

Belief in God, finally, provides a basis for hope that, in spite of all the delays, the human race will finally act so as to save itself from suicide. Belief in an omnipotent creator, by contrast, often leads people to believe that the fate of civilization is out of our hands, so that it will be saved if, and only if, Gawd wants it to be saved. Atheism, by contrast, easily leads people to hopelessness. But according to panentheism, God is calling people all over the planet to exert their utmost to save a livable climate for future generations. This belief provides a basis for hoping that now, at the last hour and against all odds, we will respond. No certainty, of course, but hope.

CONCLUSION: ANATHEISM

This book supports what Rupert Sheldrake has called *anatheism*, "returning to a belief in God after passing through the purifying fires of atheism."[28] Having begun with belief in Gawd, many people have completely rejected the idea of a divine reality, coming to see this idea as both false and destructive. But after Gawd has been rejected, often angrily, and after atheism has been found unsatisfactory, people are often led to look for a third alternative. By lifting up a number of features of our experience and world that contradict both atheism and traditional theism, this book shows that there *is* a third alternative, thereby encouraging anatheism.

ENDNOTES

1. David Ray Griffin, *Unprecedented: Can Civilization Survive the CO2 Crisis?* (Clarity Press, 2015).

2. Max Fisher, "Americans Are Less Worried about Climate Change than Almost Anyone Else," *Washington Post*, 27 September 2013; "Climate Change: Key Data Points from Pew Research," Pew Research Center, 2 April 2013.

3. Ed Stetzer, "In a Dramatic Shift, the American Church Is More Evangelical than Ever," *Washington Post*, 14 May 2015; "Evangelicals Support Some Climate Change Policies," *Conservation Magazine*, June 2013.

4. Senator James Inhofe, *The Greatest Hoax: How the Global Warming Conspiracy Threatens Your Future* (Washington, WND Books, 2012), 70–71.

5. Brian Tashman, "James Inhofe Says the Bible Refutes Climate Change," Right Wing Watch, 3 August 2012.

6. "God Won't Allow Global Warming, Congressman Seeking to Head Energy Committee Says," Raw Story, 11 November 2010.

7. David Edwards, "Limbaugh: Christians 'Cannot Believe in Manmade Global Warming,'" Raw Story, 14 August 2013.

8. David Crowe, "Katrina: God's Judgment on America," Beliefnet, September 2005.

9. Natash Noman, "Sandy Hook Senator Just Summed Up the Reality of Sending 'Thoughts and Prayers,'" News.Mic, 2 December 2015.

10. Sean Davis, "God Responds to the New York Daily News," *The Federalist*, 3 December 2015.

11. Dan Delzell, "New York Daily News: God Already Fixed This," *Christian Post*, 8 December 2015.

12. Alex McFarland, "'God Is Not Fixing This;' Well, What Do We Expect?" CNS News, 3 December 2015.

13. Ibid.

14. Delzell, "New York Daily News: God Already Fixed This"; Chip Hardwick, "The NY Daily News Is Wrong," Presbyterian Church (U.S.A.) Blog, 4 December 2015.

15. Dr. Katharine Rhodes Henderson, "Why the New York Daily News Headline about God Is Right—And Wrong," Huffington Post, 4 December 2015.

16. James Martin, S.J., "God's Isn't Fixing This? No, We're Not Listening," *America*, 3 December 2015.

17. Frank Newport, "In U.S., 46% Hold Creationist View of Human Origins," Gallup, 1 June 2012.

18. "Anti-Evolution and Anti-Climate Science Legislation Scorecard: 2013," National Center for Science Education, 20 May 2013; Katherine Stewart, "The New Anti-Science Assault on US Schools," *Guardian*, 12 February 2012.

19. Revelation 21:1; 1 Corinthians 15:52.

20. David C. Barker and David H. Bearce, "End-Times Theology, the Shadow of the Future, and Public Resistance to Addressing Global Climate Change," *Political Research Quarterly*, June 2013.

21. It is sometimes said that the rejection of belief in a divine reality does not necessarily imply atheism, because there is another option: agnosticism, according to which one neither affirms or denies the truth of every form of theism. It is true that self-identified agnostics are usually less confident and dogmatic about their absence of belief than self-identified atheists. But if atheists are simply those who do not accept any form of theism, then agnostics should be considered relatively uncertain and undogmatic atheists.

22. John Mackie, *Ethics: Inventing Right and Wrong* (New York: Penguin, 1977), 17, 70–80.

23. James Hansen et al., "The Case for Young People and Nature: A Path to a Healthy, Natural, Prosperous Future," From James Hansen, 5 May 2011.

24. Bernard Williams, *Ethics and the Limits of Philosophy* (Cambridge: Harvard University Press, 1985), 182.

25. Ibid., 53.

26. Bill McKibben, "Global Warming's Terrifying New Math," *Rolling Stone*, 19 July 2012.

27. Many thinkers have said that this negative formulation of the golden rule, commonly called the "silver rule," is a universally accepted moral principle. See, for example, Hans Küng, *A Global Ethic for Global Politics and Economics* (New York: Oxford University Press, 1998), 98–99.

28. Rupert Sheldrake, "News Release from Rupert Sheldrake Online," 14 February 2014, referring to an audio-taped lecture entitled "Finding God Again: The Rise of Anatheism."

Acknowledgments

As the index shows, this book is indebted to a great number of scholars, most fully—beyond Whitehead—Thomas Nagel.

Aside from my first wife, who died this past year, and my parents, my longest-term indebtedness is to John Cobb, who was the ideal professor for me some 50 years ago and then the ideal colleague at Claremont School of Theology, Claremont Graduate University, and the Center for Process Studies.

In writing this book, I was greatly aided by Tod Fletcher, who had been my friend and colleague for several years. Being committed to learning to the very end, he told me—when he knew that his death was just a day away—that he was grateful for all he learned by helping me with this book. This statement reflected his conviction about a topic touched upon in Chapter 5—that his intellectual and spiritual life would continue after his bodily death.

Following Tod's death, I was lucky to get philosopher-and-musician Daniel Athearn to critique and proofread the final version of the various chapters.

I am also indebted to Carol Christ, Gary Dorrien, and Daniel Dombrowski, three very busy scholars who took time to write blurbs for this book.

In addition, I am grateful to a little "process group," which has been meeting in our home monthly for several years, for reading and critiquing the manuscript, especially Diana Thomas, Thomas Heck, and Ernie Tamminga. I owe a special thanks to physicist Timothy Eastman, who gave me much good advice with Chapter 14.

Finally, my highest indebtedness over the past 30 years is to my wife, Ann Jaqua, who makes my work possible, while she and our daughters and grandsons keep me in touch with the real world.

INDEX

action at a distance, 50, 52, 97–99, 101, 155

Ahern, M.B., 36, 38

Alcock, James, 102–03

Alston, William, 57

Anselm, 2

anthropic: principle, 277–79, 286–88, 292; cosmology (philosophy, reasoning), 277–79

Apel, Karl-Otto, 3

apparitions, 106–12

Aquinas; *see* Thomas Aquinas

Archimedes, 5, 169

Aristotle, 46, 47, 48, 141, 154, 171, 247–48

atheism, 2, 6–7, 13, 14, 28, 45, 56, 57, 61–69, 101, 118–19, 121, 124, 125, 130, 132, 132–33n2, 148, 184, 187, 188, 189, 190, 191–92, 193, 225, 285, 301n39, 307, 312–15, 316–18, 319n21

Augustine, 22–24, 26, 33, 38, 148, 226, 245

bacteria, 82–87, 210, 224, 247, 260, 264, 294

Baker, Gordon, 76–77

Baldwin, Emily, 153

Barnes, Luke, 278, 280, 289

Barrett, Sir William, 158

Barrow, John D., 278, 279, 283

Becker, Carl, 118

Benacerraf, Paul, 144, 146, 148, 152, 165, 172n21, 180, 182, 188, 192, 193, 207

Bentham, Jeremy, 198

Bergson, Henri, 92n45, 157, 260

Berkeley, Bishop, 33, 148

Big Bang cosmology, 65, 258–59, 261, 282, 285, 290–91, 301n39, 303n61

biocentric universe, 277, 293, 316

Bohm, David, 158

Borg, Marcus, 111

Born, Max, 167

Boyle, Robert, 51, 52–53, 97, 99, 155

Broad, C.D., 103–04, 156, 157

Made in the USA
San Bernardino, CA
21 August 2016